POSTMODERN
CHRISTIANITY

POSTMODERN
CHRISTIANITY

John W. Riggs

TRINITY PRESS INTERNATIONAL
A Continuum imprint
HARRISBURG • LONDON • NEW YORK

Trinity Press International, P.O. Box 1321, Harrisburg, PA 17105
Trinity Press International is a member of the Continuum International Publishing Group.

Cover art: *Improvisation #7*, Vasily Kandinsky, Tretyakov Gallery, Moscow/SuperStock.

Cover design: Wesley Hoke

Library of Congress Cataloging-in-Publication Data

Riggs, John W. (John Wheelan), 1950-
  Postmodern Christianity : doing theology in the contemporary world /
John W. Riggs.
    p. cm.
Includes bibliographical references and index.
  ISBN 1-56338-364-0
  1. Postmodern theology. 2. Liberation theology. I. Title.
  BT83.597 .R54 2003
  230'.046—dc21
                            2002156523

Printed in the United States of America

03 04 05 06 07 08   10 9 8 7 6 5 4 3 2 1

In memory of my parents,
Bobby Riggs
and
Priscilla Riggs

CONTENTS

PREFACE

This study began as a lecture presented to the students and faculty of the five St. Louis area seminaries that convened at Concordia Theological Seminary on February 12, 2000. That day was a "Day of Theological Conversation" in which students and faculty took up the topic "Entering the Conversation: Speaking the Gospel into Postmodern Ears." The five schools that gathered were Concordia Seminary, a seminary of the Lutheran Church—Missouri Synod, which called and hosted the event; Kenrick-Glennon, the seminary of the archdiocese of St. Louis; the Aquinas Institute of Theology, a Dominican graduate school open to religious, priests, and lay men and women; Covenant Seminary, the national seminary of the Presbyterian Church in America; and Eden Theological Seminary, a seminary affiliated with the United Church of Christ. A representative from each school lectured on the topic for the day, and small group discussions and a panel discussion also took place.

The title of the conversation reflected the views of many who participated that day, and it reflected three of the five lectures given: There is a postmodern world that is in terrible shape and we, the church, have a solution if only the world would listen to us. My lecture and one other suggested that instead of a monologue, a dialogue between the postmodern world and Christianity was a more adequate model since there might be things that both sides might learn.[1]

The book that evolved from that lecture has been designed for seminary students, lay education groups, and pastors. It presupposes an interest in church history and theology, but only some rudiments of philosophy, theology, and history. It is an introduction to how church history, Christian theology, and philosophy have led to the current conversation between a postmodern world and Christianity, including Christian appropriation of postmodern insights. The basic argument is that postmodernism has some things to teach the church, such as the plurality of views and the historically conditioned character of Christian doctrine; and, Christian theology has something to teach postmodernism and those Christians who have adopted postmodern conceptual resources, such as the idea that some assertions about the structure of reality itself must be made in order to have meaningful claims about vital topics such as ethics and God. The fourth chapter picks up one of the significant but overall less influential directions of twentieth-century philosophy—a direction associated with people such as Peirce James, Bergson, and Whitehead—and agues for a way to include both pluralism and transcendental assertions about reality so that ethics and inter-faith dialogue might profit.

Two other general comments are in order. First, three terms will be used that may need general definitions. "Metaphysics" simply means the philosophical investigation of the structure of reality itself. "Transcendental" refers to that which rises out of a class or group, so that transcendental concepts mean those concepts that have moved from features of particular human experiences to what must be true for any experienced world. Finally, "universal" refers to a property that can apply across contexts but is concretely exemplified this way or that. Second, by covering church history, history of theology, history of philosophy, constructive theology, and theological ethics, this study covers many issues and figures about each of whom there is careful scholarly debate. The details of such discourses cannot be given here nor should they be given in an introductory work. Numerous secondary authors have been cited who often provide the discussions and scholarly notes necessary to follow the details of individual debates. Often the notes indicate scholars whose positions differ. In the section on the history of philosophy I have typically tried to cite the classic surveys on philosophy by B. A. G. Fuller and Frederick Copleston, as well as some classic and recent studies (such as Cornford's classic *Before and After Socrates*). Finally, all Scripture citations are from the New Revised Standard Verion (NRSV).

Many people have been a great help in turning that lecture into this book. Henry Carrigan at Trinity Press has been encouraging and patient because another project had to be finished prior to finishing this book for Trinity. Numerous scholars have helped along the way, most especially Phil Devenish, Steve Patterson, Deborah Krause, Joretta Marshall, and Cindy Bumb, all of whom read key sections and gave me helpful, constructive suggestions. Once again the staff at the Luhr Library, under the direction of Laura Rein, has been helpful and gracious. Missouri also has an interlibrary loan system called "Mobius," which gives computer access to all the libraries in the state and allows one to order books via the Internet. The books are delivered to your home library within a few days. Thanks to those who created and sustain the Mobius system. Finally, my family has been a source of joy to me, always reminding me of what truly is important about life. My deepest thanks go to Cindy, Andrew, and Abigail. They have been patient with my long hours and distracted thought patterns as I mulled things over. They were gracious by giving up more than one family vacation so that I could finish this project during the school year and the summer.

NOTES TO PREFACE

1. See John W. Riggs, "Protestants Speaking the Gospel into Postmodern Ears," *Concordia Journal* 27 (2001): 124–33. The journal contains all five lectures from that day.

INTRODUCTION

In Christian churches, and in theological discussions, two perspectives currently clash. There are Christians who argue that all theological claims are context bound, and thus can only be made and judged adequate by those within a specific community; but there also are Christians who believe that such theology is mere relativism—anyone or any group can believe whatever it wants and call it Christian—and what is needed is the clear assertion of those Christian claims that are objectively true, regardless of one's faith community. Here are some examples.

A wide variety of theological books have been written that have developed strictly from a particular context. There are books on African American theology, written not from within the canons of Eurocentric theology but from within the experiences, narratives, and community of African American Christians. African American women are writing womanist theologies. These theologies come from a community of people whose experience of being marginalized three times—being people of color, being women, and being economically disenfranchised—makes for different experiences, narratives, and communities than does most African American theology. Feminist theology is written by women and has a variety of shapes, such as Christian or post-Christian, political, or aesthetic. There also is lesbian feminist theology, which grows from a somewhat different set of experiences, narratives, and communities. African Christians are writing African Christian theology that develops from their unique experiences. Latin American theologians have been at the forefront of writing liberation theology from the experiences, narratives, and communities of the poor in Central and South America. Latina women are writing *mujerista* theology grounded in their particular experiences. In the words of the Yale theologian David Kelsey, we find Christians engaged in this "Christian thing," where "Christian" serves as a "placeholder" for a given community that identifies itself as Christian and is faithful to its interpretation of what Christian means.[1]

At the same time as contextual theology flourishes, there also are theologies being written that criticize this theological direction. The complaints come from

1

several perspectives. Some theologians point out the inherent relativism: if "Christian" means that a group calls itself Christian, and norms itself according to its own traditions, then being Christian can mean anything. On the humorous side, I have heard it argued that we ought to have Baseball Christian theology, because surely those who love baseball have their own experiences, narratives, and community. On the serious side, others argue that this perspective allows a wide variety of Christian communities to be authentically Christian even if, like the German state church under Hitler or American Christian Identity churches, these communities promote anti-Semitism, racism, and violence.

Another claim made against the variety of current contextual theologies is that such theology actually begins not with God's Word but with the human condition, and the human condition is plagued by sin. If David Kelsey represents the liberal wing of theology at Yale, his colleagues Hans Frei, Brevard Childs, George Lindbeck, and Paul Holmer developed what has become a quite conservative type of theology. Since all experiences are bound to a "cultural-linguistic" context, Christians are to look only to the cultural-linguistic world formed by the Bible for their theological claims. To look anywhere else is to look to contexts of sin. Indeed, a student of these scholars, Paul McGlasson, argues in *Another Gospel: A Confrontation with Liberation Theology* that the current theological movement to experiential context and pluralism amounts to capitulation to the powers of this world, and abandonment of the one gospel that has been given us.[2]

Within Roman Catholicism we can see something of the same split between contextual theology, with its inherent pluralism, and official Roman Catholic activity and teaching. In the face of widely diverse forms of liberation theology, written by Catholic theologians from Central and South America, Africa, and Asia, and faced with the interreligious dialogue between Christians and those of other religions, the Vatican has made several interesting responses.

The Roman Catholic Church beatified Pope Pius IX whose papacy (1846–1878) saw challenges to traditional church teachings and authority. First, there was a three-century long debate about papal authority in France. Some favored decentralized church authority, with more recognition of the bishops and the national church. Others favored centralizing church authority and had suggested that the pope not only was infallible on dogmatic questions but in political and ethical matters as well.

Second, papal authority was being challenged by modernity in numerous ways. Within Christianity, scripture scholars were beginning to show that the Gospels were not eyewitness accounts but edited and sculpted narratives drawn from previous sources. Critical historical scholarship was being done on the origins of the church, and historians knew that papal authority had, in the past, often been far less centralized. And, finally, theologians were finding new ways to express old doctrines since the modern mind found so many of the old views impossible to believe.

Outside the church other changes were at work. Three hundred years after the Polish mathematician Copernicus (1473–1543) had successfully shown that the solar system was heliocentric, not geocentric as the Bible taught and the tradition of the church interpreted, Charles Darwin (1809–1882) published his treatise *On the Origin of the Species.* Darwin showed that the world had developed through evolution, not through the direct intervention of divine power. No longer was God in complete control; a natural process accounted for our development. In the socioeconomic world the industrial age had begun, bringing massive production of goods, employing tens of thousands of people in factories on regular schedules, and seeing the land as a source for industry rather than life supporting food. The extended family on the land diminished and the so-called nuclear family, with the father working his way up in the economic world, took shape. The Western world seemed adrift in a vast sea of change.

In response to these challenges, Pius IX in 1854 published a document *(Ineffabilis Deus)* that declared the doctrine of the immaculate conception, which was the claim that Mary herself had been free from original sin since the moment of conception. Although this had been a disputed point among theologians for almost eight hundred years, Pius IX promulgated the doctrine anyway. The significance was not so much the issue of Mary, but that official dogma was made simply by papal authority.

Fourteen years later Pius IX called the First Vatican Council, which met from 1869 through 1870. Numerous issues were considered there, the chief among them the issue of papal infallibility. With his successful test of papal authority in promulgating the doctrine of the immaculate conception, based as it was in papal infallibility, and with adroit political activity at the council, Pius IX had no trouble guiding the council to a near unanimous vote that defined papal infallibility without reference to other divinely authorized sources of authority within the church.

If we step back and see Pius IX in the context of church power, modernity, and papal authority, we have a new perspective on his beatification. Confronted at the present moment by challenges from ecumenism, postmodernism, and contextual liberation theologies, the Vatican beatified a predecessor who helped give the papal office the authority needed to fight the doctrinal dangers to the Roman Catholic church.

A second example comes from the year 2000. On September 5 the Vatican issued a document *(Dominus Iesus)* that was a conservative blow to ecumenism and pluralism. The document declares that outside Christianity other religions cannot, in principle, have salvation. The document also asserts that within Christianity the fullness of salvation is realized within the Roman Catholic church, while those Christian churches "which have not preserved the valid Episcopate and the genuine and integral substance of the Eucharistic mystery, are not Churches in the proper sense." Those baptized in these other churches, however, have "a certain communion, albeit imperfect, with the Church." Faced with contextual theology within Christianity, and ecumenical dialogues that have claimed that Christianity is one true religion among others, the Vatican drew a firm line in the sand.

Let me turn to one other example of the current split in Christian theology and religion between contextual theology and theology derived from a divinely issued, inherent external authority (Bible, canon, or pope, for instance). Take my own Protestant denomination, the United Church of Christ. According to the UCC Bylaws the Executive Council of the national church "shall embody the commitment of the United Church of Christ to be a multicultural and multiracial Church, reflecting the racial and ethnic diversity of society with a balance of leadership between women and men, open and accessible to all." Among the council members, therefore, are representatives from groups deemed "historically under-represented." These eight, historically under-represented groups are the Council for American Indian Ministry; the Council of Hispanic Ministries; Ministers for Racial, Social, and Economic Justice; the Pacific Islander and Asian American Ministries; the United Black Christians; the United Church of Christ Coalition for Lesbian, Gay, Bisexual, and Transgender Concerns; the UCC Disabilities Ministries; and the Council for Youth and Young Adult Ministries.[3] Theologians from these various groups, both lay and academic, argue their own contextual, pluralistic theologies; and the church is quite pluralistic in its national office and synod makeup.

And yet there are people and local churches in the UCC that wonder what the church stands for other than being "politically correct." Are there not some theological truths that unite us and that apply across cultures and contexts? Can it be that anything that a group believes has equal validity with that of anyone else—a pluralism that has slid down the slippery slope to mere relativism? Not surprisingly the UCC, like other American Protestant, old-line denominations, has an active minority advocating a return to biblical authority, this done either through the old "full and verbal" inspiration theory of Scripture or narrative ideas about canonical authority. Like other American Protestant denominations, the UCC also has an active "Confessing Christ" movement that takes its stance against the waves of relativism by holding to the traditional creeds and confessions of the church, both Protestant and ecumenical.

In short, whether it be Protestant and Roman Catholic theology, or Protestant and Roman Catholic church life, the current scene finds two vocal and opposing groups, with many people wondering where they fit. Do we choose for the contextual theology that leads to full Christian and religious pluralism? If so, does that not dissolve into complete relativism or pespectivalism? But if we Christians believe in something objectively and universally true, does this mean we have to choose for the inherent external authority of the Bible, or the Vatican, or of ancient creeds and dogmas? If so, what happens to critical human thought, personal conviction that things are true, and acknowledgment that experiences and contexts not only vary but shape our language and thought?

This essay argues for a middle ground that will be called inclusive liberal theology. On the most general level the word "liberal" contrasts with "conservative" and points to those North American Christians who generally have lined up on the side of contextual, pluralistic theology. More specifically the word "liberal" refers to a particular type of theology that is associated with Friedrich Schleiermacher (1768–1834). More will be said later about this type of theology. The word "inclusive" simply refers to being inclusive of certain features from both sides of the current discussion over context-bound theological pluralism and objective claims that are universally true. The argument here supports the liberation and contextual theologies named above, but does so not by denying the validity of claims about reality as such. Rather, there are some claims strictly universal in scope that, by their nature, rule out no particular theological embodiment—thus allowing for contextual theology—while also enabling such theologies to avoid the charge of moral and theological relativism. This is what the word "inclusive" intends to signify in the phrase "inclusive liberal theology."

In order to make this argument, however, and to understand fully the current theological and church scene, we first need to enter the world of postmodernism because it provides the context for the current debates and the tools by which most contextual theology makes its claims. What does "postmodernism" mean?

To begin briefly, the postmodern world is, obviously, that period which seemingly comes after the modern world. In postmodernism we find appeals to particular individual and group experience, rather than appeals to standards of reason; appeals to particular contexts with their politics, rather than appeals to universal truths; appeals to language and how it functions to shape and express human experiences, rather than appeals to systems of thought and their transcendental arguments; and appeals to creative novelty that blurs accepted boundaries ("hybridity"), rather than appeals to traditional categories and organization. In short, postmodernism makes appeal to context-bound situations and voices skepticism over claims about reality itself.

Now these arguments likely seem new or even foreign to most people outside academia, but the postmodern world is already with us. Let me take some examples from everyday American culture. A university English department has a serious discussion about whether or not comic books ought to be considered classics and assigned for reading. This material represents the worldview of specific communities of people, expressing their identities and culture. By what standard should the writings of an alcoholic "macho-man" like Hemingway be considered classics while comic books are not? If we argue that Hemingway's writings embody enduring values, do we not really mean that they embody white, male, Eurocentric values?

In popular music there is not just cross-fertilization of traditions—jazz, classic, rock, Latino, rap, calypso, and so on. There are also artists like David Byrne (from Talking Heads), who does not just blend traditions but invents new forms of performing art. To experience his current performances, with his variety of costumes (including a skeleton suit) and the mesmerizing dancing of Mr. Byrne and a woman who dances with him, in the context of category-blurred music, is to experience cutting edge performing art. But how does one classify it?

Or again, the Oscar-winning movie *The Matrix* questions what is real, and it argues that what we know as reality is merely an illusion constructed by an unseen all-controlling power that reveals itself as three equal people (the "agents"). Conversely, on the side of the good is a white woman, dressed in black leather, named "Trinity." Furthermore, the movie unfolds in scenes that fascinate the senses as people seem to defy the natural laws of the physical universe, thus artistically blurring the distinction between computer science, technology, and art.

One last example comes from Springfield, Missouri, the home to Evangel University and the national headquarters of the Assembly of God Church and its seminary. In Springfield there is the Bass Pro Shop, which has vast buildings containing all manner of outdoor equipment. In the hat section, near the large rooms stocked with firearms and hunting bows, one can find a baseball cap that says, "If it flies, it dies." On an upper floor is a McDonald's restaurant that serves the usual American fast food. One of the servers at the McDonald's is a young man with an unusual and exotic name. His hair is blond and black, partly spiked, and cut in that Caligula of Rome style popular among many younger men. There are earrings in his ear and exotic rings on his fingers. He wears jet-black nail polish. But he also gives polite, efficient, and intelligent service. No one in the Bass Pro Shop visibly bats an eye at his appearance, whose only sure categorization could be "McDonald's employee" because he sports the standard McDonald's uniform. The best categorization for this entire eye-popping experience would be, let me suggest, "postmodern."

Postmodernism has had, and continues to have, its effects on Christianity, although they are hard to classify ahead of time since this cultural phenomenon itself argues for creativity that blurs categories and defies traditional classification. First, postmodernism has challenged the idea that there is historically anything like a single, normative meaning to "Christianity" or "church," except in the broadest sense of using such names as "placeholders" that point to self-designation by people in the Christianities and churches that have marked Christian history concretely. The vast erudition of people like Martin Marty, and the excellent historical work done by women and people of color, have shown this to be true. Such scholarship shows the effect of the postmodern insistence on contextual experiences and narratives. There are an irreducible pluralities of contexts and Christian theologies. Second, postmodernism has challenged some long held Christian ideas, among them ideas such as the inner nature of the Trinity (the so-called immanent Trinity) and the idea of divine omnipotence as classically conceived.

Yet another important effect of postmodernism has been to equip many liberation theologies, such as mentioned in the beginning of this introduction, with the conceptual tools that enable them both to discard traditional theological approaches and to construct new, context-fitting approaches.

At the same time, Christianity has something to offer postmodernism itself. Consider the postmodern assertion that in principle all claims are context bound and that no claims can apply to any conceivable context. The word "good" can then be given virtually any meaning a particular community sees fit, and the content to such a word as "good" would be as infinitely variable as the plurality of human communities. It is good to gas six million Jews, and several million Russians, gypsies, Poles, Slovaks, gay men, lesbian women, and disabled people. It is good to force genital mutilation on women, as is done several hundred thousand times a year even today, because certain communities say it is good. It is good to purchase African men and women, and then enslave them to work in the Americas. One can object that, in his or her opinion, these are atrocities, but that is just an opinion and other groups have their opinions.

By contrast, Christian claims about the structure of reality can, in principle, lay the foundation for moral claims, and thus social justice and liberation theology as well. The key is to name and describe these metaphysical claims in such a way that explains, rather than restricts, the plurality of Christian voices.

The remainder of this essay will proceed as follows. Chapter 1 traces the development of Christian thought, showing how Christians have always borrowed conceptual tools from philosophy as they argue what their claims mean and how they might be true. Chapter 2 traces Western philosophy, with particular attention to the question of those claims that pertain to the structure of reality itself. The peculiar anti-speculative rationalism of modernity stands out as the forerunner of postmodernism. Chapter 3 then takes up postmodernism by discussing some of its major contributors and their claims. The discussion then engages postmodern theologies that borrow conceptual tools from postmodernism. Two positive contributions to Christian theology are discussed: Christianity as interpretive from the start, and the historically conditioned character of traditionally held doctrines. By contrast the refusal to credit claims about reality itself is shown to be a problem for these theologies. Chapter 4 begins by showing the possibility of making such claims. It then applies this approach to the apostolic encounters with Jesus and discusses the way that Jesus was revelatory and the character of the God so revealed. This leads to a discussion of two currently controversial ethical issues—same gender sexual ethics and abortion rights—and to a discussion of interreligious dialogue. The final chapter looks back, pulling together the argument, showing how the theology developed might provide an inclusive theology that holds together the interpretive, contextual theology of current liberals and the claim from more traditional Christians that there must be some universal ideas and norms.

NOTES TO INTRODUCTION

1. David Kelsey, *To Understand God Truly* (Louisville: Westminster John Knox, 1992).
2. Paul McGlasson, *Another Gospel: A Confrontation with Liberation Theology* (Grand Rapids, Mich.: Baker, 1994).
3. "Bylaws of the United Church of Christ," nos. 220–21. The Bylaws can be found through the UCC website at http://www.ucc.org/aboutus/constitution.htm

CHAPTER ONE
THEOLOGY'S LONG ROAD

Within both Roman Catholic and Protestant theology and church life two vocal groups oppose each other. Postmodernist Christians argue for strictly contextual theology that preserves the plurality of Christian voices and challenges traditional theologies. More traditional Christians fear that this may be sheer perspectivism that needs some external, universally applicable standards for Christianity to mean anything at all. Many Christians find both sides to have compelling points and wonder where they fit.

Because this issue concerns the intersection between Christian theology and current philosophical claims, understanding where these two paths have been will help understanding how they meet now. This chapter looks broadly at Christian history, highlighting those features most helpful. The first section introduces historical background to the Jesus Movement. We can observe two important things about Christianity. First, there is an aspect to apostolic Christianity that has given it the flexibility to survive long after other reform movements within Judaism at the time of Jesus have died out. Second, the social conditions in ancient Palestine and the nature of the Jesus Movement will cast into bolder relief the tasks of current liberation theologies.

The second section moves briefly through a history of Western theology as it developed from the Jesus Movement through the eve of the Protestant Reformation. During this period classical theism developed and flourished. Greek philosophy was blended with the scriptural narratives about the personal God of Abraham and Sarah, and the narratives about the God revealed through Jesus. The end of the section describes the religious ethos of the late medieval period so that the third section can begin with the theology of the Protestant Reformation. Without avoiding classical theism and its inherent problems, the Protestant Reformers turned first not to philosophy to explain Christianity but to the Scriptures and the anxious and disquieted heart. For the classical Reformers the gracious Word of the personal God was spoken not just once through Jesus but again through Jesus, putting the heart at rest while at the same time empowering good deeds that reformed both self and the world.

The fourth section then tracks this correlation between inner piety and outer scriptural witness as Western Christianity moved through periods known as orthodox Protestantism, pietism, liberal Protestantism, and neo-orthodoxy. The final section turns to the twentieth century and describes two great projects in Christian theology: the demythologizing of the Gospel during the first half of the century, and the de-ideologizing of the Gospel during the second half of the century.

HISTORICAL BACKGROUND TO THE JESUS MOVEMENT

Domination over Israel

At the time of Jesus, the people of Israel had two conflicting experiences of what it meant to be Israel. On the one hand, the people of Israel had a collective narrative of their independence from servitude, being governed by Yahweh as their one ruler and, in return, being God's chosen people.[1] On the other hand, there was the history of mortal kings both within Israel and over Israel. When the Philistines, outfitted with the weapons of the Iron Age (1200–1000 B.C.E.), expanded their seacoast conquests in Palestine, advanced into the hill country, and threatened Israel, the people of Israel looked for their first king and chose Saul. David eventually defeated the Philistines and centralized power around the new capital, Jerusalem. Yet David's reign produced two open revolts. King Solomon was David's son, and at the end of his reign ten tribes withdrew and formed their own monarchy in the north, called Israel. The monarchy that David had established (the "Davidic Monarchy") was called Judah and lasted four hundred years in the south.

For two and one-half millennia the story of the Israelite people became the story of foreign conquest. The northern kingdom fell to the Assyrians in 722 B.C.E. In 587 B.C.E. the southern kingdom fell to the Babylonians, who had conquered the Assyrians. King Cyrus of Persia conquered Babylonia in 539 B.C.E. and Persian rule over Babylonian was to last almost two hundred years. When Persia restored the captive Israelites, it encouraged Israel to become a temple-oriented community. And so Israel did, and temple taxes supported the temple sanctioned by the Persians.

When Alexander the Great conquered the world, he brought with him an imperial and cultural legacy unlike the Western world has seen or likely will see again. Historians, geographers, and biologists, among others, went with Alexander, whose personal tutor had been the philosopher and scientist Aristotle. Alexander founded Greek cities throughout the empire, and his efforts, building upon the hellenization that had already occurred through the powerful city states of Greece, produced a common cultural base throughout the Western world.

With the death of Alexander that part of the Greek empire that eventually ruled over Palestine, the Seleucid Empire, continued to force Greek culture on the Jewish people, with some measure of compliance from the Jerusalem aristocracy. Eventually Jerusalem was attacked and Sabbath worship, temple sacrifices, and Jewish festivals were forbidden. An altar to Zeus was erected over the altar of burnt offering in the Jerusalem temple.

The populace longed for divine intervention, wanting God to end the old age and bring the eternal rule of God. Apocalypticism developed. Soon a man named Judas Maccabee, from the Hasmonean family lineage, stepped forth. The Hasmoneans used guerilla tactics and the assistance of the peasants—both as soldiers and financial support—to defeat the great generals and armies of the Seleucids in two key battles. Eventually the temple was purified, and Israel seemed restored.

Although Judas was killed in battle by a large Seleucid army in 160 B.C.E., the Seleucids found that they could rule only through a coalition of Hellenistic Jewish aristocracy and Hasmonean leaders. From 152–76 B.C.E. the Hasmoneans gradually seized control back from the Seleucids and established a policy of dictatorial Judaism throughout Judea. They conquered Samaria, Galilee, and the Jordan river area, extending by force Jewish rule throughout the old Israel, and forcing Judaism upon the Hellenistic cities and peoples there.

Pompey conquered Palestine in 63 B.C.E., liberating Jerusalem and the Hellenistic lands that were under Hasmonean rule. Two decades of political warfare ensued between Hasmonean and Roman armies vying for control of the area. Through Roman conquest and reconquest of territories, Palestinian towns were destroyed, and inhabitants enslaved or crucified by the thousands. In 37 B.C.E. Herod finally subdued the Jewish peoples with the help of the Roman armies, and had himself established as the Roman client king over Palestine.

Herod the Great continued to promote Greek culture and he founded numerous Greek cities dedicated to Caesar Augustus. He built Greek theaters, baths, and schools throughout the cities, including Jerusalem, and Herodian buildings are considered fine examples of Roman architecture. These building campaigns were supported through taxation of the peasants, who also paid religious taxes and were taxed by Rome. Herod and the priestly aristocracy dominated temple politics and were enmeshed with Roman politics. Popular rebellion was always possible under such politically and economically harsh conditions, and Herod maintained his rule through a virtual police state.

Upon Herod's death in 4 B.C.E. his kingdom was divided between his three sons: Philip, Herod Antipas, and Archelaus. Because of political turmoil, the territory ruled over by Archelaus was made an imperial district in 6 C.E., which meant that Archelaus was replaced by a "prefect" who ruled through military control and reported directly to the emperor. The prefect during the time of

Jesus' ministry was Pontius Pilate, who was known to be stubborn, greedy, and brutal. Pilate was eventually removed from imperial office because of his violent leadership, and he had to report to Rome, where he was forced to commit suicide in 36 c.e.

Patronage and Extreme Wealth

Life under Roman rule had several general characteristics. First, society was organized according to the rules of patronage. Patronage was a fundamental structure of the premodern Western world. Its organization was based on patron-client relationships rather than on a centralized democratic government with universalized equal rights.[2] The patron had the political and economic resources needed by clients, and clients reciprocated by offering loyalty. Solidarity and honored obligations were crucial.

Society from top to bottom was organized in this manner; and the civil government worked this way as well. Once you became the patron over an area you were expected to provide benefits for that area and the people in that area. They in turn showed you loyalty and paid for access to positions of power. It was a common saying among the civil elite that to retire as a successful gentleman from government you had to make three fortunes: the first to secure your office; the second to fund the infrastructure and charity projects that went with the office; and the third to maintain your retirement. Pliny the Younger gave away almost one million denarii—(one denarius was a day's wage for a worker)—of his own money on public infrastructure and well-being.

The ultimate source of all this money was agriculture. To be sure there was commerce, industry, and trade, but the backbone of the economy was agriculture, and the basis of all the great wealth was land possession. Great estates and land barons of ancient patrician families owned all of Italy, and from that economic base owned in an absentee manner great tracts of land within the empire. Pliny the Elder claimed that six landlords owned half the land in Africa. The produce and profits from the land belonged to these small number of elite families. Simply put, a small number of very wealthy people, arranged in a patronage system, controlled Roman social, economic, and political life.

Reform Movements in Israel

Given the national memory of an independent people whose one ruler was Yahweh, and the experiences of a conquered people that had undergone foreign rule, not surprisingly reform movements were common prior to and during the time of Jesus.[3]

Social banditry was one type of reform activity. As the people were forced from their lands by the economic oppression that took their lands as tax payment, or as they became indentured servants on their own land, or as they were threatened with immanent sale of family and self into slavery, they fled to the countryside. There they grouped together and raided Roman trade routes or raided border areas. Consider the stories of Robin Hood in England or the history of Pancho Villa in Mexico. In Palestine, these groups of bandits dated to the conquest of Pompey and the rule of Herod the Great, and the numbers and force of social banditry increased significantly after the great famine in the late forties of the common era.

Popular rebellion within Judaism itself was capable of developing into messianic rebellion, another type of reform movement. The activity of Judas Maccabee in 170 B.C.E. has already been mentioned. Between 66 and 70 C.E. Simon bar Giora galvanized a messianic movement to restore Israel as the true kingdom of God. His rebellion lasted two long years until the Romans, led by the Emperor Titus, finally broke a five-month siege of Jerusalem. In September of 70 C.E. Jerusalem was stormed; the temple was destroyed; countless Jews were slaughtered by the soldiers; and the city was burned. The third revolt of the Jewish people occurred under the leader Simeon bar Kochba (132–5 C.E.). There must have been significant public and peasant support for this rebellion. For three years the Israelites kept the Romans out of Judea and ruled themselves. During this period they minted coins inscribed, "Year I of the Liberation of Israel."

Three other reform movements had roots within the Maccabean revolt. The Essenes seem to have been a part of the purifying movement under the Maccabee family and their descendants—the Hasmoneans. When it became clear that the Hasmonean dynasty was not about to restore the temple priesthood to its rightful bloodline, but instead merged the high priest with the Hasmonean imperial ruler and military commander, the Essenes withdrew to the Dead Sea. There they settled at Qumran and produced the literature known as the Dead Sea Scrolls. They lived a very structured, disciplined life waiting for the cosmic battle between God and forces of evil. After this cosmic battle God would restore the true Israel through the Essenes, the one faithful remnant.

The Sadducees were the priestly family that supported the Hasmoneans and provided the high priest for the Hasmoneans and Romans. Their claim was to be of the lineage of Zadok, the high priest of David, a lineage that, according to Ezekiel and Ezra, was to provide the high priest. During the Roman occupation, the Sadducees were known for their efforts to keep the temple and its worship life pure according to the written law, striving to resist the hellenizing of the temple.

A third group whose origins can be traced to the Maccabees were the Pharisees. Instead of withdrawing from society in order to renew Judaism, as the Essenes did, and instead of holding to the written law in order to preserve the purity of the temple, thus consolidating political power in and around Jerusalem, like the Sadducees did, the Pharisees became a religious avocation within society in general. The Pharisees believed themselves to be of the direct lineage of Moses and, similar to the Essenes and Sadducees, believed themselves to have the proper interpretation of the Torah. The Pharisees also believed that anyone who kept the purity laws that the temple priests kept could have the direct presence of God in his home, and at his eating table, just as in the temple.[4]

Two later developing reform movements need final mention. First, we have John the Baptist. Set in the Judean wilderness, according to the gospel traditions, the baptist movement consisted of baptism and repentance, rigorous diet and fasting, prayer, a strict moral life, and expectation of the immanent end time. Some scholars connect John the Baptist with the Essenes who lived in the area and had similar ways of living. It is also quite possible that Jesus began his ministry with John the Baptist, only to become disenchanted with both the apocalypticism and asceticism.

Finally there was the reform movement brought by Jesus, which current scholarship calls the Jesus Movement. As Jesus wandered through Palestine teaching, healing, and sharing an inclusive and joyous table, some people felt that the reign of God was upon them. All people were equal before God, and one needed no patron to be accorded such worth. Relationship to God was unbrokered. In terms of the reform of Israel after centuries of foreign domination, some people who came into contact with Jesus felt that they had been encountered by the presence of God, so that through his teaching, healing, and table sharing the true Israel was known.

The twofold structure of the Jesus Movement that continued after his death was that of charismatic itinerant preachers who traveled from village to village, and local supporters, called householders, who gave these itinerants shelter and food while they taught, healed, and shared table in the local town. Historical evidence shows that this earliest structure to the Christian church survived well into the second century in rural Palestine, a time by which both Judaism and the followers of Jesus had realized that the Jesus Movement no longer represented a reform movement within Judaism but rather a separate religion.

CHRISTIAN THEOLOGY TO THE PROTESTANT REFORMATION
The Words and Deeds of Jesus

Among these many reform movements, why should the Jesus Movement have become so successful within a world so pervaded by foreign power and patronage? Other reform movements were larger, better organized, and more widely known in the Roman world. Why the success of the Jesus Movement?

Part of the success of the Jesus Movement was its appeal to those who were poor, outcast, foreign, unclean, women, and slaves. When Roman writers parodied Christianity as a religion of women and slaves, they were right. As Christianity spread from rural Palestine throughout the Mediterranean basin through a process historians call the Christian missionary movement, the Jesus Movement's inclusiveness of diverse, often socially marginalized people found its own form. In the communities founded by the apostle Paul, we see people of various strata (though not perhaps the very rich or the very poor), who were "mis-fits" in larger society, and who found the meaning for which they were searching.[5]

As time passed, and Christianity grew from fifty thousand Christians at the turn of the first century, to five million Christians by the year 300, and to thirty million Christians by the year 400, dubious means of making conversions accounted for Christianity's success: scaring people with fear of eternal damnation, wowing them with exorcisms and miracle stories, patronage relationships requiring conversion to Christianity, and the outright persecution of non-Christians.[6] Yet, one still needs to ask what else about Christianity might have given it the flexibility that allowed a rural, Palestinian reform movement within Judaism to spread through the Mediterranean basin and take root in places as diverse as rural Asia Minor and sophisticated urban Alexandria. Almost seventy-five years ago the Anglo-American mathematician, philosopher, and theologian Alfred North Whitehead (1861–1947) made an insightful comment about Christianity:

> We do not possess a systematic detailed record of the life of Christ; but we do possess a peculiarly vivid record of the first response to it in the minds of the first group of his disciples after the lapse of some years, with their recollections, interpretations, and incipient formularizations. . . .
>
> The reported sayings of Christ are not formularized thought. They are descriptions of direct insight. The ideas are in his mind as immediate pictures, and not as analyzed in terms of abstract concepts. He sees intuitively the relations between good men [sic] and bad men [sic]; his expressions are not cast into the form of an analysis of the goodness and badness of man [sic]. His sayings are actions and not adjustments of concepts. He speaks in the lowest abstractions that language is capable of, if it is to be language at all and to the fact itself.[7]

In other words, when we turn to the earliest apostolic testimony that we have to Jesus, we discover that Jesus bequeathed us not doctrines but sayings, teachings, and parables that, when they encountered people, made some people realize what was true about God and life. In the encounter with the person Jesus, they felt themselves encountered by God, and so they called Jesus "Sophia" (God's Wisdom), or "the Son of God," or "the Prophet," or "the True Vine," or whatever terms they inherently used to experience and interpret their encounter with the divine.[8]

Early on, as Christian missionaries carried this renewal form of Judaism through the Mediterranean basin, they tried to communicate this religion to people who were not rural Palestinians. An interesting thing happened, if we take the letters of the apostle Paul as evidence for the Christian missionary movement. No parables or sayings of Jesus appear, and only the hint of Jesus' teachings. Instead we have what has been called the "Christ kerygma," a scholarly term signifying that Christian proclamation consisted in the proclamation that God's chosen one (the "Christ") was crucified and raised from the dead. The new age had begun and no one *need* pass through the Torah (circumcision, diet, teaching, and so on) to be reckoned among God's children. A person only had to trust God with his or her life.

Paul was sure this was the cornerstone that he needed to put down, but he also knew that from this simple cornerstone people would build very different houses. Some of these religious edifices may not be so good and may not survive judgment day, yet the builders themselves would be saved (1 Cor 3:10–15). Paul also recognized that Christian proclamation must always take different forms in order to express the truth within different cultures. And so to the Jew he became as a Jew, to the Greek as a Greek, to the weak one who is weak. Why did Paul "become all things to all people"? In order, said Paul, "that I might by all means save some" (1 Cor 9:19–23).

The point about apostolic testimony to Jesus' words and deeds, and its reinterpretation by the Christian missionary movement as typified by Paul is simple. Jesus gave us not highly conceptualized theology but the encounter with God through his words and deeds. This meant that Christianity was not rooted in any thought system, but rather in human experience as such, within which a relationship to the divine must be present. Therefore, once the Jesus Movement was gone (either in time or location) all subsequent Christian people were freed to experience, proclaim, and defend their Christian witness using the language and context that was theirs.

Adapting Jesus' Words and Deeds

Early in the New Testament period, there is a simple, clear example of Jesus' words and deeds being adapted to new contexts. We know that when Matthew and Luke composed their canonical gospels they used an earlier gospel, which scholars have named "Q." This earlier gospel was a collections of sayings and teaching by Jesus; and the existence of Q has been confirmed both by the internal evidence of Matthew and Luke and by the discovery of the *Gospel of Thomas*. Both Matthew and Luke, however, adapted Q and positioned Jesus' sayings and teachings in their own gospels according to their need to proclaim the meaning of the gospel to their own communities.

Or again, by the end of the first century we see that the Fourth Gospel turned to Gnosticism, an early conceptual system, in order to proclaim the gospel. Fifty years later, by the middle of the first century in the common era, the erudite and sophisticated Christian Justin Martyr borrowed concepts from Stoicism to explain how the God who self-revealed through Jesus the Word was the same God who could not fail to be revealed in the life of any given person. The Word (Logos) of God, by which all things were created, scattered seeds of the Logos throughout creation. The Word took flesh in order to make clear to all what already was true about people's lives but which they did not yet fully understand. This was an appropriate explanation of John's Gospel and its prologue (John 1:1–5).

Even those theologians who objected to borrowing concepts from philosophy to explain Christianity borrowed from non-Christian sources. The North African thinker Tertullian (c. 155–220 C.E.) borrowed from Roman property law to explain what he thought were key Christian ideas. When it came to questions of how God could be one substance yet three persons, for instance, Tertullian may well have adapted Roman property law to give his defense of a Trinitarian doctrine.

To sum, one of the reasons that the Jesus Movement became successful was that the teachings, sayings, and activities of Jesus were not theology at high levels of abstraction, but the immediate re-presentation, through simple words and deeds, of the divine presence that could not fail to be present already in and to human experience. Later generations of Christians, from Paul and the gospel writers onward, experienced and interpreted Jesus' words and deeds within their own contexts and languages. And if Christians claimed that what they believed was true, then recourse to the most adequate conceptual tools available in those contexts was not only permissible but essential in order to show what Christian claims meant and why they should have been believed.

Classical Theism

In the early centuries of Christianity, through the medieval period of the Latin West and even through the Reformation, the conceptual system most used to explain Christian truths was that of the Greek philosophers. More specifically the thought of Plato, Aristotle, and Neoplatonism influenced most Christian thinkers of the first five centuries, including Augustine of Hippo (354–430). Scholars have given the name "classical theism" to the theological project that explained the God of the biblical narratives by use of Greek philosophy. Careful study has shown Philo of Alexandria (ca. 20 B.C.E.–ca. 50 C.E.) to have been the first great theologian to attempt this synthesis. The appeal to Greek philosophy was understandable.[9]

First of all, Plato and Aristotle, and Neoplatonism, were essentially monotheistic: there was a divine reality that was the source behind the truth and purpose of human life. Indeed, with Neoplatonism all creation longed for its return to the state of contemplating the divine reality from which it had emanated.[10] Second, since there was a single divine reality behind the truth and purpose of life, life was to be oriented to that divine reality. Human life was to be "teleological" (from the Greek *telos* meaning goal or end point) because only by aiming life at the divine reality would someone truly understand what it meant to be a human being. Think for a moment of Mark's narrative of the so-called Great Commandment (Mark 12:29–31, NRSV):

> Jesus answered, "The first is 'Hear, O Israel: the Lord our God, the Lord is One; you shall love the Lord your God with all your heart, and with all your soul, and with all your mind, and with all your strength.' The second is this, 'You shall love your neighbor as yourself.' There is no other commandment greater than these."

These gospel verses repeat and interpret Deut 6:4, and if they are taken to be the heart of the Christian life, as Mark would suggest, then one can see why Greek philosophy that was monotheistic and that aimed one's life at God would seem useful to Christian thinkers. On these points there was a fit between Christianity and Greek thought, and Greek philosophy then supplied Christianity with the conceptual tools that were lacking in the words and deeds of Jesus. In other words, Greek philosophy supplied Christianity with a "metaphysics"— that is, a technical and integrated understanding of reality itself.

Over the coming centuries, through the Reformation and into the modern era, Christian theology continued to use Greek philosophical tools to render Christian claims intelligible. Even if some Christian claims were beyond reason and needed to be revealed, such revealed truths were themselves open to being organized by reason. So, for instance, Thomas Aquinas (1225–1274) thought that there were three classes of truths: those that reason can prove because their concepts derive from the bodily senses; those that reason can prove but which also are revealed, such as the existence of God; and those truths that are beyond all reason but must be revealed, such as the Trinity or the incarnation. In this third category we find what are usually called the "mysteries of the faith."

What Christian theologians gradually have come to see since the modern era is that the use of Greek philosophy to provide a metaphysics for Christianity has rendered Christian theology ultimately nonreasonable. The fundamental problem was the insistence among Greek thinkers that what was most real did not change and stood "outside of time." This assumption naturally carried to what was considered the perfection of what was real, God. God did not change in any way, nor was God involved within time.

Two basic problems arise. First, there are inner contradictions within classical theism.[11] For instance, we have the God of the biblical narratives who knows and reacts, and thus is affected by the world. By contrast, the God of Aristotle and Neoplatonism cannot be affected. Consider the problem of whether God can literally know the world as it truly is. If God knows that which changes, then God's knowledge also changes when that which is known changes. God therefore changes. A second problem with classical theism is that modern people, both by self-awareness and reason, reject the idea that what is most real exists beyond time and change. Our deepest sense of self, and the world of which we are a part, is that of change and growth.

THEOLOGY IN THE PROTESTANT REFORMATION

"Paradise lost" is the leitmotiv for the Middle Ages.[12] Augustine bequeathed to the medieval period the notion that Adam had not been able to sin.[13] Adam could live as he so chose because his desires were ruled by his will and his will was ruled by his knowledge of what God desired. After the fall, however, humankind found itself in the predicament of not being able not to sin. How did that happen? Medieval theologians speculated that Adam had a special grace that was lost.

For Augustine the incarnation had the power to heal the human will so that the restorative process might begin for people. Since the church was the body of Christ and continued that work of Christ, the church too possessed the means of healing grace. By forgiving sin and administering the sacraments that conveyed grace, the church helped people actually become healed, better people and thus progress in their journey back to the paradise that had been lost.

For the church of the Middle Ages, baptism washed away original sin and any actual sins, and it weakened the inclination to sin. After baptism Christians who sinned could go to the sacrament of penance, confess their sins thereby showing their contrite hearts, receive priestly absolution for the guilt that their sins incurred, and then do penance in order to make restitution to the injured parties, including God.[14] The penance converted the punishment that would have occurred in eternity into the temporal realm, lessening the punitive time that one would spend in purgatory later.

It was the teaching of the medieval church that when someone was in a state of grace, so restored through baptism and penance, the good works done by them received merit ("condign merit") toward their salvation. In the cycles of sin, absolution, penance, grace, and good works, steady progress was made on the journey back to paradise. But human beings are imperfect and not only continue to sin but wonder about when, and where, and how they have sinned. How would people know the length of time they would spend in purgatory prior to being cleansed enough to enter heaven? For that matter, how would people know whether they were ever going to make it to heaven? Christian spiritual life that was described as a pilgrimage was rather like a spiritual treadmill.

The anxiety about going to heaven was exacerbated by numerous factors in the late medieval period. One crucial event to the medieval psyche happened because of the prosperous merchant economy of the later Middle Ages. During the thirteenth century Genoa had established a trading post called Caffa (now the resort city of Feodosiya, Ukraine) in southeast Crimea, a peninsula in southern Russia that juts into the Black Sea. In 1347 Mongol forces besieged the trading post and practiced biological warfare by catapulting into the town dead bodies infected with a disease that had come from Asia. From Caffa the bubonic plague spread via trade routes throughout Europe. Turkey and Sicily were infected first. Within a year the plague spread through the Balkans, Italy, Spain, France, and up to England. By 1348 it had worked its way into central Europe and within two years had spread throughout Scandinavia. Where the death rate was highest, at least two-thirds of the population died. The overall death toll was somewhere between 25 and 30 million people, with an average death rate of about one-third.

The results of the plague, lesser plagues, and severe famines were complex.[15] Agriculture all but shut down in many areas. With so few workers to work the land labor costs increased. At the same time there were also fewer people needing food, so that decreased demand produced decreased revenue. As salaries for urban artisans increased because of low supply relative to demand, peasants increasingly left the land for better jobs in the cities. This slowed the agrarian economy more. Later efforts by the nobility to help their revenue stream by raising taxes on the peasants and restricting their mobility only fostered peasant revolts in France and England in the mid-fourteenth century.

The late medieval religious psyche was also affected by the physical hardships of wars, famines, poverty, and the plague. Why did the black death happen? Popular piety believed that God was angry and the God who once had not hesitated to cleanse the earth and its babies with the flood apparently had no problem in once again cleansing a large portion of western Europe. Given that modern people have made the unconscionable interpretation of AIDS as God's punishment for sexual orientation, how seemingly natural in premodern Europe that people interpreted the plague as a sign of God's wrath. More than that, people reckoned that if God was so angry as to threaten the mortal life of every man, woman, and child, how much more might God be threatening their immortal lives.[16]

Obsession with going to heaven and avoiding hell became ever more central for what it meant to be Christian. Great efforts were made at appeasing this angry God and purifying one's guilty conscience. The old practice of flagellation, for example, became an enormous personal and social enterprise, as groups of flagellants traveled throughout Europe. Comprised of men and women, clergy and lay, these flagellants twice a day would whip themselves with leather thongs, sing from their flagellant hymnals, and proclaim that only flagellation would secure one's salvation. The early medieval shift in Lent from a season that joyously anticipated Easter to one of penance was given even greater emphasis. The dour and sacrificial piety associated with the Lord's Supper, still dominant in many old-line Protestant traditions, was distinctly medieval. And perhaps most of all, in the late medieval period there were indulgences to purchase and, of course, indulgences to sell by a Western church enmeshed in the surplus capital economy that had developed in Europe during the late Middle Ages.

Furthermore, the Latin West throughout this period was simply not a safe, secure place or time to live. A sensitive person could only be anxious about life. Consider what John Calvin said about his era:

Innumerable are the evils that beset human life; innumerable, too, the deaths that threaten it. We need not go beyond ourselves: since our body is the receptacle of a thousand diseases—in fact—holds within itself and fosters the causes of diseases—a man cannot go about unburdened by many forms of his own destruction, and without drawing out a life enveloped, as it were, with death. For what else would you call it, when he neither freezes nor sweats without danger? Now wherever you turn, all things around you not only are hardly to be trusted but almost openly menace, and seem to threaten immediate death. Embark upon a ship, you are one step away from death. Mount a horse, if one foot slips, your life is imperiled. Go through the city streets, you are subject to as many dangers as there are tiles on the roofs. If there is a weapon in your hand or a friend's, harm awaits. All the fierce animals you see are armed for your destruction. But if you try to shut yourself up in a walled garden, seemingly delightful, there a serpent sometimes lies hidden. Your house, continually in danger of fire, threatens in the daytime to impoverish you, at night even to collapse upon you. Your field, since it is exposed to hail, frost, drought, and other calamities, threatens you with barrenness, and hence, famine. I pass over poisonings, ambushes, robberies, open violence, which in part besiege us at home, in part dog us abroad. Amid these tribulations must not man be most miserable since, but half alive in life, he weakly draws his anxious and languid breath, as if he had a sword perpetually hanging over his neck?[17]

Where to turn to have piety nourished and to know restoration and security with the God of Jesus Christ? Not to penance, which participated on the spiritual treadmill of the late medieval church. Furthermore, the sacrament of penance itself had become monastic and unworkable for late medieval people.[18] People hardly found sufficient nurture in Sunday worship either. The mass was said in church Latin which the laity did not understand. The Lord's Supper had become too awesome a sacrament to take because church teachings on, and scrupulosity about, the materialistic presence of Christ combined with lay feelings of unworthiness. The result was reluctance and fear to take the Supper despite the church requirement that eucharistic participation occur at least once a year. For the laity, the crowning moment of Sunday mass was the elevation, when the priest holds high the elements and they become the literal body and blood of Christ. *Seeing* became the key moment and the ringing of the church bell at the moment of elevation was to help the laity pay attention. Eventually the bell-ringing took on the function of calling people in from outside or, if at some distance from the church, to turn to the church and watch during the key moment. Turning and seeing the church at the sound of the bell could earn one three hundred days' indulgence.[19]

Some people turned to mysticism, which was a common theme during the Middle Ages.[20] Mystical practices and writings crossed boundaries of gender, class, and education. There were many practitioners but few true mystics. Overall medieval mysticism was of two types: a Christ-centered mysticism that focused on conforming one's will to Christ and thus being conformed to God's will; and a God-centered mysticism that focused on study and ascetic practices that would eventually reveal that part of the soul was divine. Both types of mysticism depended on an old Platonic idea that "only like can know like." To know God immediately one first had to become like God in some way. In the end mysticism, like the more regular church means of grace, the sacraments, became merely another futile way to satisfy spiritual longing. In the case of mysticism more and more righteous works would be required in order to become like God and have that longed-for mystical experience. True mystics, however, were rare while the unsuccessful work of securing one's piety through mystical practices was far more common.

In short, what has sometimes been portrayed as Luther's psychological troubles and hyper-sensitivity about sin turns out to be the sadly normal, spiritual condition of the late medieval Christian. She or he lived with a terrified conscience.[21]

It was to the point of *personal* contact between God and humankind, between divine goodness and the human conscience, that the Protestant Reformers addressed their theologies. Theological issues derived first from philosophical constructs were no longer the key to doing theology. Discussing how one knew, and how one knew God, required a turn not to universals but to the personal God, described in Scripture, who addressed humankind. Discussing what divine power was like required not the distinction between absolute divine power and covenanting divine power, but holding to the scriptural proclamation that God's powerful mercy was unfailingly bound to Jesus Christ.

This means that the same God whose self-revelation through Jesus Christ comes to us through Scripture still comes to people in the present moment with the grace that sets the heart at peace. Thus piety or, more carefully put, reflection on the experience of one's relationship with God, served as a second source for theology. "Experience alone makes a theologian," said Luther, and he took his stand on Scripture and experience.[22] So also Calvin called Scripture "spectacles" that helped clarify for us the God we already were seeing but needed help to see clearly.[23] Zwingli personally internalized Christianity in 1519 through a near-death experience with the plague. The Zürich Anabaptist Conrad Grebel took his stand on Scripture and the conversion of his hardened heart through the confrontation with a God who yielded the divine heart on the cross. And the direct experience of God that came with mysticism affected a number of the more radical Protestant Reformers.[24]

FROM THE PROTESTANT REFORMATION TO THE TWENTIETH CENTURY

Scholars give the name "classical Protestantism" to the period of the Reformation that spanned the first several generations and went into the last third of the sixteenth century. As Protestantism moved from the last third of the sixteenth century into the seventeenth, and as the second generation of great Reformers died, classical Protestantism moved into the period of orthodox Protestantism.[25] When the Formula of Concord (1577) formalized the division between Lutheranism and the Reformed tradition, new challenges arose. The two traditions needed to be defined carefully, pastors needed to be trained in those traditions, and Protestantism needed to defend itself against Roman Catholicism. The task of formalizing the Reformation insights fell on the Lutheran side to men like Johann Gerhard (1582–1637), Abraham Calov (1612–1686), and Johann Andreas Quenstedt (1617–1688). For the Reformed tradition, the work was carried on by Theodore Beza (1519–1605), Amandus Polanus (1561–1610), Johannes Wolleb (1586–1629), Johann Heinrich Heidegger (1633–1698), François Turettini (1623–1687), and others. Although these two Reformation trajectories carefully distinguished themselves one from the other, they shared certain features while other features were distinct.

Protestant orthodox theologians produced multivolume systems of theology. These systems were arranged in carefully derived categories that covered all conceivable options within any given topic. The philosophy of Aristotle was often employed in making the many subtle distinctions that were made. While this may seem like a retreat from the Reformation back to the medieval captivation of theology by philosophy, orthodox theologians insisted that Christian theology was only to be done by believers, with a focus on Christ and the religious life that ensued. Luther's phrase comes to mind that one could turn to philosophy if first one were a "fool for Christ."

Protestant orthodoxy turned its systematic eye first toward Scripture, following the Protestant principle of "Scripture alone" *(sola scriptura)*. Scripture was fully and verbally inspired by God, meaning that Scripture was divinely inspired with everything needed for salvation ("fully inspired"), and that the Holy Spirit inspired not just the teachings but every word of Scripture ("verbally inspired"). Some Protestant orthodox theologians thought that the vowels that later Jewish scholars added to original Hebrew text (which consisted only of consonants) were also directly inspired. There was thus an extremely close connection between the word of God and the actual text itself, despite an attempt to distinguish the two with distinctions such as the "form" (what God wants to tell us) and the "matter" (the actual letters) of the text. Orthodox theological systems typically treated the inspiration of Scripture at or near the beginning of the work.

A principle characteristic of Lutheran orthodoxy was the interest in upholding the confessional nature of Lutheranism. When the *Book of Concord* (1580) formalized Lutheran teaching, resolving disagreements within Lutheranism and distinguishing the tradition from Reformed Protestantism, Lutheran teaching took on a fixed quality. When this confessional teaching was undergirded by Scripture, which was seen as fully and verbally inspired, the confession itself could easily be seen as divine truth governing most of the church's life.

Reformed orthodoxy became keen on upholding, and discussing in subtle detail, divine predestination. Beginning with thinkers such as Jerome Zanchius (1516–1590) and Theodore Beza (1519–1605), and continuing through the Syod of Dort (November 1618–May 1619) and thinkers such as François Turretini (1623–1687), Reformed theology treated divine predestination as one of the given attributes of God, discussing the precise sequence of divine decrees in the mind of God. One crucial issue was whether God's decision to elect was made prior to ("supralapsarian election"), or subsequent to ("infralapsarian election"), the fall of Adam and Eve. Another important issue was whether Christ's atoning death had positive effect for all people or whether God applied its benefits only to the elect ("limited atonement").

When the surety of Protestant orthodox teaching was coupled to the organization of the church, and to the regularizing of liturgical patterns, some Protestants felt that Christianity had become too much a religion of external authority imposed upon people as the theological and spiritual truth. When Protestant and Roman Catholic rulers alike used true Christianity as a justification for the Thirty Years' War (1618–1648), the decimation of central Europe resulted. German population dropped from 16 million to 6 million people. The heart of Christianity seemed to be missing.

Philip Jakob Spener (1635–1705), a devout Lutheran, sought to return the sense of inner authority and spiritual life to Christianity. This was an attempt to restore the relationship between inner piety and external authority that had tilted too far toward the external. Spener's *Pia Desideria* (1675) marked the beginning of pietism, and in that book Spener outlined six pious desires: small house meetings to study Scripture; the priesthood of all believers within these groups; Christianity as a total experience of faith, attitude, and life, not mere correct doctrine; controversies carried out with charity; the training of pastors beyond technical theology to encompass parish practice and devotional, Christian life; and the pulpit for inspiring and nourishing, not doctrinal debate. When in 1702 Samuel Wesley organized his parish at Epworth along similar lines, he gave his sons John (1703–1791) and Charles (1707–1788) a model for the balance between the inner piety that came from the experience of the Spirit and the external authority known through the Word as revealed through Scripture.

A century later in Germany, a young boy and budding theologian tried to balance the external authority of Scripture and church teaching with the internal piety that came from his experience of Jesus. Friedrich Ernst Daniel Schleiermacher (1768–1834) was born the second of two children to Katharina-Maria and Gottlieb Schleiermacher. Friedrich's father was a Reformed army chaplain who had found his spiritual life renewed through contact with the Moravians. As a boy Schleiermacher attended Moravian schools, where he was spiritually formed by this distinctive pietist tradition. His problem was that he found traditional Christian *doctrines* hard to believe. Schleiermacher went on to study at the University of Halle. From there he served as tutor for a noble family in East Prussia; he then served as assistant pastor before moving to Berlin in 1796, where he was a hospital chaplain.

While in Berlin (1796–1802) Schleiermacher came to know the German romantic writers, and along with Friedrich Schlegel (1772–1829) he began the translation of Plato into German, a project he would complete alone some years later. Schleiermacher's best-known work of the period was *On Religion: Speeches to Its Cultured Despisers* (1799). There he argued that to be interested in the human condition without being interested in religion was to end up with an insufficient view of the human person. Religion was at the heart of being

human, and organized religion fundamentally concerned the religious association that people had since the human person was fundamentally social.

After Berlin Schleiermacher served another pastorate. He then spent a short
term teaching at the University of Halle (1804–1806). Eventually he became
professor at the new University of Berlin in 1810, which he helped found and
where he remained until his death in 1834. Among his many and wide ranging
writings, Schleiermacher's crowning work was his book *Christian Faith (Der
Christliche Glaube)*. Always the preacher and churchman as well as the scholar,
Schleiermacher influenced the study of aesthetics, Plato, philosophy of religion,
hermeneutics, ethics, and Christian theology. He also was active and influential
in the life of the German church under Frederick III.[26]

Upon self-reflection, asserted Schleiermacher, all people have a "feeling of
absolute dependence." By this terminology Schleiermacher did not mean a particular emotion, but rather an awareness, or sense, or consciousness, underlying
all selfhood that the self and world were not only mutually related but also
absolutely dependent. The "feeling of absolute dependence" was itself the awareness of being immediately related to God. This original revelation of God lay
behind all religions, and in Christianity it was called forth, named, and shaped
by the decisive revelation of God in the Redeemer, Jesus Christ.

> If it be the essence of redemption that the God-consciousness already
> present in human nature, though feeble and repressed, becomes stim-
> ulated and made dominant by the entrance of the living influence of
> Christ, the individual on whom this influence is exercised attains a
> religious personality not his before.[27]

Rejecting the classical formulation of Christ's two natures, Schleiermacher
instead argued that Christ had perfect "God-consciousness." The power of this
consciousness was mediated to others through his physical existence, exerting
redeeming influence upon them. The God-consciousness of Christ remained
available through those whose lives he had redeemed and who proclaimed him
as their redeemer.[28] The church, therefore, not only derived its existence from
Christ, but the God-consciousness that was his was passed on to the church,
which continued his activity:

> On the one hand, as the organism of Christ—which is what Scripture
> means by calling it [sc. the Christian Church] His body—it is related to
> Christ as the outward to the inward, so that in its essential activities it
> must also be a reflection of the activities of Christ. And since the effects
> produced by it are simply the gradual realization of redemption in the

world, its activities must likewise be a continuation of the activities of Christ Himself.[29]

Simply put, through the church Christ himself still evoked and shaped the "feeling of absolute dependence," which for Christians was known only in the experience of redemption through Christ. *Christian Faith* was a reflection upon faith from within Christianity and addressed the Christian community.

Part of Schleiermacher's significance comes from the merging of two trends that this chapter has traced. First, he restored the relationship between piety and scriptural witness to Jesus Christ, which was so characteristic of the classical Protestant period. And second, Schleiermacher was an Enlightenment theologian, inheriting the tradition of critical humanist thought that passed from humanism through Protestantism into the modern era.[30] Schleiermacher began the process of casting off the conceptual system of classical theism in favor of new ways of thinking about God, Christ, and the world.[31] Much debate has occurred over how much, if at all, Schleiermacher's theology was determined by prior commitments to philosophical issues such as philosophy of religion, or determined by various philosophers such as "Spinoza, Kant, Fichte, Schelling, and Jacobi." Schleiermacher himself thought the alternatives were hardly ordinary language or some philosophical system. One ought to be able to use whatever ideas are best suited.[32]

Looking back from the twenty-first century it seems inevitable that Schleiermacher's careful (and sometimes difficult) formulations would become loosened until what remained on a popular, cultural level was but a mere caricature. The fully human Jesus who had complete God-consciousness became the moral man who followed God's ethical teaching. The transcendent yet relational God became the kindly father who wished for human growth. The organic and mystical body of Christ that was the church became merely the place where good morals were taught. And the reign of God as the reality transforming the world, yet resisting sin and not being of the world, became identified with the social progress of Western civilization.

The debasement of God's revelation through Jesus Christ into "cultural Christianity" was the direct result, thundered Swiss theologian Karl Barth (1886–1968), of Schleiermacher's turn to subjective human feeling. What resulted was "talking about God by talking about 'man' in a loud voice." As a young man, Barth studied at Bern, Bonn, Tübingen, and Marburg, where he learned the theology of Schleiermacher and was influenced by liberal Protestant thinkers such as Adolf von Harnack (1851–1930) and Wilhelm Herrmann (1846–1922). From 1911 to 1921 Barth served as pastor in a local working-class Swiss parish, Safenwil, where the horror of the Great War and the economic oppression of the poor led to his gradual abandonment of the liberal theological tradition in which he had trained. During this period he was also influenced by Christoph Friedrich Blumhardt (1842–1919), son of Johann Christoph Blumhardt (1805–1880) whose exorcisms and spiritual healings and renewals eventually centered at Bad Boll in southern Germany. The younger Blumhardt, also a Lutheran pastor, continued these efforts and for a period combined them with a political interest in the workers' party. Through the preaching of Blumhardt, Barth became aware of the power of Christ, as God's present Word revealing God to us.

During his pastorate in Safenwil the young Barth discovered a poverty in his preaching. What did Christianity have to say during such a cataclysmic period in European history? He turned to the Epistle to the Romans where he discovered a lifeline. His commentary on Romans brought a new voice to theology which, Barth believed, was the true Reformation voice. God not humankind stood at the center of the scriptural world so that, following Luther, we should "Let God be God."

As Barth reappraised the liberal Protestantism in which he had been raised and with which he first agreed, he drew the line sharply between liberal Protestant theology and the path he thought he should take:

> Until better instructed, I can see no way from Schleiermacher or from his contemporary epigones, to the chroniclers, prophets, and wise ones of Israel, to those who narrate the story of the life, death, and resurrection of Jesus Christ, to the word of the apostles—no way to the God of Abraham, Isaac, and Jacob and the Father of Jesus Christ, no way to the great tradition of the Christian church. For the present I see nothing here but a choice. And for me there can be no question as to how that choice is to be made.[33]

Barth went on to argue for a radically Other God who in sovereign freedom came to us in Jesus Christ. As the Son of God, Jesus Christ was the electing God; as the Son of Man, he was the elected human. Thus Jesus Christ inclusively displayed the sum of the gospel—the unmerited, gracious acceptance of all people. This was God's eternal, predestining will whose content was not obscure in the traditional sense. A person could accept this election by God into the covenant of grace, and live by receiving its promise, or the individual could reject the election, which rejection itself was overturned and rejected in Jesus Christ. All people lived confronted by the divine offer and their own decision. God's gracious and eternal election remained.

Barth is often assumed to have been entirely against the use of philosophy in discussing theology but this is not quite accurate.[34] Barth knew that there had to be some contact point between the Word of God and the human person, but he objected to the human specification of what that meeting point would be. Inevitably, asserted Barth, Christianity was handed over to some preconceived human thought system. We should let the Word of God come to us and create for us its own ground of understanding. There where God points us we might safely use this or that conceptual system, never committing Christianity to any one thought world. In this basic process, some recent interpreters of Barth have seen him as postmodern: God's Word continually destabilizes this world, always making for new creative possibilities in the presence of the Word.

This brings us to the twentieth century and here I want to take up what I take to be the two most important developments of twentieth-century theology—demythologizing the gospel and de-ideologizing the gospel.

TWO IMPORTANT TWENTIETH-CENTURY DEVELOPMENTS

Modernity

The essence of modernity is the claim that all ideas are open for public criticism, according to some appeal to human experience and reason, so that no claim is to be believed simply because some putative authority says that the given claim is true. There is no inherent external authority over the human person, and people are set free for thought and self-determination. As the history of the Enlightenment program shows, what the Enlightenment thinkers used this new found freedom for, and a telos which they bequeathed to the nineteenth and twentieth centuries, was the improvement of the human condition through the natural sciences, the social sciences, the human arts, and politics.[35] However much people may criticize this Enlightenment program, given problems such as horrific world wars, genocides, Western individualism, consumerism, environmental rape of the planet—and a host of other problems that to many show the failure of the Enlightenment—the historical reality remains that since the Enlightenment the Western world has been shaped by this modern commitment.

Demythologizing the Gospel

Western culture's quest for freedom, and its turning to the human and natural sciences, had its effect on Christianity. Modern Western people increasingly found it difficult if not impossible to accept the biblical worldview. The world was not flat, domed by heaven with God sitting above, and Sheol lying dark and cold below. Americans may have laughed at Russian cosmonaut Yuri Gagarin (1934–1968), who, in humankind's first space flight on April 12, 1961, proclaimed that he did not see any God up there. But Gagarin's comment was telling. Long ago Western consciousness, in varying ways, had deconstructed and reconstructed the biblical worldview so that people no longer thought that God was "up there" somewhere. We knew there was a God and only stupid Russian atheists who did not know better thought that "He" was "up there."

Among twentieth-century theologians, Rudolf Bultmann (1884–1976) gave the most careful articulation to this program of "demythologizing" the gospel. By demythologizing, Bultmann meant the two-sided task of deconstructing the mythological worldview of the ancients and reinterpreting this worldview through existential reconstruction according to the biblical myths themselves. To this day Bultmann's program is often misunderstood or misrepresented, so it would be appropriate to summarize briefly what he meant by demythologizing.[36]

By the word "myth," Bultmann had in mind a worldview that comprised three elements. First, the real but numinous experience of God was objectified into categories of time and space. What is not truly an object open to the senses becomes an object. And so, for instance, when the ancients conceived of God's transcendence by way of space, they thought of God as "up," and when they conceived of God's transcendence by way of time, they thought of God "coming at the end time." Second, myth provides the answers to the origins of things around us, from the creation itself to the reason that there was an altar at Bethel (because God appeared there to Joseph while he slept with his head upon a rock for a pillow). And third, the natural result of these first two ideas about myth is that a "double-history" is conceived: a divine history above, and a human history below, with divine intervention into our history. The New Testament worldview, as Bultmann carefully showed, was mythological in just this sense.

Bultmann thought there were three problems with this mythological worldview. Foremost, Bultmann thought that it compromised God's otherness. While the biblical writers knew that human life was ultimately rooted in a reality transcendent to anything within the world of human control, they spoke of God as one great being among other lesser beings. Myth makes what is qualitatively different into something that is merely quantitatively different. A second problem with the mythological worldview concerns faith. As long as Christian faith is taken to be belief in a mythological worldview, rather than what the New Testament writers take it to be, radical trust in God in each and every moment, then Christian faith is compromised. Naturally this faith event comes to us, and comes to expression, through a given worldview; but one should not confuse faith as the unified event of trust and loyalty with the conceptual framework through which the event takes place. Works-righteousness as correct beliefs can too easily be confused with the faith that clings only to God. Finally, a mythological worldview compromises human credibility. For instance, we go to doctors and dentists when illness occurs; but in the biblical view such illnesses are the result of sin.

For Bultmann deconstruction was only half the project of demythologizing. There was also reconstruction. Here Bultmann argued that the New Testament itself warranted demythologizing and reconstruction. For one thing, the New Testament writers themselves saw that the point to the mythological language was not the worldview but how one intimately understood oneself in life, standing before God and neighbor. Also, the New Testament itself deconstructed and reconstructed: Paul thought the end time was immanent; Luke thought it would occur someday, who knew when; and John thought that it already had happened as a quality of life now.

Therefore, argued Bultmann, we must interpret this mythology for ourselves, according to the understanding of human existence, which the New Testament itself expresses through these myths. And what the New Testament proclaims to us is this: that what it means to be human, in the face of the divine reality, is always a living question for us. And we continually give the answer by our own actions.[37]

Liberation Theology

While the program of demythologizing might be seen as the significant theological movement in the first half of the twentieth century, the articulation of liberation theologies was the most significant development in the second half of the twentieth century. Where demythologizing addresses the question of how to believe in a world that is foreign to the biblical world, liberation theologies address the question of how to be in a world whose social, political, and economic forces produce brutality not unlike that which the Jesus Movement itself tried to reform. I want to look briefly at three theologians who stand as forebears in recent feminist, African American, and Latin American liberation theology: Valerie Saiving, James Cone, and Gustavo Gutiérrez. I pick these three theologians not because they are the only voices in their respective liberation theologies, nor because they are the first voices. Rather, each of these theologians has made a distinct effort to credit the concrete experiences of his or her own community—understanding this as a political act—and each of these three is looked to as influential and ground breaking by other liberation theologians.

When Carol Christ and Judith Plaskow edited the well-known collection of feminist essays entitled *Womanspirit Rising*, they wrote in an opening essay that:

[Valerie] Saiving's essay, a landmark in feminist theology, was ten years ahead of its time. Published in 1960 before the second wave of the women's movement, its author seems to have been aware of her own audacity in criticizing theology from the perspective of "feminine experience." "I am a student of theology," Saiving begins her article, "I am

also a woman. Perhaps it strikes you as curious that I put these two assertions beside each other." Curious, it was revolutionary! In putting the two
statements together, Saiving set forth what was to become the basic
premise of all feminist theology: that the vision of the theologian is
affected by the particularities of his or her experience as male of female.[38]

Saiving described the modern era as characteristically masculine. In the free
market West, dominated by science, secularism, and consumerism, the modern
person has been called to achieve and accumulate. Do more. Have more. And
thus be more. Extended families and communities have become de-emphasized
while the role of individual achievement through hard work has been emphasized. No wonder, then, that male theologians have characterized the human
condition as one of anxiety. No wonder that modern life is an estranged life and
that sin has been described as pride. But does this describe the human situation
as such, or rather the male situation and sin? In a characterization that has had
lasting impact on the theological consciousness of many modern liberation theologians, Saiving asserted:

> For the temptations of woman *as woman* are not the same as the temp-
> tations of man *as man,* and the specifically feminine forms of sin—
> "feminine" not because they are confined to women or because women
> are incapable of sinning in other ways but because they are outgrowths
> of the basic feminine character structure—have a quality which can
> never be encompassed by such terms as "pride" or "will-to-power." They
> are better suggested by such items as triviality, distractibility, and dif-
> fuseness; lack of an organizing center or focus; dependence on others
> for one's own self-definition; tolerance at the expense of standards of
> excellence; inability to respect the boundaries of privacy; sentimentality,
> gossipy sociability, and mistrust of reason—in short, underdevelopment
> or negation of the self.[39]

Within a decade other feminist theologians would make their contribution
to the second wave of feminism. The Roman Catholic theologian Mary Daly
argued for reform within the church, hoping that the changes wrought by the
Second Vatican Council might lead toward a more egalitarian church. She soon
came to argue that for women the problem with Christianity lay at its center
symbol systems, such as "God the Father," which themselves had to be challenged. With this insight, Daly became "post-Christian."

At almost the same time, Rosemary Radford Ruether pointed toward the
breakdown of tribal culture, with its holistic view of women and men, goddesses
and gods, body and soul, all webbed together with the rhythms of the earth.

Western cultures with their dualisms of mind and body, heaven and earth, eternal and perishing, male and female, would replace the earlier worldview. Women were the first of the many who would be oppressed by the dualisms of patriarchy.[40] Ruether, like Daly and Saiving, asserted that a woman's experiences and redemptive needs as a *woman* make a difference in how theology is done.

In 1970 James Cone first published *A Black Theology of Liberation*, considered by other liberation theologians to be a classic that helped spawn black theology, and liberation theology, in wide-ranging communities.[41] In his opening chapter, Cone concluded simply that "truth for the black thinker arises from a passionate encounter with black reality. Though that truth may be described religiously as God, it is not the god of white religion but the God of black existence."[42] And so the source for theology become black experience, black history, and black culture. Revelation as ongoing encounter with Jesus was thus "a black event," and the Scriptures and tradition had to be properly read. Norms for doing theology were the liberation of blacks and Jesus Christ so that "the norm of all God-talk which seeks to be black-talk is the manifestation of Jesus as the black Christ who provides the necessary soul for black liberation. This is the hermeneutical principle for black theology which guides its interpretation of the meaning of contemporary Christianity."[43]

In his preface to the 1986 edition, Cone noticed several weaknesses in this book, one of which was his dependence on the theological framework of Karl Barth. He also mentioned that his "colleague and friend" Gayraud Wilmore had, from the start, been critical of Cone's use of Barth's theology:

> he was the first to point out the limitations of my perspective on black theology, especially in terms of my dependence upon the neo-orthodoxy theology of Karl Barth . . . and he challenged me to develop black theology from the religio-cultural resources of African people on the continent and in the United States.

Cone contended that God's revelation comes concretely in and to those working for the liberation of the poor, and that theology as such is the second-order reflection on such ortho-praxis.[44]

In 1971, and contemporaneous with the writings of Daly, Ruether, and Cone, we find the groundbreaking essay on liberation by Gustavo Gutiérrez, *Teología de la liberación: Perspectivas* (published in English in 1973 as *A Theology of Liberation*).[45] Whereas European theology has addressed the *non-believer* who lived with a non-mythological Enlightenment worldview, liberation theology had become "aware that our partners in the dialogue are the poor, those who are '*non-persons*'—that is, those who are not considered to be human beings with full rights, beginning with the right to live and to freedom in various spheres."[46]

For Gutiérrez, becoming fully human amid human history was itself the Christian vocation. This meant that working for a just society, the building of the kingdom, *was* participating in the work of Christ, *was* participating in the church as the sacrament of salvation to the world, and indeed *was* already salvific.[47] Thus, as a corollary for Gutiérrez,

> the first state or phase of theological work is the lived faith that finds expression in prayer and commitment. To live the faith means to put into practice, in the light of the demands of the reign of God, these fundamental elements of Christian existence. Faith is here lived "in the church" and geared to the communication of the Lord's message. The second act of theology, that of reflection in the proper sense of the term, has for its purpose to read this complex praxis in the light of God's word.[48]

In what would become a major theme of liberation theology, Gutiérrez argued that prior to doing liberation theology as such, one must first live liberation by taking up the Christian vocation wherein we have "direct knowledge of the reality of oppression/liberation through objective engagement in solidarity with the poor."[49]

Here, as with the contemporaneous liberation theologies of Daly, Ruether, and Cone, one's experience under a particular form of bondage is the primary source for theological reflection. This insistence has helped lead forth a great wealth of liberation theologies from various lived experiences. Among new perspectives, for instance, we find Christian theology done from the experiences and perspectives of African American theology, Latin American theology, feminist theology, womanist theology (theology as articulated by women of color), *mujerista* theology (Hispanic feminist theology), African theology, Asian theology, lesbian theology, gay theology, and theology as articulated by those who are disabled. Even within these broad groups, we find theologies, not merely one single theology.

PIETY, SCRIPTURE, AND CONCEPTUAL SYSTEMS

In the millennium that had passed since David was king, Israel had been ruled by Assyrians, Babylonians, Persians, Greeks, and Romans. Christianity was born during the violence and poverty of Roman rule over Western civilization. Where was the true Israel and the temple where God dwelled? Two Jewish movements during the first century of the common era, Pharisaic Judaism and the Jesus Movement, had answers to the question of the true Israel and God's dwelling place. By the second century, these two Jewish reform movements had distinguished themselves one from the other as two different Mediterranean religions—(rabbinic) Judaism and Christianity.

Jesus' words and deeds were drawn from the everyday life of Mediterranean peasantry. His rural, itinerant ministry practiced table sharing, and healing and teaching. The teaching, which came in pithy sayings, or in parables, was typically taken from ordinary scenes or images. The collections of Jesus' teachings that formed the earliest Christian gospels (such as the *Gospel of Thomas,* and Q—an early gospel used by Matthew and Luke) were good examples of what is known as "wisdom literature." The teachings invited reflection on life and one's native relationship with God. Words such as "what say ye," and "let the one who has ears hear," which follow Jesus' teaching, show that the gospel writers knew the conversation with God was beginning not ending.

As Christianity grew in vast numbers and began to be socially embedded in the Roman Empire, Christian thinkers necessarily reached to various conceptual systems in order to explain what Christian claims meant and how they might be true. By the second century, Justin Martyr had reached for ideas from Stoicism. Alexandrian thinkers used Neoplatonism. And even the anti-philosophical North African thinker, Tertullian, probably used legal terms to help explain how Christian theology could be true. Classical theism, which blended Greek philosophy with biblical narratives, dominated for almost two millennia.

The Protestant Reformers inherently retained the conceptual heritage of classical theism but tried to be appropriate to the biblical narratives of a personal God, whose personal relationship with humankind was ultimately gracious. External authority was lodged in Scripture alone *(sola scriptura)* because Scripture pointed us to Jesus Christ *(Christus solus)* and the self-revelation of God. External authority correlated to the inner piety realized in one's relationship to this God *(sola gratia, sola fide).* Technical tools from philosophy could be used "without danger to the soul" so long as they appropriately fit the God known through Scripture and piety.

Protestant theology worked within the balance of these two poles, doing "theology within the limits of piety": from Protestant orthodoxy and its lean toward the external, to pietism and its lean toward the internal; from high liberal theology with its lean toward the internal, to high neo-orthodoxy with its lean toward the external. Certain people and moments seemed to strike a good balance. Among them would be the Anglican priest and father of Methodism, John Wesley; the German churchman and Reformed theologian Friedrich Schleiermacher; the German New Testament scholar and Lutheran theologian Rudolf Bultmann; and liberation theologians such as Rosemary Radford Ruether, James Cone, and Gustavo Gutiérrez, who look to the experience of God among those who experience suffering and oppression, while looking also at the liberating God revealed to Israel and revealed through Jesus.

To put this another way, Christian theology negotiates between the God who self-revealed through Jesus and the same God who self-reveals in and to human experience as such. Cardinal to this theological task is that the technical tools used to explain the meaning and truth of the Christian witness of faith must be an appropriate fit to the character of the revealed God. Here Barth's comments in his *Church Dogmatics* remain sound, even if applied a bit differently than he would have had in mind: one must have "fidelity in all circumstances to the object reflected in the words of the prophets and apostles."[50]

The question now arises about how this issue stands in a postmodern world where theology turns to postmodern tools to explain the meaning and truth of Christian claims. In order to work toward an answer, a brief history of philosophy needs to be sketched, particularly with an eye toward the issue of "universals"—claims that transcend context and thus necessarily apply in any given situation.

NOTES TO CHAPTER ONE

1. For the best scholarly description of the histories and cultures that made the background for Christianity, see Helmut Koester, *History, Culture, and Religion of the Hellenistic Age* (2d ed.; Berlin: Walter de Gruyter, 1995). Also see Ramsay MacMullen, *Roman Social Relations* (New Haven: Yale University Press, 1974); idem, *Paganism in the Roman Empire* (New Haven: Yale University Press, 1981); Richard Horsley with John S. Hanson, *Bandits, Prophets, and Messiahs* (Harrisburg, Pa.: Trinity Press International, 1999). For a brief summary of the historical background, see Dennis C. Duling and Norman Perrin, *The New Testament* (3d ed.; New York: Harcourt Brace, 1994), 35–63.

2. See Halvor Moxnes, "Patron-Client Relations and the New Community in Luke-Acts," in *The Social World of Luke-Acts* (ed. Jerome H. Neyrey; Peabody, Mass.: Hendrickson, 1991), pp. 241–68. Also see John Dominic Crossan, *The Historical Jesus* (San Francisco: HarperSanFrancisco, 1991), 59–71; and MacMullen, *Roman Social Relations*.

3. See, for instance, Dulling and Perrin, *The New Testament*, 35–63; Horsley, *Bandits, Prophets, Messiahs;* Koester, *History, Culture, and Religion*, 197–35.

4. On the interesting views of the Pharisees, see Jacob Neusner, *From Politics to Piety* (Englewood Cliffs, N.J.: Prentice-Hall, 1973); idem, "The Pharisees: Jesus' Competition," in *Judaism in the Beginning of Christianity* (Philadelphia: Fortress, 1984), 45–61. One group connected to the Pharisees was the so-called Fourth Philosophy. This group developed from the Pharisaic movement as a more active, political wing. Viewing tax payments to the Romans as an act of slavery and of idolatry since Yahweh alone was ruler, the Fourth Philosophy seemed to have openly resisted Roman rule. It encouraged nonviolent resistance to Roman taxation and some of its adherents suffered persecution at the hands of the Romans. According to the Fourth Philosophy, it was better to die free than to live a slave, all the more so because its adherents believed that their activities were part of God's activity to intervene and restore the true Israel.

5. See, for instance, Abraham J. Malherbe, *Social Aspects of Early Christianity* (2d ed.; Philadelphia: Fortress, 1983); and Wayne A. Meeks, *The First Urban Christians* (New Haven: Yale University Press, 1983).

6. For the population figures, see John W. Riggs, "The Sacred Food of Didache 9–10 and Second-Century Ecclesiologies," in *The Didache in Context* (ed. Clayton N. Jefford; Leiden: E. J. Brill, 1995), 266–67, esp. 267 n. 47. On the issues of Christian means of conversion, see Riggs, "The Sacred Food of Didache 9–10," 267–69 for a summary of the arguments and bibliographic references.

7. Alfred North Whitehead, *Religion in the Making* (New York: Macmillan, 1926), 56–57.

8. For an introduction to Marxsen's work, see Willi Marxsen, *Jesus and the Church: The Beginnings of Christology* (selected, translated, and introduced by Philip E. Devenish; Philadelphia: Trinity Press International, 1992). On the particular point about encountering God in the encounter with Jesus, and then bestowing titles on Jesus that reflected this encounter, see Marxsen's groundbreaking essay, "Jesus Had Many Names," in *Jesus and the Church*, 1–15.

9. For Philo, see Harry A. Wolfson, *Philo: Foundations of Religious Philosophy in Judaism, Christianity, and Islam* (rev. ed.; 2 vols.; Cambridge, Mass.: Harvard University Press, 1948). For the clearest and most readable English explanation of the insights of Socrates, Plato, and Aristotle, see Francis M. Cornford, *Before and After Socrates* (Cambridge: Cambridge University Press, 1932).

10. For the classical study on the Neoplatonism of Plotinus, which was so influential on Christian theology, see Émile Bréhier, *The Philosophy of Plotinus* (trans. Joseph Thomas; Chicago: University of Chicago Press, 1958). Also see B. A. G. Fuller, *A History of Philosophy* (rev. ed.; 2 vols.; New York: Henry Holt, 1945), 1:306–61; Lloyd P. Gerson, *Plotinus* (London: Routledge, 1994); Lloyd P. Gerson, ed., *The Cambridge Companion to Plotinus* (Cambridge: Cambridge University Press, 1996).

11. For a helpful discussion of these basic problems, see Schubert M. Ogden, *The Reality of God and Other Essays* (New York: Harper & Row, 1966), 44–70. Also see Charles Hartshorne's 1976 Aquinas Lecture at Marquette University, *Aquinas to Whitehead: Seven Centuries of Metaphysics of Religion* (Milwaukee: Marquette University Publications, 1976); idem, *Omnipotence and Other Theological Mistakes* (Albany: State University of New York Press, 1984), 1–44; Charles Hartshorne and William L. Reese, *Philosophers Speak of God* (Chicago: University of Chicago Press, 1979), 1–25.

12. For two excellent but divergent overviews of the late medieval period and reformation Europe see, Steven Ozment, *The Age of Reform* (New Haven: Yale University Press, 1980) and Euan Cameron, *The European Reformation* (Oxford: Clarendon, 1991). For an overview of scholarship placing the Reformation in its medieval setting, see Steven Ozment, *The Reformation in the Cities* (New Haven: Yale University Press, 1975), 2–14. For a summary of interpretation of the Reformation, see Steven Ozment, *Protestants: The Birth of a Revolution* (New York: Doubleday, 1992), 218–19.

13. See Reinhold Seeburg, *Text-Book of the History of Doctrines* (trans. Charles E. Hay; Grand Rapids, Mich.: Baker, 1964), 1:341–45. On the following issues of late medieval piety, this essay

follows Ozment, *The Age of Reform*, 22–32, 190–222, 231–39; idem, *The Reformation in the Cities*, 22–32. Note the differing views by Cameron, *European Reformation*, 292–13; and Thomas N. Tentler, *Sin and Confession on the Eve of the Reformation* (Princeton: Princeton University Press, 1977). Compare Ozment's replies to Tentler, *The Age of Reform*, 218–19.

14. See the helpful chart in Cameron, *European Reformation*, 80.

15. On the following issues of late medieval piety, this essay follows Ozment, *The Age of Reform*, 190–222; idem, *The Reformation in the Cities*, 22–32. Note the differing views by Cameron, *European Reformation*, 292–313 and Tentler, *Sin and Confession on the Eve of the Reformation*. Compare Ozment's replies to Tentler, *The Age of Reform*, 218–19.

16. For some insight into the fear of hell, and the power of Satan, see the artwork reproduced throughout Ozment, *The Age of Reform;* and Heiko Oberman, *Luther: Man between God and the Devil* (trans. Eileen Walliser-Schwarzbart; New Haven: Yale University Press, 1989).

17. John Calvin, *Institutes of the Christian Religion* (2 vols.; ed. John T. McNeill; trans. Ford Lewis Battles; LCC 20–21; Philadelphia: Westminster, 1960), 1:223 (1.17.10).

18. Ozment, *The Age of Reform*, 190–222; idem, *The Reformation in the Cities*, 22–32.

19. See Joseph Jungmann, *The Mass of the Roman Rite* (2 vols., trans. Francis A. Brunner; Westminster, Md.: Christian Classics, 1986), 2:206–10, 359–67.

20. Ozment, *The Age of Reform*, 115–34, 239–44.

21. Ozment, *The Age of Reform*, 204–31. Also see Randall C. Zachman, *The Assurance of Faith: Conscience in the Theology of Martin Luther and John Calvin* (Minneapolis: Fortress, 1993).

22. Throughout his books Ozment argued that Protestantism aimed at reforming late medieval piety. Inwardly the Christian heart was secured by the proclamation of the gospel, while outwardly the Christian attempted to reform both personal life and social structures. See the already mentioned *The Age of Reform* and *The Reformation in the Cities;* also see *When Fathers Ruled: Family Life in Reformation Europe* (Cambridge, Mass.: Harvard University Press, 1983), and *Protestants*.

23. On Calvin's theological project done within the limits of piety, see B. A. Gerrish, *The Old Protestantism and the New* (Chicago: University of Chicago Press, 1982), 196–207. Also see B. A. Gerrish, *Grace and Gratitude: The Eucharistic Theology of John Calvin* (Minneapolis: Fortress, 1993), in which he argued that the structure of Calvin's eucharistic theology is that of his theology overall—divine grace and human gratitude.

24. Steven E. Ozment, *Mysticism and Dissent: Religious Ideology and Social Protest in the Sixteenth Century* (New Haven: Yale University Press, 1973).

25. For a survey of scholarly views on orthodoxy, and a very brief definition of orthodoxy, see Richard A. Muller, *Christ and the Decree: Christology and Predestination in Reformed Theology from Calvin to Perkins* (Durham, N.C.: Labyrinth, 1986), 1–13. For an extended discussion and bibliography on Protestant orthodoxy, see Markus Mattias, "Lutherische Orthodoxie," *TRE* 25 (Berlin: Walter de Gruyter, 1995), 464–85; Olivier Fatio, "Reformierte Orthodoxie," *TRE* 25 (Berlin: Walter de Gruyter, 1995), 485–97.

26. See Martin Redeker, *Schleiermacher: Life and Thought* (trans. John Wallhauser; Philadelphia: Fortress, 1973), 94–100, 151–208.

27. Friedrich Schleiermacher, *The Christian Faith* (Philadelphia: Fortress, 1976), 476, [§106.1].

28. "The difference is simply that the self-revelation of Christ is now mediated by those who preach Him; but they being appropriated by Him as His instruments, the activity really proceeds from Him and is essentially His own." Schleiermacher, *Christian Faith*, 490–91 [§108.5].

29. Schleiermacher, *Christian Faith*, 589–90 [§127.3].

30. See Ozment's discussion and notes in *The Age of Reform*, 290–317.

31. That classical theism still remained can be seen by turning to the section in the *Christian Faith* that takes up the attributes of God such as omnipotence. The translator of Schleiermacher's work into English, the remarkable and little known theologian John Oman (1860–1939), took up the task of constructing a theology in which God was conceived as *strictly personal reality—* able to influence but unable to guarantee results. See Stephen Bevans, *John Oman and His Doctrine of God* (Cambridge: Cambridge University Press, 1992).

32. B. A. Gerrish, *Tradition in the Modern World: Reformed Theology in the Nineteenth Century* (Chicago: University of Chicago Press, 1978), 29, 31–32. For Schleiermacher also see Gerrish, *The Old Protestantism and the New*, 179–207; idem, *A Prince of the Church* (Philadelphia: Fortress, 1984); Richard R. Niebuhr, *Schleiermacher on Christ and Religion* (New York: Charles Scribner's Sons, 1964).

33. Karl Barth, *The Theology of Schleiermacher* (ed. Dietrich Ritschl; trans. Geoffrey W. Bromiley; Grand Rapids, Mich.: Eerdmans, 1982), 271–72.

34. See Mark I. Wallace, *The Second Naiveté: Barth, Ricoeur, and the New Yale Theology* Macon, Ga.: Mercer University Press, 1990), 59–67.

35. See Peter Gay, *The Enlightenment: An Interpretation* (2 vols.; New York: Knopf, 1967–1969).

36. For the best entrance to Bultmann's thought, see Schubert M. Ogden: *Christ without Myth* (New York: Harper, 1961).

37. To see this to be the case is also to see that mythological language is not the only way of expressing the human condition, and Bultmann turned to the existential tools of the philosopher Martin Heidegger (1889–1976) as means for the modern person to grasp how the mythological texts address her or him.

38. Carol P. Christ and Judith Plaskow, *Womanspirit Rising: A Feminist Reader in Religion* (San Francisco: Harper & Row, 1979), 20.

39. Valerie Saiving Goldstein, "The Human Situation: A Feminine View," *The Journal of Religion* 40, no. 2 (1960): 108–9.

40. For Mary Daly, see her reformist book *The Church and the Second Sex* (New York: Harper Colophon, 1975), her first post-Christian and classic work, *Beyond God the Father: Toward a Philosophy of Women's Liberation* (Boston: Beacon, 1973), and the mythologically world-creating *Pure Lust: Elemental Feminist Philosophy* (New York: Harper Collins, 1992). For Rosemary Radford Ruether, see *Sexism and God-Talk* (Boston: Beacon, 1983), and the more recent, *Gaia and God: An Ecofeminist Theology of Earth Healing* (San Francisco: HarperSanFrancisco, 1992).

41. James H. Cone, *A Black Theology of Liberation* (twentieth anniversary ed.; Maryknoll, N.Y.: Orbis, 1995). In this volume, also see the critical reflections by Gayraud Wilmore, Robert

McAfee Brown, Pablo Richard, Rosemary Radford Ruether, K. C. Abraham, and Delores S. Williams, 145–95.

42. Cone, *A Black Theology of Liberation*, 19.

43. Cone, *A Black Theology of Liberation*, 21–39.

44. Cone, *A Black Theology of Liberation*, xviii–xix, 200.

45. Gustavo Gutiérrez, *A Theology of Liberation: History, Politics, and Salvation* (rev. ed.; ed. and trans. Sister Caridad Inda and John Eagleson; Maryknoll, N.Y.: Orbis, 1990).

46. Gutiérrez, *A Theology of Liberation*, xxix, italics added.

47. Gutiérrez, *A Theology of Liberation*, 39–46, 83–106, 143–61.

48. Gutiérrez, *A Theology of Liberation*, xxxiv.

49. So, Leonardo Boff and Clodovis Boff, *Introducing Liberation Theology* (Maryknoll, N.Y.: Orbis, 1989), 22–42.

50. Karl Barth, *Church Dogmatics* I, no. 2, trans. G. W. Bromiley (Edinburgh: T & T Clark, 1975), 725, §21.2.

CHAPTER TWO
PHILOSOPHY: THE TRAVELING COMPANION

The prior chapter argued that Christianity began when the words and deeds of Jesus evoked the presence of God for some people. Not surprisingly, for instance, the earliest Christian gospels, which themselves preceded the four gospels found in the Bible, were examples of Wisdom literature. Rather than literary narratives that gave a life of Jesus, they were collections of sayings, teachings, and parables that worked through reflection to uncover the God who was already working in people's particular contexts.

As this religion became instantiated in various cultures, and in various degrees of social development, people reflected on the God revealed through these Scriptures and encountered in their piety. In order to explain what Christian claims meant and why one ought to believe them to be true, Christians borrowed conceptual tools. The end of the last chapter raised the question of how theology might use the conceptual tools available in this period of postmodernism.

Two comments would be helpful as introduction to this chapter. First, two learned scholars, quite independent of each other, argue similarly about the Enlightenment and subsequent modern era. Peter Gay, whose field is European intellectual history, argued in his magisterial work on the Enlightenment that this period was fundamentally not about reasoned discourse concerning the structure of reality as such.[1] Rather modernity concerned the omni-competence of public criticism for the improvement of the greater good. The mathematician and philosopher Alfred North Whitehead made a similar observation in his work *Science and the Modern World*. Modern thought took a turn to the critical and the historical, but not to the metaphysical—not to matters of the very structure of reality as such.[2] That two scholars of such skill, from different perspectives and unrelated to each other, should argue much the same point about the Enlightenment can seem puzzling since this period so often is called the Age of Reason. More recently John Cobb's essay on Whitehead, which appeared in a collection of essays on the "founders of constructive postmodern philosophy," cites Whitehead's passage from *Science and the Modern World* at length.[3] Cobb discusses the ways that postmodernism actually continues this "anti-rational rationalism." In the same collection of essays David Ray Griffin comments ironically that, for several technical reasons, postmodernism really ought to be called *most*modernism.[4]

This leads to my second introductory comment. Individual scholars have written erudite volumes on the history of philosophy.[5] What can this short introductory chapter hope to accomplish? Not only will philosophical movements be overlooked, important philosophers will be bypassed, and those philosophers mentioned will often be summarized very quickly. The goal here is to sketch a broad yet appropriately accurate picture of how Western thinkers have, and have not, made assertions about the structure of reality itself. The main outline takes up the theme from Gay and Whitehead: modern thinkers have not reasoned about reality as such but have been critical about human experience, language, and history. In this move modern thinkers have both gained and lost as compared to prior periods of thought. In the West, the ancient Greeks bequeathed to us the matter of universals and the fundamental structure of reality, shaping the discussion for over two millennia.

FROM THE PRE-SOCRATICS THROUGH AUGUSTINE OF HIPPO

In the sixth century B.C.E., on the southwest coast of what now is Turkey, lay the prosperous Ionian seaport city of Miletus. According to Aristotle, the Milesians had the wealth and leisure time to think philosophically about the world. We might also add that people who lived in a thriving seaport would also become accustomed to the religions and myths of many different peoples and easily become skeptical about religious explanations for the origin of the universe. The thinkers of Miletus, notably Thales and the students who followed him, Anaximander and Anaximenes, thought "scientifically" about the world and its origins. The origin and continuance of the world lay not in mythic tales of gods and goddesses, not in heavenly councils and divine rivalries, but within the natural order itself. Individual events were part of a greater natural process and were to be explained not by appealing to myth, but by appealing to publicly made observations of the world and systematic thought about those observations.[6]

These Milesian thinkers helped begin a tradition of Western thinkers, given the name of pre-Socratics, who examined the origin and the nature of the universe. Turning away from reliance upon supernatural beings to explain the world, they instead looked to the world itself. They observed, discussed, and then devised theories that explained how the original oneness of the universe produced the various effects that we call the world, including the human person.

Socrates (ca. 470–399 B.C.E.) reported that he studied these thinkers and became dissatisfied with how they did philosophy. Knowledge of the origin and material structure of the cosmos was, argued Socrates, ultimately not helpful since it did not tell the purpose toward which we are headed. Socrates turned philosophy from cosmology and science to humankind: Where are we going? What is the purpose toward which we direct our lives? No doubt this partly had to do with the Persian wars of independence (500–449 B.C.E.), followed by the Peloponnesian wars between Athens and Sparta (431–404 B.C.E.). The people of Athens turned attention to the point of life and the organization of humankind.

During the time of Socrates there arose a school of practical philosophers called Sophists who really were itinerant teachers. They made their living from teaching practical wisdom about how to get along in a rapidly changing world. The Sophists had an interest in learning the how-to (the *arete*) of getting along in life and a skeptical mistrust of absolute knowledge of any kind, whether it be scientific (hot and cold) or moral (good and bad). Everything depended on the given arrangement of atoms, or of given human relationships. The famous Sophist, Protagoras, argued that "the person is the measure of things," meaning that the way I see things is all right for me, while the way you in your circumstance see them is all right for you. Some opinions may work better or worse, but truth is relative and subjective.

For the Sophists, pragmatism had displaced truth claims, and this meant that social law was a matter of social contract—and Sophists interpreted this variously, from contract ideas to "might makes right."

Socrates directly challenged the Sophists' idea that they could teach skill at living *(arete)* and that nothing universal could be said about life, including any universal knowledge or truth claims. According to Socrates, there are words that we use, often unreflectively, to talk about universal qualities: virtue, knowledge, even *arete* (the how-to), for example. If these words have no universal meanings they ought not be used since that only leads to confusion. If they have universal meanings, then we need to ask what such meanings might be. Socrates went about this process by asking people questions until he found examples for various terms. He then would compare these examples of a term to see if a general definition—a common quality, or nexus of qualities—could be generated from them that would account for them. He believed we ought to stop using words for which common qualities could not be found because they are meaningless.

The Sophists, argued Socrates, were either illogical or moral anarchists. If there were a common meaning to the skill of human living *(arete)*, which they taught, then they contradicted their insistence that there were no universal truths. In contrast, if there were no such universal meaning to human *arete*, then individuals should and could do whatever they want to do because that is their own particular nature.

Plato (428–348 B.C.E.) was a student of Socrates and about thirty years old when Socrates drank the cup of hemlock and died. He also lived during the last days of the Peloponnesian War and Sparta's defeat of Athens. The internal political life of Athens was tumultuous. The social fabric of Athens needed to be restored; and Plato tried to show how wisdom and life in community might work for the common good. Thus in his mature years, Plato wrote *The Republic*. He tried to take up Socrates' task against the Sophists, who claimed nothing universal could be said, including ideas, laws, and structures. Plato also attempted to defend the city-state, giving it structure and laying its foundation in a transcending reality.

Plato developed Socrates' idea of universal ideas. What do we mean when we say that something is "good," whether it be a good athletic achievement or a good piece of fruit? Either there was a universal meaning to the word "good," which various people shared, or we literally could not communicate with each other. Plato's answer was that there was an eternal *idea,* or form, of which the earthly form was a real but imperfect example. These ideas, this world of forms, existed outside ourselves, untouched by space or time and forming a coherent vision of reality. People knew the eternal *idea* for something when their senses drove them inward and their soul, which likewise was eternal and once dwelled in the realm of the forms, re-cognized the reality at hand.

Here Plato leaned directly on the Pythagoreans with whom he had lived and from whom he had learned. The soul was eternal and a part of the World Soul, and earthly realities reminded the soul of what it knew but had temporarily forgotten. How the eternal realm of *ideas* and our earthly realm related was a struggle for Plato to explain. Sometimes he used myth and sometimes he used metaphors: a pattern and a constructed model, or a play written by an author and its particular acting out by actors.

When Plato was sixty years old, a young man from northern Greece, whose father was the physician to Philip of Macedon, came to study with him. For the next twenty years, Aristotle (384–322 B.C.E.) remained at the Academy, leaving after the death of Plato. In 343 B.C.E. Philip of Macedon appointed him tutor to the young Alexander the Great. Aristotle eventually returned to Athens, founding there a famous school (the Lyceum) one of whose specialties became biology. Beginning and ending with the concrete entity that one observed was characteristic for Aristotle, and his philosophy always seems most at home when applied to biological models. Aristotle's curiosity for, and love of, the created world also made him deeply suspicious of Plato's ideas about an eternal realm of forms. If true universals existed somewhere, where was that? Metaphor and myth were unsuitable approaches for finding the best answer. In a similar way, Aristotle rejected the idea that numbers constituted reality and were anything other than abstractions that the mind made from concrete things. This also represented a turn from Plato whose time with the Pythagoreans had convinced him that numbers and ratios were of the very structure of the cosmos.

But without Plato's universals, how could one explain the sensible ordering and development of creation? Why didn't ducks hatch from eggs laid by chickens? Why didn't pine trees grow from acorns? Aristotle's simple answer was that the universal—the Form—particular to every entity was inherently a part of that entity. It received this universal from that which was its biological parent. The universal of a chicken was given to the egg from the parents. The universal of an oak tree was likewise given to an acorn from an adult oak tree. Given normal conditions the egg or the acorn would eventually develop into a duck or an oak tree as their potential developed.

Aristotle's ideas about universals and potential growth were also applied to human ethical activity. What was the universal to which human beings were aimed so that their potential would develop in a way appropriate to the human species? Since reason was the distinctive human capacity, a life lived according to reason, and aimed at the virtues embodied in the lives of virtuous people, resulted in the happiness that comes from fulfilling one's purpose in life.

Following the deaths of Alexander (323 B.C.E.) and Aristotle (322 B.C.E.), and the shift from the city-state organization *(polis)* to the empire that Alexander had constructed in the political world, two overall trends appeared in philosophy. A brief word about Hellenism, however, might first be helpful. Hellenism refers to the cosmopolitan Greek culture that spread throughout Alexander's empire. While the Hellenistic period strictly ended with the rise of Roman power under Octavian (Emperor Augustus) at the battle of Actium in 31 B.C.E., Hellenism lived on as a cultural force that merged with the many local cultures within Alexander's empire.

The first of the two overall trends of philosophy during the Hellenistic period is that Greek philosophy itself split into various schools that competed to give the most practical philosophy for everyday living. The most notable schools were Skepticism, Epicureanism, and Stoicism.[7]

Second, the city of Alexandria became the cultural center of the new Hellenistic empire. There Greek philosophy, the ancient Greek and Hebrew texts, and philosophies from the East, all converged in religious dialogue and cross-fertilization. The greatest of the Alexandrian thinkers was the Jewish thinker Philo of Alexandria (Philo Judaeus, ca. 10 B.C.E.–50 C.E.) whose synthesis of Greek philosophy and Hebrew texts—a synthesis usually called "classical theism"—became the basis for all Western theology for almost two thousand years.

Skepticism usually is traced to Pyrrho (360 B.C.E.–272 B.C.E.), who was a generation younger than Aristotle. Believing that one should avoid philosophical beliefs in order to find peace, Pyrrho bequeathed this tradition to students but obviously not to writing, since committing such ideas to writing would imply beliefs that ought to be followed. Since thinkers have always argued for all sides of any issue, and argued for a wide variety of views about reality itself, and since people obviously are widely divergent in what they think and perceive, what we think is merely the conventions in which we ourselves have been raised and live. Pyrrho denied that we could objectively know things as they were in themselves. The way to human peace came from not making claims about a reality one could not know. It may well be that Pyrrho was influenced by Indian thought when he traveled to India with the advance of Alexander the Great.

By the early third century B.C.E. Skepticism was taken up by Plato's Academy and argued against the Epicureans and especially the Stoics. As this Academic Skepticism ran its course through the next two centuries, the skeptical approach was taken up outside the Academy. The best known and last in the lineage of these Skeptics was Sextus Empiricus, who lived during the early third century of the common era. Sextus, who was a physician, firmly attacked all speculative systems and took to arguing against all positions. His written works not only give us historical insight into ancient Skepticism but were influential in the Latin West when some of his ideas were published during the sixteenth century.

Throughout the history of Skepticism, Stoicism was a major opponent. Beginning with Zeno the Stoic (ca. 335–263 B.C.E.), Stoicism held that reality was composed of passive matter and active reason, both of which were corporeal. Reason moved throughout all matter organizing reality and giving to each entity its distinctive nature. The human mind participated uniquely in this universal, energizing reason. For the human person this meant that to think correctly was to be grounded in reality itself; indeed, grounded in the divine reality, which is what this universal, enlivening reason was. At the same time, this meant that one was to lead a virtuous life, contributing to the well-being of the reality of which one was a part. The human person thus could become an embodiment of reality itself in which the divine reason organizes all parts for the good of the whole.

Stoicism remained influential well into the second century of the common era, a notable example being the work of the Roman emperor Marcus Aurelius (121–180 C.E.), whose *Meditations* exemplifies most of traditional Stoic teachings. By appealing to the structure of reality itself, and the human ability to mirror that reality through the right exercise in reason, Stoicism provided a way of living amid the tumultuous crumbling of Alexander's empire and the violent rise of the Roman Empire. The Roman philosopher, statesman, writer of tragedies, and Stoic, Seneca (4 B.C.E.–65 C.E.), was a dominant voice of reason under several unbalanced emperors.

The third philosophical school that arose in Hellenism was Epicureanism. Epicurus (341 B.C.E.–270 B.C.E.) argued a position quite the opposite of that held by the Stoics, and thus the particular ongoing controversies between these two schools. Epicurus was influenced by the teachings of the pre-Socratic philosopher Democritus, for whom the basic unit of the universe was the *atomos*—a small, indivisible unit of matter. Atoms were countless in number and associated randomly throughout space. The world as we have it was then produced not by some universal, divine reason but by the random collocation of these atoms. For practical reasons, people organized themselves into societies, and within human societies values such as goodness or justice were mere conventions rather than instantiations of some universal truth. Only pain is evil and avoiding pain is good, and here human beings have continuity with other creatures. Pleasure is the absence of pain and brings with it serenity.

Such views led to a relatively austere life for the Epicureans, but also a life that was less socially conventional. Women, and even slaves, could study at the Garden—the school founded by Epicurus. People could lead simple lives that matched the simple physical desires of creaturehood, avoiding the sufferings that came from mistakenly thinking the world was something that it was not.

Of these three schools that predominated the Hellenistic period Stoicism was most naturally looked to by Christian thinkers in the early centuries of Christianity. The Skeptics' refusal to make claims about the structure of reality was not a good fit for Christians, nor was the atomistic construction of reality that was fundamental to the Epicureans. Stoicism fit Christianity better because of its idea of an embodied and divine-like universal reason that organized and energized the universe. Justin Martyr's interpretation of Jesus as this divine Logos, combined with Platonic ideas of a transcendent God in whose mind were eternal forms, not only rendered John's Gospel and its prologue intelligible, it echoed the widespread early Christian tradition that Jesus was Sophia, God's wisdom incarnate. It also accounted for the seemingly contradictory Christian claims for monotheism *and* Jesus as the divine presence. Further, Justin could situate Christianity within the pagan realm and Jewish realm by showing that the Logos not only planted seeds of truth throughout the pagan world in people such as Socrates, but was also present as God's self-revelation in the Hebrew writings.

Of the philosophical options open to Christian thinkers in the early church, the most influential was just developing when Justin wrote in the middle of the first century of the common era. During the century prior to the common era there was a renewed interest in the classical period of Greek philosophy. The philosophy of Plato was taken up again and blended with Aristotle's idea of a God who was the unaffected, unmoved mover of the cosmos. Out of this eclectic revival of classical thought arose Neoplatonism, a philosophical movement that had profound effect upon Christianity.

By the third century of the common era the Roman world seemed to be passing into irretrievable decay. The economic infrastructure was failing, internal imperial politics and external wars produced political instability, and long dead were the intellectual giants of prior centuries who could help interpret the world. In the fertile, creative environment of Alexandria, however, Neoplatonism arose as a kind of religious philosophy, or we might say philosophical theology, that the theologians of Christianity would embrace. The greatest Alexandrian Neoplatonist was Plotinus (205–270).[8]

Above and beyond all things, said Plotinus, and describable only by negative language in which God was unknowable and ineffable, was the One. The One contemplated itself and in so doing contemplated the Intellect (divine mind) in which existed the metaprinciples or fundamental structures of all reality. The World Soul then proceeded from the Intellect, embodying the structures of the Intellect in matter, and thereby also ensouling itself in the created order that naturally flowed from this threefold spiritual realm.

The world therefore was an overflow or natural emanation from the One, with a hierarchy of being descending from the spiritual realm down through the created realm. Evil came from the entrapment of Soul in matter, yet the world itself was intimately connected with the One through the presence of the Soul as it longed to return to the spiritual realm and mystical union with the One. This means that just as there was a descending movement created through the World Soul there was also an ascending desire of all creation. Plotinus's philosophical theology not only gave religious explanation to the decaying, third-century world, but gave voice to a religious desire for its transcendence through fulfillment of its deepest reality.

The Christian embrace of Neoplatonism was firm and sensible. Once the connection between the Intellect and Jesus as God's Word (Logos) was made— and a good conceptual fit it was, considering the Gospel of John—everything else fell into place. The Alexandrian theologian Origen (185–254) developed an influential form of Neoplatonic Christianity. In the East he influenced all the great defenders of orthodoxy, from Athanasius (293–273) through the great Cappadocian thinkers (Basil the Great [329–379], Gregory of Nazianzus [330–389], and Gregory of Nyssa [335–394]). However, this Neoplatonism was to have its greatest effect on the West through its effect on the greatest theologian of the ancient church, Augustine of Hippo (354–430), who was born in North Africa one century after Origen's death.[9]

Augustine's early life and education was in Thagaste and Carthage. He was a bright student and young scholar, and he built a career teaching rhetoric, eventually landing an important job in Milan teaching under imperial appointment there. From an early age Augustine was interested in the problem of evil and its connection both to a divine reality and to the human heart. Early in his life Manichaeism provided a good and arguable answer to evil. According to the teachings of Mani (216–274), the good human spirit could be released from its imprisonment in evil matter through a life of renunciation and purification. Augustine became disenchanted with Manichaeism, however, because its answer to the problem of evil seemed to have shallow views of both God and the human heart. In a system where the good was conceived as Light, the divine reality was merely passive in the face of evil. At the same time, Manichaeism failed to talk about conscience and how the heart participated in evil through its own longing. Augustine found a far better home in Neoplatonism.

For Augustine the source of moral evil was the decision by Adam, whose soul already tended to internal disorder, to chose freely against God. Adam's choice then sent the human person into further internal disorder of which temptation was one of the consequences. On the divine side of the divine-human relationship God was the active force for good, not some mere Manichaen "light" passive in the face of evil. On the human side, the human heart knew both guilt for human sin that caused moral evil and the inevitable and incessant longing for its one true goal of mystical union with God.

Along with this Neoplatonic cosmology and religion, Augustine embraced and passed on a fundamentally Platonic theory of knowing (epistemology). For Augustine there are two connected realms, one heavenly, one earthly. The heavenly realm contains the "universals"—those eternal forms that shape everything—while the earthly realm has only shadowy approximation of these forms. We know something only when our senses turn to the memory and a universal form is recognized by our mind. For Augustine, the way that the mind knows these eternal forms, and thus could know anything, is because the Word (Christ)—the second person of the Trinity—illumines the mind with the eternal forms that exist in God's mind. Thus all knowledge, not just religious knowledge, comes from divine illumination.

THE WEST FROM AUGUSTINE THROUGH THE PROTESTANT REFORMATION

Not long after the death of Augustine, the Latin West moved from what is known as the period of the church fathers (the patristic era) into the medieval period. Medieval Europe typically is divided into three periods. The early Middle Ages extended roughly from the fall of Rome (476) to the split between the Western Latin church and the Eastern Greek church (1054). The high Middle Ages then continued through the middle of the fourteenth century, sometimes dated to 1309, which was the year that the papacy moved from Rome to Avignon, France. The late medieval period is usually thought to run until the Renaissance and Italian humanism of the fourteenth century, or to the opening European encroachment of the Americas by Columbus in 1492, or to the clear split between the Roman Catholic church and the newly emerged Protestant churches in the middle of the sixteenth century.

The early Middle Ages were a time of peasants, soldiers, and feudalism amid a chaotic, underdeveloped European landscape. Benedictine monasteries particularly carried on the religious and cultural inheritance of the patristic era. The most noted thinker of this period was the Roman aristocrat and statesman Boethius (480–525), who translated into Latin the works of Aristotle and Porphyry (232–305), the great student of Plotinus. During the high Middle Ages the seat of learning in the Latin West moved from the monasteries to the urban schools where scholarship suddenly took on new methods of logic and dialectic, and moved to new depths and breadths of thinking. The standard name for this intellectual movement is Scholasticism and the eleventh century saw the birth of two of the most famous early thinkers of the high Middle Ages, Anselm of Canterbury (1033–1109) and Peter Abelard (1079–1142).[10]

Anselm is best known for the development of two important ideas, the atonement of Christ and the so-called ontological proof for the existence of God. In his proof for God's existence, Anselm made an important intellectual discovery. He argued that if we mean by the word God "that than which nothing greater can be conceived," then we cannot conceive of this entity in any way other than existing. Anselm's argument is that the concept of "God" has a peculiar logic to it: to be able to conceive *what* God is is to be able to know *that* God is. The *idea* of God, alone among ideas, cannot fail to be realized in existence.

Anselm's argument basically goes like this. Were God to exist and God's nonexistence able to be conceived, then God's existence would be contingent. Contingent existence—that something might or might not have come to be—is the type of existence that creatures exhibit. Such existence is dependent on this or that particular cause, or chance, and some other actuality might have been realized instead. If God's existence were of this contingent type then God would be dependent upon some cause, which then would be greater than God. Thus if God is "that than which nothing greater can be conceived" God's existence cannot be contingent but must be necessary. God necessarily exists.

Whether Anselm was ultimately successful in his particular ontological argument cannot occupy us here. The important point to learn, which Anselm discovered, is that the discussion of God's existence is properly a discussion about the character of the ideas as such, not a discussion about empirical realities such as the beauty of creation or the existence of evil. Anselm's argument is an argument that applies to any conceivable reality, not an argument that depends on this or that particular creation. The category of strictly necessary ideas, which cannot fail to apply to any conceivable state of affairs, becomes important when the question is asked, Can anything be said that transcends particular contexts of time and place?

In the Middle Ages Peter Abelard raised to new heights a different type of argument, which becomes important for this book. As a young French philosopher and student of logic, Abelard looked at the ancient Greek discussion about whether universals existed. He developed a middle ground between two of his teachers, Roscelin (1050–1125) and William of Champeaux (1070–1121). Attacking the position of Boethius, Roscelin had argued that universals were mere words and had no reality other than being the puff of wind from one's mouth. This position was called nominalism because a universal was a mere name (*nomen* in Latin) and no reality as such. By contrast, William of Champeaux was a "realist" who defended the Platonic tradition of Boethius with his own line of arguments. As teacher at the cathedral school of Notre Dame, and later its head, William argued that universals had an existence of their own. All human beings, for instance, possess the substance "humanity" and differ from each other in their accidental qualities such as height, weight, or hair color.

Abelard applied his relentless logic to the issue and developed what we might call a philosophy of language. A universal is not a reality that exists somewhere, argued Abelard, but instead refers to a category of words such as common nouns like "horse." This word can be applied to all individual horses whereas the word "Trigger" is a proper noun and can be applied only to the horse that Roy Rogers rode. Yet these universals have meaning attached to them and are not mere puffs of wind able to be used interchangeably. We cannot say that "horse is a cowboy." The meaning for these universals comes from their describing common likenesses between things, and they are formed when we concentrate on one aspect of something and disregard the other aspects.

A century later Thomas Aquinas (1225–1274) altered the shape of Western theology when he elegantly merged the Neoplatonic theology of Augustine with newly found writings of Aristotle.[11] Among many issues that Aquinas took up in new and creative ways was how we know something, and this discussion included the concept of universals. For Aquinas universals existed in three ways. A universal existed in the mind of God prior to a given concrete entity as part of the divine activity of contemplating all things. It then existed in that entity itself, as an aspect of its concrete reality. And third, it existed in the human mind, which abstracted it from its concrete reality. Here Aquinas borrowed from Aristotle and developed a theory of how we know that differed from Augustine's traditional teaching.

Thomas's theory of knowledge began with the concrete entity and ended with it, but in the process the intellect passed through three steps. First, there was sensation in which the senses gathered data and passed this data to the "passive intellect," the mind at rest. This data was a fuzzy picture of individual things—phantasms—which nevertheless had some identifiable features. Second, the mind itself took an active part and abstracted out from these phantasms the universal aspects that it found in the particular images it received. Third, the mind took this abstracted universal ("intelligible species," as Aquinas called it), and applied it to the particular object at hand. At that moment someone knew someone or thing.

A century later much of the method and content of Thomas's theology was questioned by the English theologian William of Ockham (1285–1347), whose approach can be characterized by his famous dictum that "plurality should not be posited without necessity": in other words, fewer words and concepts are preferable to more, and simpler explanations are preferable to more complex.[12] And so, when it came to how one knows Ockham rejected both the theories of Augustine and Aquinas, which depended on universals that really existed in God's mind. On the most basic level, argued Ockham, we know because we directly experience particular things. Others can experience these things also. On the more complicated level, said Ockham, we can remember our experiences of particular things so that we know them even though our senses do not now experience them. From our experiences of concrete things, and from our memories, we then abstract out universal ideas that allow us to think and communicate.

Another area where Ockham challenged older traditions was in his concept of God. For Ockham God was primarily the covenant-making God who, through gracious will, promised to be the God of this natural order and of God's people. God no longer was fundamentally the Unmoved Mover who at a distance knew and caused all that was. This also meant that the world itself was no longer conceived as imperfect embodiments of universal forms in the divine mind. The world was fully real. This was God's world and the people of Earth were God's contracted partners here on Earth. This naturally led to valuing human experience; valuing experimentation, trial and error, and the rudiments of modern science; and viewing social history as just that, social history rather than a history of continual divine intervention. Experienced reality became the basis for making judgments.

In contrast to this sympathetic view of Ockham's theology, which was advanced with force by the Dutch Reformation scholar Heiko Oberman, stands an older view of Ockham, which argues that his logic and skepticism contributed to the decline of Western theology and culture.[13] The significant voice for this view was the Roman Catholic scholar Etiénne Gilson. Here it was argued that Thomas Aquinas produced a great synthesis that combined nature and grace, reason and revelation, and state and church.[14] Under the influence of Ockham and his followers (late medieval nominalism), this theological vision of a unified reality gradually gave way to speculative works that reduced theology to subtleties and incessant logic. This speculative theology was an important contributor to the Western split into religious and secular cultures: the one looking to revelation and religion for what was true; the other looking to reason, philosophy, and science for what was true. However much this view has needed correction, there remains much that is insightful.

Taken to its logical conclusion Ockham's empiricism, and his denial that universals were anything other than concepts abstracted from experience, could lead to denying a wide range of traditional Christian doctrines such as the existence of God or the Trinity. Using Ockham's approach to reflect on more ordinary human experiences could deny the basic idea of cause and effect: all we really know is that one thing follows another, and so we say that one is the cause and the other is the effect. Followers of Ockham at the University of Paris who taught in the middle of the fourteenth century, such as John of Mirecourt and especially Nicholas of Autrecourt, developed such ideas in their own ways. Nicholas, for example, denied causality as such. Practically speaking we may observe and comment that X causes Y, but this sureness lasts only as long as sensory experience lasts.

What made coherence real in the world, and coherence between the world and our knowledge, was that God made it be so not that we can know such coherence in and of itself. This would imply that absent the idea of an omnipotent God, what would remain would be a skepticism based in experience and logic. Little wonder that Ockham would influence later British empirical thinkers or that much later Nicholas would be thought of as the David Hume (1711–1776) of the late medieval period.

Ockham's challenge to the late medieval church was perhaps nowhere stronger than his challenge to the concept of church. Without the idea that universals were the most real entities, one no longer had to conceive of the church as an (imperfect) incarnation of a reality existing in the mind of God and literally mediating divine grace. Instead the church was the body of the faithful who pledged themselves together as the people with whom God has covenanted. The pope thus was an administrator of this faithful body. The church could err, as could the pope, as could church councils. What was needed, said Ockham, was a reading of Scripture with proper humility, and use of reason that was faithful to God.

The young Luther studied at the University of Erfurt, which had chosen for this "new way" of doing theology.[15] Luther not only spoke about Ockham as his "master," but he felt free to challenge Ockham's teachings all the while acknowledging that he had absorbed them. Little debate among scholars exists here. In what ways late medieval nominalism influenced Luther's own theology, and merged with other influences such as Scripture, humanism, and mysticism, remains much debated. However, when Luther took his Reformation stand on Scripture (because it preached God's grace—"Christ crucified") and experience (because there we experience this same God through faith), he was a nominalist.[16] Thus, Luther's call to "Scripture alone" *(sola scriptura)* was never meant to be a call to biblical fundamentalism. Rather, the Scripture principle was, on the one hand, a priority of Scripture over other religious authorities, such as creeds, councils, or popes. On the other hand, "Scripture alone" was expressly linked to experience by the principle of "by grace alone, by faith alone" *(sola gratia, sola fide)*. As the greatest Reformation historian of the second half of the twentieth century aptly commented about Luther, "At the end of the road to becoming a reformer stood the discovery that the Scriptures confirmed what he had sensed, sought, and seen with increasing accuracy by living with the God of the Scriptures."[17]

Luther's great theological disciple, John Calvin (1509–1564), had much the same approach.[18] For Calvin, theology was to be done within the limits of piety, that sure and certain, heart-felt knowledge that God was the "source of all goodness" and our "gracious 'Father.'" Careful study has shown that for Calvin knowledge of God came not just from Scripture but also from the experience of faith in the God that Scripture proclaimed. Likewise the doctrine of God, for Calvin, was not merely to be found in his theological writings on God, but also in those that concern human faith in God.

MYSTICISM, EXPERIENCE, AND THE PROTESTANT REFORMATION

The medieval period had seen a blossoming of mysticism. Not unlike the desert monks of the fourth century who sought a purer form of Christianity than the institutional church provided, the medieval mystics turned inward to seek the real truth of Christianity.[19] What the dogmaticians could only write about, the mystics actually sought and sometimes experienced. Broadly speaking medieval mysticism was of two types. One focused on God and through rigorous study and meditation the mystic discovered that a part of the human soul itself was connected to God. A second type of mysticism, which became increasingly popular in the fifteenth century, focused on Christ. Here the mystic conformed the human will to that of Christ's will. Since Christ had conformed his will to that of God's, the mystic whose will followed Christ was literally in touch with the divine will and lived according to it.

Luther himself thought well of the theology of the late medieval mystic Johannes Tauler (ca. 1300–1361), who was a student of the famous (theocentric) mystic Meister Eckhart (ca. 1260–ca. 1327). Luther also oversaw the publication of a fourteenth-century, German mystical treatise called "German Theology," which he said had taught him more about God, Christ, and humankind than anything other than Augustine and the Bible. From these mystical sources Luther drew on the experience of both misery and ecstasy, knowing both one's own broken, sinful condition that resists God, as well as the joy that comes with the experience of God's liberating grace. Luther's own spiritual mentor, and vicar general of the Augustinian Observant congregation, Johannes von Staupitz (1468–1524), can be added to this influence of mysticism. Staupitz had written about Christ taking upon himself our guilt, and we taking upon ourselves divine righteousness and experiencing a piece of eternal life. So, also, in Luther's famous essay "The Freedom of a Christian." Luther wrote in traditional, mystical language about the Christian and Christ being as the bride and the bridegroom who exchange property with each other. Christ takes on our sin and misery, we take on Christ's righteousness and life.[20]

Several important scholars have suggested that this German mystical tradition was influential on Luther and on the Protestant Reformation in Germany.[21] Other scholars have pointed to the differences between Luther and the mystical traditions that preceded him.[22] The principle difference hinges on this: that the medieval tradition conceived, in its Platonic way, that only like can know like. In order for a person to have a mystical experience of God, some part of that person (a part of the soul, or a conformity of the will) must first be like God. Here Luther expressly turned the tradition on its head. Precisely in the human distance from God, as a sinner, the experience of God was known; and it was known through God's Word, which awakened our dormant faith. Faith grasped God's grace and in so doing knew both the misery and distance from God, and knew the ecstasy and closeness of God. In the moment of faith, we could be like Adam and Eve in paradise, wrote Luther in "The Freedom of a Christian."[23]

Recent study has also shown the influence of (christocentric) mysticism on John Calvin (1509–1564). Not only was Calvin's education at the Collège de Montaigu done in an ethos that looked back to Thomas à Kempis (1379–1471), who wrote the influential devotional book *The Imitation of Christ,* but Calvin's sacramental theology was influenced by the mysticism of Bernard of Clairvaux (1090–1153). Bernard had described the mystical union of the soul and Christ as that between bride and bridegroom. According to Calvin, in the sacraments the Christian could have mystical union with Christ through the power of the Holy Spirit working in human faith and the divine Word. Calvin described this union as an engrafting into Christ more intimate than that between the human body and its head. Calvin also called this engrafting a sacred marriage with Christ, or a wondrous communion with Christ, or mystical union with Christ.[24]

Study has also shown that the mystical tradition was influential on the Reformation's more radical leaders such as Thomas Müntzer (d. 1525), Hans Hut (d. 1527), Hans Denck (ca. 1500–1527), Sebastian Franck (ca. 1499–ca. 1542), Sebastian Castellio (1515–1563), and Valentin Weigel (1533–1588).[25] Here mysticism functioned as an authority that authorized Scripture, and all other authorities for that matter, since it was the internal experience of God that allowed one to see what was true about God in the external authority. This ultimate relationship thus naturally carried a relativizing view toward all penultimate religious institutions.

HUMANISM AND THE PROTESTANT REFORMATION

There was another historical influence that valued human experience, the Renaissance.[26] As the late Middle Ages came to a close, the term "Renaissance" has typically been given to a period in which the classical learning of Greece and Rome was rediscovered, feudalism waned, the printing press was invented, and scientists began to understand that the earth as well as other planets revolved around the sun.

The movement known as humanism was part of the Renaissance, and the usual interpretation is that the modern mind was first birthed in this period. As the late medieval church and the Holy Roman Empire no longer provided conditions for creative, cultural growth, thinkers in Italy turned to the human person and the human spirit as a source for study. Medieval Christian culture, with its negative view of human nature and centuries of dogma to buttress that view, finally was shrugged off. The human person and the dignity, creativity, and critical ability of the person were now emphasized. The hegemony of the medieval synthesis was giving way to moral autonomy and the modern, secular mind.

Quite an opposite view of Italian humanism has also been proposed. This school of thought argues that Italian humanism had as its adversaries not the medieval church, with its worldview, which it imposed and interpreted to secular and religious society. Rather, Renaissance humanism championed the older, Augustinian traditions of the church, especially as renewed by Albertus Magnus (1200–1280) and his student Thomas Aquinas. The opponents were late medieval thinkers who pushed Aristotle and science, paganizing the older Latin-Catholic tradition.

Given a seemingly irreconcilable gulf between these two positions, and given the seemingly protean character of Renaissance humanism, many scholars have accepted a third view on humanism. Rather than signifying a commitment to a particular philosophical position, humanism was a movement that focused on rhetoric and good scholarship, and in so doing tapped into a long-standing Western tradition that reached back to the Greeks. What were important were classical studies in Greek and Latin, based on historical and linguistic principles.

These are not the only views on Renaissance humanism, to be sure. For instance, one would also have to discuss the hotly contested view of humanism as fundamentally part of Italian politics during the start of the fifteenth century. Still, the three main views on humanism—the onset of modernity, the defense of medieval Christian culture and values, a rhetorical phase of Western culture—not unfairly summarize the state of scholarship on this late medieval phenomenon. How did this movement affect the Protestant Reformation? This question also is widely debated.

At the University of Erfurt, where Luther studied, humanism and the theology of the medieval period (so called "scholastic" theology) existed harmoniously. Luther learned Hebrew at Erfurt and later was taught Greek by Philipp Melanchthon (1497–1560). His ease with the classical languages, and his ability to criticize the Latin Bible of the medieval church (the Vulgate), owe to his education at Erfurt. The student Luther was remembered as a lover of classical literature.

At the University of Wittenberg, where Luther took over the chair of biblical theology, which had been held by Staupitz, the older theology typified by that of the Dominican Thomas Aquinas or the Franciscan Duns Scotus (ca. 1266–1308) was dominant.[27] The effect of humanism was present but quietly conservative. This changed from 1518 onward when Luther and Melanchthon began to reform the curriculum there. Two years later the curriculum was quite different with the ancient languages (Hebrew and Greek) given new status. Old methods of doing theology and studying Aristotle were replaced by more historical approaches and lectures on classical authors.

The effect of humanism on other Reformers is also quite well known. Zwingli was trained in humanist studies and held Erasmus in great respect. Although the relationship between Zwingli's humanist background and his Reformation turn is much discussed, there can be little doubt that humanism left a major effect on Zwingli's approach to theology.[28]

Calvin also began as a humanist scholar.[29] With his first book on Seneca's treatise *On Mercy*, Calvin was headed toward a career as a noted French Christian humanist. In his major work, *The Institutes of the Christian Religion*, Calvin carefully argued in Book One that knowledge of God has always been present to all people and cultures. Among other things, this explains why some cultures are more advanced than others and why certain people are better than others. The problem was that people have always taken credit for such goodness without understanding that God was the source of all goodness whatsoever. By contrast, this meant that Calvin understood sin as fundamentally a religious mistake in which people failed to acknowledge God and acknowledged themselves instead. This also explains why Calvin's metaphor for Scripture was that of "spectacles." Scripture allowed people to see that God was already a part of their lives but they had not realized it because they could not see with the clarity they needed.

One of the world's most noted Renaissance scholars has even argued that the Protestant Reformation carried on the course of humanism, and that Reformation preaching embodied the Renaissance ideals.[30] This may be an exaggeration, but it surely is an exaggeration in the direction of the truth. The most sensible explanation is that where the late medieval scholars used intellectual tools from Aristotle to explain the truth of Christianity as fully as possible, the Protestant Reformers used the tools of Renaissance humanism.[31]

FROM THE PROTESTANT REFORMATION THROUGH THE ENLIGHTENMENT

Why has the discussion spent so much time on the Protestant Reformation? Students of philosophy and Christian theologians who are not Protestant might rightly wonder. There are a variety of views on the Protestant Reformation.[32]

Some scholars have seen the Protestant Reformation as essentially a political event. Where Protestantism was dominant, secular rulers were able to take back power from the church insofar as the church had been organizing secular society. Or from another perspective, modern revolutionary movements find their origin in the ability of people to risk all they have for an ideal, such as the Calvinists in France or the Puritans in England.

The work of the sociologist Max Weber points to another view of the Reformation. It was an unintended revolution, Weber argued.[33] By providing a means for people to relieve their anxiety about their religious status through hard work, Protestantism paved the way for modern capitalism. This social development then promoted a view that looked back and made more of the Protestant Reformation than it really was.

On an even less positive view of the Protestant Reformation, a variety of scholars have seen the Protestant Reformation as a step backward, accidentally producing violence and authoritarianism. Some have argued that in sixteenth-century Germany the nascent forms of decentralized democracy that the plague had produced were overcome by German aristocracy as they appealed to Luther's Two Kingdoms idea. The church is given by God to rule over people's spiritual lives; rulers are given by God to give order to civil society. Other thinkers have argued that Protestantism looked back to old worldviews and stood in the way of modern science and learning. Still others have argued that once traditional religion was removed by Protestants without a suitable replacement, magic and witchcraft increased. The witch holocausts were a result of Protestantism.

Many historians think of the Protestant Reformation as producing minor local adjustment to religious views. On the one hand, civil magistrates tended to work with forms of Protestantism that fostered their own agendas. On the other hand, the reforming religious forces were swallowed up in the larger social, political, and economic forces at work in the society.[34]

On the other hand, some scholars see the Protestant Reformation as the single most important event of the sixteenth century—a view, say these scholars, with which the people of the sixteenth century would have agreed. Picking up a theme from Renaissance humanism, as well as from late medieval nominalism, Protestantism insisted that each and every individual be convinced in his or her own heart of that which was true. This inward appeal to human experience was balanced by the outward appeal to Scripture because Scripture told us about

Christ. No wonder then that Protestant ideas influenced and were argued over by the common person in the sixteenth century. On this view, Protestantism continued the critical advance of humanism, and demanded that people critically reflect on, and personally appropriate religious ideas. In so doing, Protestantism help provide a link between the earlier humanist movement and the Enlightenment that began at the end of sixteenth century classical Protestantism.[35]

The term Enlightenment refers to the European intellectual and cultural movement in the seventeenth and eighteenth centuries whose principle theme might be summed by the sentence, borrowed from Immanuel Kant (1724–1804), "Have the courage to think for yourself." Some scholars use the term Age of Reason for both centuries, reserving the term Enlightenment for the more wide-spread cultural effects of this movement in the eighteenth century. The Enlightenment is typically described as a movement committed to critical reflection on the human arts such as philosophy, science, politics, religion, and art. Its aim was to leave behind the authoritarianism of the late medieval period, strangely echoed in the sixteenth-century movement known as Protestant orthodoxy.[36]

A full defense of the Enlightenment, giving a fair appraisal of its strengths and weaknesses, can hardly be done here. A few sensible observations and comments, however, can be made. First, as odd as it may sound, given the near universal application of the term, the Age of Reason may not be the most appropriate description of the Enlightenment. René Descartes (1596–1650) is typically considered the first great "rationalist" of the Enlightenment.[37] He worked by deriving principles which themselves had been derived from other well-reasoned principles and he was a noted mathematician. And yet it must also be noted that Descartes's fundamental philosophical principle, the so-called *cogito* (*Cogito ergo sum*—"I think therefore I am"), was itself not rationally derived. Furthermore, as the *cogito* illustrates, Descartes prescinded from discussing the structure of reality as such, focusing instead on the mind's ability to establish the existence of the self and then to grasp the essential qualities of the material world. This basic approach of being rational up to a point and then assuming an external world that we cannot know in itself set a framework for the great modern thinkers.

Gottfried Wilhelm Leibniz (1646–1716) was an exception here.[38] A wide-ranging thinker, Leibniz worked avidly on technical devices such as pumps and carriages; he observed both the heavens and the earth (sometimes being counted among the inventors of geology as a result); and wrote not just of philosophy but also of history. What set Leibniz apart from most other Enlightenment thinkers, however, was that he was keenly interested in the very structure of reality itself, positing that reality consisted of "monads" that were the basic units capable of perception. Some realities were aggregates in which these monads existed together without a central perception, like a rock; other realities were compound individuals in which a "dominant monad" gave all the monads unity of perception and purpose.

Other than Leibniz, who applied reason to the issue of reality itself, the Enlightenment ushered in not an "age of reason" as such but an age of reasoned criticism. No longer taking the authority of the church to be the rule, Enlightenment thinkers worked from history and observation of nature and self.

Descartes and Leibniz are usually compared and contrasted with thinkers given the description "empiricist." John Locke (1632–1704) carried on that practical, critical, experience-based mode of thinking we already have seen in the late medieval nominalist William of Ockham.[39] Locke was a physician with Aristotle-like devotion to that which is observable—recall that Aristotle's father was a physician. Locke believed that all knowledge came from experience. From our senses come sensations, and from thinking about these sensations we derive the more technical ideas that govern our lives.

Just as we saw Ockham's insistence upon experience and reflection evolving into the more skeptical reflection on experience by Nicholas of Autrecourt, so too Locke's thought eventually evolved into the great empirical skepticism of David Hume.[40] Hume was well-read in the ancient Greek thinkers—this was a general trademark of the Enlightenment thinkers—and he was an heir to the skepticism of Pyrrho and Sextus Empiricus, whose thought had directly influenced a forerunner of the Enlightenment, Michel Montaigne (1533–1592). Basic human assumptions, argued Hume, simply cannot be proved by reason. If all we know we know by sense experience, all that we truly know is our experience. Is there really a world "out there"? Does one thing cause another, even as simply as one ball causing another to move? What we really know, said Hume, is that the mind has developed certain habits and we feel compelled to view things a certain way. We say that one ball caused another to move because we have become habituated to a certain sequence of events. The repeated force of nature overcomes an empirical skepticism that otherwise knows better. At the end of the day, this skepticism finds relief merely in the experiences that one has and the common sense assumption that there is reality out there.

If Descartes is often named as the first of the great Enlightenment thinkers, Immanuel Kant is named as the great thinker at the end of this period.[41] Keenly interested in answering the skepticism of Hume, Kant began by arguing that what we know we know from experience. Since experience limits our knowledge we cannot know anything in and of itself. What we have are sensations from which we derive knowledge by the application of organizing concepts (such as "substance") and intuitions (such as "time and space") that are givens in the mind. Kant defeated the skepticism of Hume by showing that the basic skeptical approach is not relevant. Experience based on sensations and organized into a world by universal structures and intuitions that necessarily existed in the mind bypass the question whether the "real world" matches our sensory experience.

Both Hume and Kant agreed that day in and day out one just assumed a world "out there." That was the ordinary way that people lived. When science and philosophy turned to examine that world they discovered rules by which the world might work, and such organizing rules were open to public discussion. From Descartes through Locke, through Hume and Kant, no great Enlightenment thinker other than Leibniz showed interest in rationally describing the structure of reality as such. The Enlightenment, with which modernity began, was not so much the "age of reason," rationally probing the depths of reality, as it was the public court of criticism for the practical improvement of the world. There was no such thing as an inherent external authority, and all claims sought validity through some open appeal to human history and experience. No wonder that the noted intellectual historian Peter Gay used Voltaire's *Candide* as the epitome of the modern project. Leibniz, who rationally described the structure of reality, was spoofed ("Dr. Pangloss"), while Candide was held up as the model of one who learned by living and experiencing the world as it was given. Summarizing the end of *Candide,* Gay noted that for Voltaire

> only Pangloss is incurable: the madness of metaphysics is too deeply ingrained to be exorcised by the realities around him, or by his own sufferings. But to his involved logical chains of argument in behalf of optimism, Candide opposes the brief, wise sentence, "That's well said, but we must cultivate our garden." Here, in that concluding sentence to the tale, Voltaire has fused the lessons of ancient philosophy into a prescription. . . . It is the task of philosophy to discover, as the Stoics had long ago, what is within our power and what is beyond it. *Candide* is thus a morality tale in the most concrete sense possible: it teaches, by example, the supremacy of realistic moral thinking.[42]

PHILOSOPHY IN THE NINETEENTH AND TWENTIETH CENTURIES

Nineteenth Century Philosophy

If during the Enlightenment thinkers made open, critical appeal to experience and reason for the improvement of humankind, the nineteenth century saw two general trends. First, we find the so-called German idealists such as Johann Gottlieb Fichte (1762–1814), Georg Wilhelm Friedrich Hegel (1770–1831), and Friedrich Wilhelm Joseph Schelling (1775–1854), all of whose philosophy was interested in metaphysics and began by turning to the human self. Religious in its outlook, the work of these thinkers suggests that reality is unified, and that the world and the human self have the character of purpose and moral will.[43]

Fichte was born in Saxony, the eldest child in a family of ribbon weavers. His early education was done at the home of a local pastor, but his academic abilities eventually led him to the universities of Jena and Leipzig. The young Fichte was influenced by the writings of Kant, and because of a printing error his first essay, on religious revelation, was mistakenly thought to be have been authored by Kant. This early critical success helped him secure a teaching position in philosophy at the University of Jena where he taught and wrote until 1799. In this highly productive period, Fichte concentrated on revising Kant's philosophical project. From 1799 onward he lived primarily in Berlin, serving late in life as the rector of the University of Berlin. While continuing his philosophical and political writings during this period, Fichte also wrote in near mystical fashion about religion. Our subjective, finite lives are aimed at knowing and loving God, the infinite I, who transcends the differentiation between subject and object.

Schelling was born in Swabia, his father was a Lutheran pastor and professor of Old Testament. Schelling entered the Protestant seminary at Tübingen at the unusual age of 15, where he was friends with Hegel and the German poet Johann Christian Friedrich Hölderlin (1770–1843). An admirer of Ficthe, Schelling joined him at Jena in 1798 where, at the age of 23, he was appointed professor of philosophy. After five years teaching at Jena, Schelling taught at Würzberg, later also at Erlangen and Munich. He eventually accepted an appointment at the University of Berlin in 1841. The time at Würzberg and Munich was important for Schelling because it put him back in touch with some of the mystical traditions of the Western church, including Meister Eckhart (1260–1320) and Jacob Boehme (1575–1624). Schelling came to argue that from the very ground of God's being came the desire for selfhood that gave rise to a process in which world, creatures, and God were in free and creative relationship. Schelling later worked on, but never finished, an elaborate system that described God's creative coming to be in history, religion, and Jesus Christ.

The third German thinker of this period who has influenced modern theology was Hegel who was born in Stuttgart, the oldest of three children whose father was a government official. His early education was aimed at the ministry, and he studied at the Protestant seminary connected to the University of Tübingen where he became friends with Schelling and Hölderlin. His first years after graduation were spent as a tutor, but in 1801 he joined Schelling at the University of Jena. He was appointed to the University of Heidelberg in 1816 and then accepted the chair in philosophy at the University of Berlin in 1818.

Hegel was interested in the history and development of philosophy, and he intended his philosophical work to build from the best of those who came before him. A traditional view of Hegel's philosophy has been that, departing from Kant, he undertook a metaphysical project that presented a unified view of reality in which the opposites such as finite and infinite, flesh and spirit, found themselves synthesized in a manner that both distinguished God and world yet held them mutually related. For Hegel, the "Absolute Spirit" becomes realized in the course of human affairs. Hegel's influence can be seen in a number of leading twentieth century theologians, among them both Karl Barth and Paul Tillich (1886–1965).

Second, and in contrast to these thinkers, we find positivist thinkers in England and France, such as August Comte (1798–1857) and John Stuart Mill (1806–1873), who were skeptical of metaphysical enterprises and concentrated instead on that which could be known from the sciences and logic.[44] Comte grew up in a period of social disorganization after the French Revolution. He conceived of "positivism" in which the procedure of scientific rules, based on observable facts, was applied to human organization. Freed from theology and metaphysics, the two stages of the human spirit prior to the positive stage, such an approach would be able to organize society in the most helpful way possible. Comte was interested in the religion of humanity.

John Stuart Mill was the son of a well-known British thinker, James Mill, who educated John in classical studies and strict discipline of thought. A child prodigy—the young Mill easily read Plato by the age of 10, and by the age of 12 read scholastic and Aristotelean logic—John Stuart Mill became the most influential British philosophy of his century. Mill was committed to those facts known by the senses and the rigorously made inferences that led from these facts to complex belief systems. In ethics, Mill reformed the utilitarian principles he had learned from Jeremy Bentham (1748–1832). For Mill happiness not only consisted of seeking pleasure and avoiding pain, but pleasure itself was understood broadly so to include spiritual and aesthetic values. Elected to Parliament in 1865, Mill worked for liberal political causes, including women's rights.

In contrast to the empirical and logical approaches of Comte and Mill, but sharing equally in the disdain for metaphysics, were two other influential thinkers of the nineteenth century, Søren Kierkegaard (1813–1855) and Friedrich Nietzsche (1844–1900).[45] Kierkegaard was the son of a successful Copenhagen businessman whose magnetic yet melancholic personality left a profound impression on Søren. Kierkegaard took a masters in theology and was ordained a Lutheran minister; yet, for a variety of complex, personal reasons, Kierkegaard spent his time writing while living off his inheritance from his father. Kierkegaard rejected the great system of Hegel which he thought dwelt in abstracts while failing to credit the intimate, concrete ways that people faced the ethical possibilities that faced them. In the risky activity of choosing, people became who they were. So too, thought Kierkegaard, Hegel had reduced

Christianity to a historical example of the Absolute Spirit as it moved through history. Gone was any sense that Christianity concerned the risk of faith. Gone too was the incomprehensible mystery that what was eternal had become time-bound.

In Germany Nietzsche came to reject both metaphysics and organized religion. In the place of conventional philosophy and religion, and the view of morality they represented, Nietzsche sought a philosophy that valued human creativity and development, in all their variations. Society would be a place that enhanced such transformation of life. But to aim at such a society philosophy would have to question relentlessly all motives for religion, philosophy, and morality. What are the contexts for the values that a society might hold? Who holds such values and to whose benefit? In his commitment to perspectivism—that all views are perspectival and that there is no single view that encompasses all the others, and in his commitment to unmasking the power relationships behind inherited value systems, Nietzsche was a founding voice for much of twentieth century philosophy.

Twentieth Century Philosophy

Given the Enlightenment's critical questioning for the practical improvement of the human condition, its philosophical turn from the structure of reality to human sensation and thinking, and the strong influence of the nineteenth century's anti-metaphysical thinkers, one should hardly be surprised that philosophy in the twentieth century was dominated by approaches that were nonmetaphysical.

Broadly speaking most of twentieth-century philosophy can be grouped into phenomenology, existentialism, analytic philosophy (logical positivism and linguistic philosophy), and pragmatism. Phenomenology had its start with the German philosopher Edmund Husserl (1859–1939) and took as its starting point for analysis that which is given, the data of consciousness, free from any scientific or metaphysical assumptions. Connected to phenomenology is existentialism, typified by Martin Heidegger (1889–1976) or Jean-Paul Sartre (1905–1980). Here focus was upon the particular individual who continually constitutes herself or himself, at each moment, as that person comes to be either open or closed to life. Logical positivism denied all metaphysical claims and sought instead to build on only those assertions that were logical or that could be verified. A. J. Ayer (1910–1989) has been the most widely known English voice here. Linguistic philosophy turned to language and asked descriptively how it functioned. As Ludwig Wittengenstein (1889–1951) argued, reflection on language, and its usage, held forth the possibility of therapeutically clearing up many of philosophy's so-called problems. In the early twentieth century pragmatism arose as a philosophical movement in America, and it is usually characterized as an approach that valued analysis of actions and their human consequences, rather than abstract theories. While there is some truth in that characterization, it hardly describes adequately the projects of pragmatism's foundational thinkers, Charles Sanders Peirce (1839–1914) and William James (1842–1910).[46]

The son of a Harvard mathematician and scientist, and himself a graduate of Harvard as an undergraduate and then a graduate student in science, Charles Peirce spent his intellectual life on the boundary of science, logic, and philosophy.[47] In thinking about the structure of reality, Peirce conceived of the universe as a symbol. On the analogy of human symbol making the universe is the product of a divine symbol maker. Through this divine creative activity we continually discover new meanings about the universe of which, for Peirce, potentiality and growth are real features.[48] For Peirce

the universe is God's great poem, a living inferential metaboly of symbols. Fragments of its meaning are accessible to the human intellect, most especially to a genuine community of inquirers devoted to discovering that meaning and governed by the principles of a valid scientific method. . . . That method commences with an act of interpretation, a reading of the signs that are presented in human experience, proceeds with the exploration and clarification of that interpretation, and then with its utilization as a rule of living, a habit of action.[49]

James likewise was more than the anti-metaphysical pragmatist he often is characterized to be.[50] A student at the Lawrence Scientific School of Harvard University, as was Peirce, James went on to Harvard Medical School, interrupted by study in science, psychology, and philosophy in Europe. James taught physiology at Harvard College and authored an influential book on psychology. He went on to study and write on philosophy and religion, teaching at Harvard and lecturing in America and Europe.

James advanced numerous ideas that ran counter to the scientific modernism that dominated his intellectual era. According to James, knowing consists of more than our sensations and rational reflections upon them. There is another kind of knowing that connects to a sense, or perception, of something there which is value-laden. The world itself consists not of mind and matter, or merely of matter, but of successive moments—drops of water—that flow one into another, yet discrete with consciousness or sense of what they led from and connected to. God exists within this creative universe, limited in absolute control but unlimited in influence and able to be affected by the world.

Finally there are two thinkers whose views are often thought of as passé since they were two of the few twentieth-century voices concerned with metaphysics:

Henri Bergson (1859–1941) and Alfred North Whitehead. The winner of the Nobel prize for literature in 1927, Bergson was educated at the École Normale Supérieure in Paris.[51] His doctoral dissertation, *Time and Free Will* (1889) was an extended argument that modern thought has "spatialized" time: it is conceived as existing in moments, or units, with neat edges dividing one moment or unit from another. By contrast, argued Bergson, time is lived as duration with the psychic quality of one moment flowing into the next. By his next work, *Matter and Moment* (1896), Bergson argued that reality itself has the quality of duration because it fundamentally consists not of matter but of pulses of energy that also had a psychic quality. They occur one after another but hold together through "memory." Notable twentieth-century physicists and scientists have found in Bergson a prescient forerunner of quantum physics. But more than that, Bergson's ideas overcame some classical Western dualities such as mind-body or spirit-matter. Reality itself was of a single quality.

In his later works, *Creative Evolution* (1907) and *Two Sources of Morality and Religion* (1932), Bergson developed an approach that linked intuition, instinct, and intelligence into an evolution from the animal kingdom to human beings. Within the human species this development continued into religion, first as closed, static, fearful, and tribal, later as open, dynamic, loving, and universalizing.

Whitehead was the son of an Anglican clergyman and studied at Cambridge as a young man.[52] He had a keen interest in mathematics and logic, co-authoring with Bertrand Russell the famous *Principia Mathematica*. Whitehead continued to teach mathematics, and to write on the subject, but gradually his interest turned to physics and mathematics, and then to basic philosophical issues. When in 1924 Harvard University offered him a professorship in philosophy Whitehead accepted the position, effectively moving to his third intellectual career—from mathematician to philosopher of science and then to a philosopher.

Most basically Whitehead conceived of reality as constituted not by substances, such as chairs or tables, but by "event"—enduring patterns of a reality more basic. The fundamental unit that comprises the world is the "occasion of experience" in which a particular event feels the events that have preceded it, and influence it, and integrates these feelings into a new creative moment. In this view, every event that comes to be once was a "subject" creatively integrating the events that influenced it. After the creative coming-to-be of this event, the event then becomes an object for subsequent events. Thus while retaining the Western distinction between subject and object, the dualistic split between the two is overcome. Since all reality is constituted by this creative becoming, Whitehead's thought overturned a series of other Western dualisms such as living spirit versus dead matter, or mind versus body. Whitehead extended his thought into the realm of religion, retaining a transcendence to God while also crediting a concrete, divine immanence in the world.

Some attention has been paid to Peirce and James, and to Bergson and Whitehead, because they stand apart from what otherwise is the development of Western philosophy. First, where Western philosophy since the Enlightenment has generally prescinded from reasoned discussion of reality itself, concentrating instead on issues such as human sensation and knowledge, Peirce, James, Bergson, and Whitehead worked at conceiving the nature of reality as such. But, second, where modern thought led to the dualism of mind versus matter, to dependence on logic and mathematics apart from inner perceptions (as compared to mere physical sensations), to a mechanistic view of the world, and to the domination of nature by humankind, these thinkers overcame the mind versus matter dualism, used reason while crediting perception and feeling, and saw the world as an open-ended adventure in which the human person was literally interwoven.

With the notable exceptions of Peirce, James, Bergson, and Whitehead, twentieth-century philosophy continued the trend since the Enlightenment that eschewed the metaphysical enterprise and turned instead to reflection on questions of *how* one knows and *who it is* that knows. The primary mode for such thought has been the examination of language—the "linguistic turn"—to use the words of the modern philosopher Richard Rorty (b. 1931).

This turn to language can largely be traced to the work of the Swiss linguist Ferdinand de Saussure (1857–1913), who helped found the discipline of semiotics, which looks at how signs work within language and society. Saussure's principles have become widely used in a variety of contexts. Jacques Derrida (b. 1930) carried twentieth-century concerns about particularity and language into postmodernism: language may function to create concrete worlds wherein meaning is found, yet upon closer inspection such world-creating closes off other meanings and suppresses other voices. Jacques Lacan (1901–1981) developed psychoanalytic theory through reflection on language and its role in the unconscious. Roland Barthes (1915–1980) helped extend Saussure's ideas into literary criticism and establish structuralism as a leading movement within postmodernism. The work of Michel Foucault (1926–1984) has shown that even our very concepts are socially conditioned and all too often serve a politically repressive function. In a different trajectory than this continental focus on language was the philosophical efforts of the Austrian born Ludwig Wittgenstein, who studied at Cambridge with the great philosophers Bertrand Russell (1872–1970) and G. E. Moore (1873–1958).

Chapter 3 examines the ways that twentieth-century thought has taken up this linguistic turn and has attempted to work without positing universal assertions about reality. The chapter then takes up the effects that this philosophical direction has had for theological enterprises. A convergence of themes will be suggested: (1) the irreducible diversity of human expression based on particular contexts; (2) the challenge to universal theological assertions and the sociopolitical power that lies behind some traditional concepts; and (3) the denial of, or at least the invalid nature of, claims about reality as such.

NOTES TO CHAPTER TWO

1. Gay, *The Enlightenment*.

2. Alfred North Whitehead, *Science and the Modern World* (New York: Macmillan, 1926), 12–14.

3. David Ray Griffin et al. *Founders of Postmodern Constructive Theology: Peirce, James, Bergson, Whitehead, and Hartshorne* (Albany: State University of New York Press, 1993).

4. Ibid., 32–33.

5. Just to mention two well-known efforts that will be referred to in this chapter, there is Frederick Copleston, *The History of Philosophy* (9 vols.; London: Burns, Oates & Washbourne, 1947–1975); Fuller, *History of Philosophy*.

6. See Jonathan Barnes, ed., *The Cambridge Companion to Aristotle* (Cambridge: Cambridge University Press, 1995); Cornford, *Before and After Socrates;* Fuller, *History of Philosophy,* 1:17–228; G. M. A. Grube, *Plato's Thought* (with new introduction, bibliographic essay, and bibliography by Donald J. Zeyl; Indianapolis: Hackett, 1980); W. K. C. Guthrie, *The Greek Philosophers* (New York: Harper & Row, 1975); A. A. Long, ed., *The Cambridge Companion to Early Greek Philosophy* (Cambridge: Cambridge University Press, 1999); W. D. Ross, *Aristotle* (New York: Barnes & Noble, 1956); Philip Wheelwright, ed., *The Presocratics* (New York: Odyssey, 1966).

7. See Edwyn Bevan, *Stoics and Skeptics* (Oxford: Clarendon, 1913); Fuller, *History of Philosophy,* 1:228–98; A. A. Long, *Hellenistic Philosophy: Stoics, Epicureans, Skeptics* (2d ed.; Berkeley: University of California Press, 1986); A. E. Taylor, *Epicurus* (London: Constable, 1911).

8. See Bréhier, *The Philosophy of Plotinus;* Fuller, *History of Philosophy,* 1:306–61; Gerson, *Plotinus;* Gerson, ed., *The Cambridge Companion to Plotinus*.

9. Gerald Bonner, *St. Augustine of Hippo: Life and Controversies* (London: SCM Press, 1963); Peter Brown, *Augustine of Hippo: A Biography* (Berkeley: University of California Press, 1967); Etienne Gilson, *The Christian Philosophy of Saint Augustine* (trans. L. E. M. Lynch; New York: Octagon, 1960); Eugène Portalié, *A Guide to the Thought of St. Augustine* (trans. Ralph J. Bastian; intro. by Vernon J. Bourke; Chicago: Regnery, 1969); Eleonore Stump and Norman Kretzmann, eds., *The Cambridge Companion to Augustine* (Cambridge: Cambridge University Press, 2001).

10. For Anselm and Abelard, see Frederick Copleston, *A History of Medieval Philosophy* (New York: Harper & Row, 1972), 72–85; Copleston, *A History of Philosophy*, 2:148–51, 156–65; Leif Grane, *Peter Abelard: Philosophy and Christianity in the Middle Ages* (trans. Frederick and Christine Crowley; New York: Harcourt, Brace & World, 1970); Charles Hartshorne, *Anselm's Discovery* (LaSalle, Ill.: Open Court, 1965); Armand A. Maurer, *Medieval Philosophy* (New York: Random House, 1962), 47–70; John McIntyre, *St. Anselm and His Critics* (Edinburgh: Oliver & Boyd, 1954); Paul Vignaux, *Philosophy in the Middle Ages* (trans. E. C. Hall; Westport, Conn.: Greenwood, 1973), 34–59.

11. For Aquinas, see Copleston, History of Philosophy, 2:302–434; idem, History of Medieval Philosophy, 178–98; Etienne Gilson, The Christian Philosophy of St. Thomas Aquinas (trans. L. E. M. Lynch; New York: Random House, 1960); ibid., *Wisdom and Love in St. Thomas Aquinas* (Milwaukee: Marquette University Press, 1951); Norman Kretzmann and Eleonore Stump, eds., *The Cambridge Companion to Aquinas* (Cambridge: Cambridge University Press, 1993); Maurer, *Medieval Philosophy,* 163–91; Vignaux, *Philosophy in the Middle Ages,* 115–29.

12. For Ockham and his followers, see Copleston, A History of Philosophy III:43–152; idem, *History of Medieval Philosophy,* 23–256; Maurer, *Medieval Philosophy,* 265–91; Arthur McGrade, *The Political Thought of William of Ockham* (Cambridge: Cambridge University Press, 1974); Ernest Moody, *The Logic of William of Ockham* (London: Sheed & Ward, 1935); Vignaux, *Philosophy in the Middle Ages,* 15–179. For a review of the revisionist work on Ockham, see William J. Courtney, "Nominalism and Late Medieval Religion," in *The Pursuit of Holiness in Late Medieval and Renaissance Religion* (ed. Charles Trinkhaus and Heiko Oberman; Leiden: E. J. Brill, 1974), 26–58.

13. Heiko Oberman had three significant impacts of Reformation studies: he helped rescue the fourteenth and fifteenth centuries from the view that they were a period of intellectual decline; he charted a new path for understanding the relationship between the Reformation and the late medieval period of which it was a part; and he argued for the social importance and impact of the Reformation on actual social conditions of late medieval Europe. With his book *The Harvest of Medieval Theology* (Cambridge, Mass.: Harvard University Press, 1963) Oberman began a rehabilitation of the fifteenth century by arguing that the century prior to the Protestant Reformation was a creative period of great harvest, not barrenness. In *Forerunners of the Reformation* (New York: Holt, Rinehart & Winston, 1966) Oberman argued that we ought to leave behind the old model of intellectual decline. The fourteenth and fifteenth centuries had diverse reforming trends that eventually, in hindsight, coalesced into both the Protestant Reformation and the so-called Counter Reformation, better conceived as the Catholic Reformation. Among his many other books, also see *The Dawn of the Reformation* (Edinburgh: T & T Clark, 1986), particularly his essay "The Shape of Late Medieval Thought: The Birthpangs of the Modern Era," 18–38.

14. For Gilson's major work see *History of Christian Philosophy in the Middle Ages* (New York: Random House, 1955). Gilson summarizes the main themes in his Richards Lectures at the University of Virginia, in *Reason and Revelation* (New York: Charles Scribner's Sons, 1938). Also see Gordon Leff, *William of Ockham: The Metamorphosis of Scholastic Discourse* (Manchester: Manchester University Press, 1975); idem, *The Dissolution of the Medieval Outlook* (New York: New York University Press, 1976).

15. For an entrance to the biographies and bibliographies on Luther, see John W. Riggs, *Baptism in the Reformed Tradition* (Columbia Series in Reformed Theology; Louisville, Ky.: Westminster John Knox, 2002), 135, nn. 33–34.

16. See Oberman's comments in *Luther,* 120–23.

17. Oberman, *Luther,* 152.

18. For an entrance to Calvin scholarship, see Riggs, *Baptism,* 141–42, nn. 23, 25–26, 28.

19. For an introduction to the issues and scholarship, see Ozment, *The Age of Reform,* 115–34.
20. See Ozment, *The Age of Reform,* 239–44.
21. Ibid., 239–40, nn. 48–53.
22. Ibid., 241–43, esp. 241 n. 57. Also see, Martin Luther, *Luther's Works* (vol. 31; ed. Harold J. Grimm; Philadelphia: Fortress, 1957), 350 (hereafter cited as *LW* with volume and page number).
23. Luther, *LW,* 31:359.
24. See Dennis E. Tamburello, *Union with Christ: John Calvin and the Mysticism of St. Bernard* (Columbia Series in Reformed Theology; Louisville, Ky.: Westminster John Knox, 1984). Calvin can describe the union with Christ using a number of biblical metaphors: God became Emmanuel that divinity and humanity might grow together (*Institutes* 2.12.1); taking our nature including sin and death, giving us his nature, grace and righteousness (*Institutes* 2.12.2–3; 2.16.6); giving us a sacred marriage with Christ (*Institutes* 3.1.3), or a wondrous communion with Christ (*Institutes* 3.2.24), or a mystical union with Christ (*Institutes* 3.11.10).
25. Ozment, *Mysticism and Dissent.*
26. The following summary and division can be found in Donald Weinstein, "In Whose Image and Likeness? Interpretations of Renaissance Humanism," *J H Ideas* 33 (1972): 165–76.
27. On Protestantism and humanism, see Ozment, *The Age of Reform,* 290–317.
28. For a brief discussion of the issues and references to the scholars, see Riggs, *Baptism,* 132 n.4.
29. For the scholarship on Calvin and humanism, see Riggs, *Baptism,* 141–42 n.26.
30. William Bouwsma, "Renaissance and Reformation: An Essay in Their Affinities and Connections," in *Luther and the Dawn of the Modern Era: Papers for the Fourth International Congress for Luther Research* (ed. Heiko Oberman; Leiden: E. J. Brill, 1974), 30.
31. See the comments by Ozment, *The Age of Reform,* 315–16.
32. This summary borrows from Ozment, *Protestants,* 218–19.
33. Max Weber, *The Protestant Ethic and the Spirit of Capitalism* (trans. Talcott Parsons; New York: Charles Scribner's Sons, 1958). Also see Robert W. Green, ed., *Protestantism, Capitalism, and Social Science: The Weber Thesis Controversy* (Lexington, Mass: Heath, 1973).
34. See, for instance, the magisterial study on Strasbourg by Thomas A. Brady, Jr., *Ruling Class, Regime and Reformation at Strasbourg: 1520–1555* (Leiden: E. J. Brill, 1978). For a very different study that in the end makes a similar point, see the careful study of witch-hunts in Scotland by Christina Larner, *Enemies of God: The Witch-hunt in Scotland* (Baltimore: The Johns Hopkins University Press, 1981.)
35. See the comments by Ozment, *The Age of Reform,* 290–317, esp. 316–17; compare the comments by Fuller, *History of Philosophy,* 2:22.
36. Three overall observations should be made. First, there was great diversity within the Enlightenment. For example, the Enlightenment was part of a relatively peaceful development in England and Germany, but was connected to sometimes violent political events in France. There were also diverse areas for reform. For some thinkers the important issues concerned philosophy and science. For others the concern was art and aesthetic theory. Still others

concentrated on economic theory. The degree of reform also varied between Enlightenment thinkers. Descartes and Locke, for example, were interested in moderate social change; the French thinkers of the late eighteenth century were interested in grander social reform. Some influential Enlightenment thinkers were religious sceptics like Hume, while others were deists like Voltaire.

Second, from the start the Enlightenment had detractors. Thinkers such as Johann Gottfried von Herder and Johann Georg Hamann were outspoken, public critics of overly rational and scientific approaches to the human person, social organizations, and religion. Edmund Burke, whose conservatism was influential in Britain and the United States, found Enlightenment thought responsible for the disasters of the French revolution. In the twentieth century defenders and critics of the Enlightenment came from various directions. While thinkers such as Jürgen Habermas and John Rawls defended a basic Kantian approach to ethics and social theory, both Alisdair MacIntyre and Michael Foucault have criticized Enlightenment social philosophy. Yet, MacIntyre has argued for more communal life and definition of virtue, while Foucault has argued for diversity and freedom communal values that define in order to control.

Third, since postmodernism has stressed issues of context and the cultural setting of any proposed claim, there is no current, non-partisan summary of the Enlightenment and review of scholarship on it. The two-volume study by Peter Gay, *The Enlightenment,* remains a classic and is unlikely to be surpassed in breadth and depth of scholarship. For a solid entry to the Enlightenment, see Crane Brinton, "Enlightenment," in *The Encyclopedia of Philosophy,* (8 vols.; ed. Paul Edwards; New York: Mac Millan, 1967), 2:519–24.

37. Copleston, *History of Philosophy,* 4:63–152; John Cottingham, ed., *The Cambridge Companion to Descartes* (Cambridge: Cambridge University Press, 1992); Fuller, *History of Philosophy,* 2:55–70.

38. Copleston, *History of Philosophy,* 4:264–332; Fuller, *History of Philosophy,* 2:105–19; Nicholas Jolley, ed., *The Cambridge Companion to Leibniz* (Cambridge: Cambridge University Press, 1995); Charles Hartshorne, *Insights and Oversights of Great Thinkers: An Evaluation of Western Philosophy* (Albany: State University of New York Press, 1983), 127–35.

39. Vere Chappell, ed., *The Cambridge Companion to Locke* (Cambridge: Cambridge University Press, 1994); Copleston, *History of Philosophy,* 5:67–142; Fuller, *History of Philosophy,* 2:120–39.

40. Copleston, *History of Philosophy,* 5:258–394; Fuller, *History of Philosophy,* 2:152–77; David Fate Norton, ed., *The Cambridge Companion to Hume* (Cambridge: Cambridge University Press, 1993); Richard H. Popkin, *The High Road to Pyrrhonism* (Indianapolis: Hackett, 1993).

41. Copleston, *History of Philosophy,* 6:180–392; Fuller, *History of Philosophy,* 2:215–72; Paul Guyer, ed., *The Cambridge Companion to Kant* (Cambridge: Cambridge University Press, 1992); John Kemp, *The Philosophy of Kant* (Oxford: Oxford University Press, 1968).

42. Gay, *The Enlightenment,* 1:201–2.

43. See Karl Ameriks, ed. *The Cambridge Companion to German Idealism* (Cambridge: Cambridge University Press, 2000); Copleston, *History of Philosophy,* 7:32–247; Fuller, *History of Philosophy,*

2:273–354; Etienne Gilson, Thomas Langan, and Armand Maurer, *Recent Philosophy: Hegel to the Present* (New York: Random House, 1962).; Quentin Lauer, *Hegel's Concept of God* (Albany: State University of New York Press, 1982); Dale E. Snow, *Schelling and the End of Idealism* (Albany: State University of New York Press, 1996).

44. Fuller, *A History of Philosophy*, I2: 384–40; Copleston, *A History of Philosophy*, 8:50-92; 9:74–98

45. See Fuller, *History of Philosophy*, 2:438–50; Copleston, *History of Philosophy*, 7:335–51, 390–420.

46. The sections on Peirce and James, and Bergson and Whitehead are indebted to the essays in Griffin et al., *Founders of Postmodern Constructive Theology.*

47. See, Peter Ochs, "Charles Sanders Peirce," in *Founders of Postmodern Constructive Theology* (Albany: State University of New York Press, 1993) 43–87; Michael L. Raposa, *Peirce's Philosophy of Religion* (Bloomington, Ind.: Indiana University Press, 1989); Hartshorne and Reese, *Philosophers Speak about God,* 258–69. Also see Copleston, *History of Philosophy*, 8:304–29; Charles Hartshorne, *Creativity in American Philosophy* (Albany: State University of New York Press, 1984), 74–91.

48. See Ochs, "Peirce," 64–67, 74–76; Raposa, *Peirce's Philosophy of Religion*, 142–54.

49. Raposa, *Peirce's Philosophy of Religion*, p. 144.

50. See Marcus P. Ford, "William James," in *Founders of Postmodern Constructive Theology: Peirce, James, Bergson, Whitehead, and Hartshorne* (Albany: State University of New York Press, 1993), 89–132; idem, *William James's Philosophy: A New Perspective* (Amherst: University of Massachusetts Press, 1982). Also see Copleston, *History of Philosophy*, 8:330–44; Fuller, *History of Philosophy*, 2:462–68; Hartshorne, *Creativity in American Philosophy*, 50–62; Hartshorne and Reese, *Philosophers Speak about God*, 335–52; Ruth Anna Putnam, ed., *The Cambridge Companion to William James* (Cambridge: Cambridge University Press, 1997).

51. Peter A. Y. Gunter, "Henri Bergson," in *Founders of Postmodern Constructive Theology: Peirce, James, Bergson, and Hartshorne* (Albany: State University of New York Press), 133–63; Copleston, *History of Philosophy*, 9:178–215; Fuller, *History of Philosophy*, 2:474–77.

52. John B. Cobb Jr., "Alfred North Whitehead," in *Founders of Postmodern Constructive Theology: Peirce, James, Bergson, Whitehead, and Hartshorne* (Albany: State University of New York Press, 1993), 165–95; Copleston, *History of Philosophy*, 9:399–401; Fuller, *History of Philosophy*, 2:491–94; Hartshorne, *Insights and Oversights*, 255–82; Hartshorne and Reese, *Philosophers Speak about God*, 273–85; Charles Hartshorne and Creighton Peden, *Whitehead's View of Reality* (New York: Pilgrim, 1981); Donald W. Sherburne, ed., *A Key to Whitehead's Process and Reality* (New York: Macmillan, 1966).

CHAPTER THREE
THE POSTMODERN TURN

The end of chapter 2 argued that by developing analytical philosophy, logical positivism, existentialism, and phenomenology, the twentieth century remained largely skeptical of efforts to talk about reality itself. The notable exceptions were Peirce, James, Bergson, Whitehead, and the philosopher of religion Charles Hartshorne (1897–2000), who spent his entire philosophical career swimming against the anti-metaphysical stream.

There was a seeming consensus that conceptual systems that credited claims about the objective nature of reality itself were at best useless, and at worst made invalid claims and were politically abusive of divergent voices. Not surprisingly, when theologians in the late twentieth and early twenty-first centuries turned to conceptual resources to explain what Christian claims meant and how they could be true, the available resources were deconstructive, context-oriented approaches to philosophy. Given these available resources, and given the de-ideologizing of the gospel during the late twentieth century, it has been natural for postmodern theology to work from these philosophies.

This chapter will look at some of the influential philosophical tools that have been used in theology. Then postmodern theologies using these resources will be grouped into three broad categories, with examples given for each. Finally, some postmodern theological assertions will be credited and one fundamental assertion will be challenged.

POSTMODERN PHILOSOPHICAL RESOURCES

Within the twentieth-century options for philosophy, the development of linguistic philosophy has been very important for postmodern theology. Admittedly this area is broadly populated and often complex so that short discussions may seem inadequate. Yet two principal names and directions surely can be given: Ludwig Wittgenstein and Ferdinand de Saussure.

Born in 1889 as the youngest of eight children to a wealthy Austrian industrialist, Wittgenstein took an early liking to mathematics and science. At a young age he became interested in the work of Bertrand Russell in logic and mathematics. Wittgenstein studied with Russell at Cambridge and he began writing his first work—and only major work published during his lifetime—called the *Tractatus*, which is only seventy-five pages long but covers a wide range of topics from language to ethics.[1] Wittgenstein later submitted this work as his doctoral dissertation, which was reviewed by Russell as well as by the British philosopher G. E. Moore who considered it a work of genius. In the *Tractatus* the young Wittgenstein argued that we can understand words and sentences because there is a correlation between the name and the object, between the picture that a sentence gives and the external reality it represents.

After Wittgenstein's death in 1951 some of the vast corpus of his writings have begun to be published, the apparent gem of which is his *Philosophical Investigations*, which was first published in 1953.[2] Most scholars agree that this later work repudiated his earlier *Tractatus* and developed a new way of thinking about philosophy and language.

In his *Philosophical Investigations* Wittgenstein argued that traditional philosophy had thought it was concerned with disclosing the very structure of reality. However, argued Wittgenstein, instead of discovering reality philosophers impose their picture upon the complex reality that they encounter. No wonder confusion reign in the world of philosophy. By contrast, philosophy ought to describe not explain, and the subject of philosophical description ought to be the way that ordinary language describes the world. Here we discover exactly how certain words are used in certain contexts, and we see how "language games" construct our everyday life. By "language games" Wittgenstein meant the way that language functions in complex everyday personal and communal life. Key to his thought is the idea that concepts relate to each other in complicated sets of meaning that often overlap with each other and form "family resemblances." Gone are the eternal forms of Plato that structure the world and give it meaning; present are complicated nexuses of meanings that allow us to structure reality and communicate. The philosopher must observe these complicated patterns of meaning, ask about their assumptions, and describe their workings from different perspectives.

Saussure was a Swiss-born scholar of language who founded what is known as structural linguistics. His academic training was in language and grammar, and as a young man he made his name with his 1879 book, *Memoir on the Original System of Vowels in the Indo-European Languages*. Saussure taught at the School for Advanced Studies in Paris (École des Hautes Études) from 1881 through 1891. He then taught linguistics and Sanskrit at the University of Geneva until his death in 1913. Saussure's principle book, *Course in General Linguistics*, which was compiled from student notes and lectures, was published in 1916.[3]

Saussure studied the elements and rules of language as such, those objective features that arrange any given language used by a given community. All language, argued Saussure, consists of signs that parse into both signifier and signified. The signifier, which can be oral or written, has the function of conveying meaning (what is signified). More importantly, signifier and signified have their relationship fixed by social convention, and the sign receives exact meaning by its relationship to other signs in the whole language system. Grammar and syntax arrange these signs into a coherent system. Structuralism (or more precisely, linguistic structuralism) is the name given to this idea that language has an objective structure, able to be analyzed and studied in and of itself, which produces a reality in which people live and understand themselves and others.[4]

Saussure's pioneering work on structuralism has had wide-ranging effects. The French psychotherapist Jacques Lacan (1901–1981) developed an approach that was something like a blend of Freud and Saussure.[5] Lacan insisted that the unconscious self lies behind all that we are and that the unconscious is structured like a language. Where Saussure had signifier and signified as the two aspects of a sign, Lacan focused on the signifier, arguing that signifiers connect to each other by differentiating themselves from the other. Signifiers do not point to external signifieds but work inwardly, structuring the self and the unconscious world. Where Freud used the term condensation to explain the unconscious blending of meaning, Lacan used the linguistic term metaphor. Where Freud used the term displacement to explain the unconscious replacement of one idea with another, Lacan used the linguistic term metonymy. In a sense, the unconscious becomes the very language of the self and this language speaks through us.

Since this linguistic world that is the human person works by absence, by signifiers distinguishing themselves from what they are not, "lack" is a fundamental structure of reality itself. The child lacks in its separation from the mother. Only by a misrecognition of itself in a mirror does it think that the self is a whole. The mother lacks primally by not having a penis. Only the father does not lack, in this symbolic sense, and so the father—or more precisely for Lacan, the *phallus*—becomes the organizing principle for the whole arrangement of signifiers that linguistically order one's world. The phallus thus holds together meaning within a system that copes with lack and therefore vulnerability.

By far the most influential thinker whose thought began with that of Saussure, and then worked outward toward new ways of thinking about language, is the Algerian-born Jacques Derrida (b. 1930).[6] Derrida studied at the École Normale Supérieure in Paris, where he later taught. He has taught philosophy at the Sorbonne (1960–1964); he directs the École des Hautes Études en Science Sociales in Paris; he has taught at Yale, Cornell, CUNY Graduate School; and he currently is professor of philosophy at the University of California, Irvine.

Derrida's work has been and remains the subject of lively debate: hundreds of dissertations have been written about his work; and in 1992, when Cambridge University wanted to give him an honorary doctorate, there was a discussion at Cambridge whether granting him an honorary degree was appropriate.

Beginning with Saussure's distinction between signifier and signified as the two aspects of a sign, Derrida deconstructs and reconstructs the basic model, overcoming the opposition between signifier and signified by pointing to a more complex process. The signifier indicates meaning both by differentiating itself from other elements and by pointing toward meanings that are still differed, put off to some indeterminate time. (Derrida invented a word for this—*différance*). For instance, "1" can be defined as the first odd integer; but you have to know what odd means in this context, which means you have to know what even means; but then you need to know what zero means, and so on. The full meaning of "1" always seems deferred until later as more and more meanings are added, the meaning to "1" becoming more polyvalent. Meaning is thus conferred by a complex, sometimes conflicting struggle that renders no predetermined solution or synthesis. All experiences come to meaning through this linguistic process and thus no stable, constant, objective state of affairs can be identified that would be the subject of philosophy. At the level of philosophy (and thus theology) what could be identified as truth, or being, or a human being?

Western thought, argues Derrida, has traditionally avoided this de-centering process by precisely positing a center, or rather many centers. This happens by thinking in terms of binary opposites such as man/woman, Caucasian/people of color, or spirit/matter. The first term invariably becomes the center point and the binary opposite becomes the margin. Think of the center of a circle where words like male, spirit, heterosexual, Caucasian, and Christian lie. The circumference then becomes female, material, homosexual, people of color, and pagan religions and atheism. Derrida's move is to de-center the center by showing how the privileged term could just as easily be the marginal, and the marginalized term just as easily be the center.

In his work *Of Grammatology*, Derrida argues in detail that the West has worked from the binary opposition of speech/written word, a bias he calls "logocentrism."[7] Speaking is presence; writing is absence (one would only write if one were absent), and Western logocentrism has thus focused on defining those realities that are eternally present as the basis of all that is—metaphysics, in other words. Derrida's project of de-centering, or deconstruction, thus argues that Western solutions to the problem of absence derive from mistakenly privileging one term in a binary opposition. All real solutions must come by dis-solving these binary oppositions: neither privileged nor marginalized, nor privileged and marginalized, but novel meaning that arises from the free play of the terms.

Working in ways similar to Barthes and Derrida was the French thinker Michel Foucault. Foucault was a star student at the École Normale Supérieure in Paris where he studied with the noted philosopher Maurice Merleau-Ponty (1908–1961). Merleau-Ponty had begun his career influenced by Edmund Husserl (1859–1938), the philosopher and inventor of phenomenology, and he developed a philosophy that looked to bodily perceptions as a key. His interests also bridged to political theory and he published two collections of essays defending Marxism.

Between 1954 and 1960 the young Foucault taught at the University of Uppsala, the University of Warsaw, and the University of Hamburg, returning to teach in France in 1960. That same year he published *The History of Madness,* which exemplified both his approach and the direction of his thought. (The English translation has the title *Madness and Civilization.*)[8] Through historical study of clinical medicine Foucault showed how the medical discourse about sanity and madness was historically situated and thus conditioned. Language about mental health reflects social and historical conditions rather than objective, positivist observations about reality. What truly is sanity and what madness? And how does putatively objective scientific language function to empower some and marginalize others?

Throughout the 1960s Foucault worked on what he called the "archeology" of social systems: analyzing social systems according to their language and categories, and trying to understand how and why concepts developed and how they were socially used. Foucault's historical interest was always existential and social. Beginning with a particular, unacceptable social condition he traced the development of those concepts and social structures that enable such current, intolerable conditions. While Foucault has sometimes been criticized for doing history that is one-sided in interest, or misrepresentative of the all data, his historical work is not so far from that of more traditional historians. Few people if any write history without an eye to the present moment, and few historians if any have mastered the many varieties of historical research that would comprise a relatively full historical account—social history, political history, religious history, economic history, history of ideas, and so on. What would seem to separate Foucault's historical work from more traditional approaches is its interest in diagnosis rather than explanation.

Not surprisingly Foucault's later interests shift toward analyzing the relationships between the "discursive systems" that he had named and the social systems that made people into "subjects" and exercise power over them.[9] Always interested in the concrete, Foucault mistrusted universals, meta-narratives, and any such attempts to generalize past the social situation being analyzed and the modes by which power is exerted. Foucault thought of his own approach as "nominalist," meaning that for concepts such as "power" only individual instances exist and must be analyzed ad hoc.

Into the same circle of radical French thinkers entered Julia Kristeva (b. 1941), who was born and raised in Bulgaria. After coming to Paris during the 1960s, Kristeva became an active participant in the Tel Quel group, a cluster of French thinkers—including Barthes, Foucault, Derrida, and others—who reflected upon and wrote about issues of language, culture, and politics. As a young student fluent in Russian, Kristeva not only was conversant with the work of Saussure but of Russian thinkers such as Mikhail Bakhtin (1895–1975), who is best known as a literary theorist who developed Saussure's ideas in new directions. Kristeva's background also includes study in Freudian and Lacanian analysis, although she has rejected both for an approach that combines her interest in language, fiction, and psychoanalysis.[10]

For Kristeva there is an early (pre-Oedipal, in Freudian terms) "semiotic" stage in life constituted by energy or drives that, although prelinguistic, usher forth in sounds and gestures that connect the child to the mother. These drives carry on through the period of separation from the mother as the child learns its "symbolic" world constituted by a sign-system rooted in a particular world. The semiotic activity continues through life, making possible the symbolic world and creatively erupting into the symbolic world. Such eruption, which expresses these semiotic drives, can happen through the poetry and literary expressions of writers. Such literary eruptions have political consequences because they disturb the order of language and thus the social system formed by that language. Repression, and thus liberation, are part of all sociolinguistic systems, and marginalized groups have their drives stilled and voices quieted in a variety of ways, all of which exemplify a larger pattern of social processes.

Besides the linguistic turn in the analytic philosophy (or "ordinary language philosophy") of Wittgenstein, and in the continental "structuralists" and "poststructuralists" we have looked at—Saussure, Barthes, Derrida, Foucault, and Kristeva—two other twentieth-century approaches have provided significant resources for postmodern theology: the phenomenology of French thinker Paul Ricoeur (b. 1913) and the pragmatism of the American philosopher Richard Rorty (b. 1931).

Born in France and raised by his paternal grandparents, Ricoeur began his higher education at the University of Rennes. He went on to the Sorbonne where he studied with the famous French existentialist philosopher and playwright Gabriel Marcel (1889–1973). At the Sorbonne Ricoeur studied the work of the existentialist philosopher Karl Jaspers (1883–1969) and the phenomenology of Husserl. Ricoeur went on to teach at the Sorbonne (1957–1967) and later at the University of Chicago.

Continuing the tradition of Husserl and Heidegger, Ricoeur argues that the task of philosophy is the descriptive task of analyzing what happens when we actually claim to know something. Such analysis shows, among other things, that the world is a reality already given to us and structured for us. All knowledge thus shows two related aspects: knowledge is historically conditioned by the world we inherit, and whatever we do know, we know from already being involved in this historical condition with others. To know is to interpret what has been historically given and what historically conditions us, and to do so in a new circumstance. Knowledge is "intersubjective" and not a matter of making true assertions about an objective reality "out there."

For Ricoeur this has important implications for biblical hermeneutics. Contrary to what may seem the case, we do not read a text and understand what the text "objectively says," after which we interpret the text. The text may indeed have had meaning given by its author, but the current meaning, which comes through the historically conditioned understanding that is always also interpretation, goes far beyond any authorial intention. A new horizon of meaning is opened.[11]

The final thinker to engage us is the American pragmatist Richard Rorty, who was born in New York city to a politically liberal, reformist, and pragmatist family. Rorty received his B.A. at the University of Chicago, studying philosophy in a department that included Rudolf Carnap (1891–1970), Charles Hartshorne, and Richard McKeon (1900–1985). He completed an M.A. at Chicago and went on to do a Ph.D. in philosophy at Yale. He then taught at Wellesley College (1958–1961), Princeton University (1961–1982), the University of Virginia (1982–1998), and he currently teaches at Stanford University. Rorty's best known book—and one whose widespread popularity surprised Rorty himself— is his *Philosophy and the Mirror of Nature* (1979) in which he challenges the idea that true knowledge is the mind's inner, conceptually correct mirroring of an external world.[12]

Rorty has avowedly taken to heart the Enlightenment task: there is no inherent external authority and all ideas are open to public and communal conversation for that which is most adequate. Modernity rightly overturned religious authoritarianism in which human endeavors were to be measured according to divine decrees revealed to and interpreted by church authorities. This was a positive step to human adulthood in which people exchanged ideas, thought for themselves, and took responsibility for their actions in relation to their community of dialogue. This maturation, says Rorty, was arrested by the philosophical tradition in the West that reverted back to a form of authoritarian submission to a nonhuman Other. This secular deity that is erected by the philosophers is the objective norms constituted by reality itself—the world out there as it really is.

The root conceptual problem, as Rorty puts it, is representation. Part of representation is the mistake that there is some correlation between the real world, out there, and its more or less accurate mirroring by our mental concepts, in here. Related is the idea that some set of conceptual terms is to be privileged because it accurately maps out the world as it is given and allows us to say things that are literally true of reality. Philosophy of this type, which Rorty can dub a "super-science," impedes human adulthood by making us subservient to a philosophical view of reality rather than being dialogue partners with each other.

Rorty's constructive offerings have several features worth noting. First, objectivity as conformity with the way the world really is should be replaced by solidarity as agreement with one's community. We should seek not truth as such but growing consensus, recognizing that the language we use must always be appropriate to the specific communal task in which the consensus is being sought.

Second, for Rorty human language can best be conceived of as a tool, in a rather natural, developmental, Darwin-like way. This has several implications. In history, for instance, the way one gets history right is to narrate for the community in a way that is acceptable and edifying. In the realms of public and private there are simply different goals for each realm, which cannot be folded into a single meta-structure. The vocabulary for the private sphere, where a goal is self-expression, can be deconstructive. The vocabulary for the public sphere, where politics is the issue, must be a different tool than deconstructive language because the job at hand is different.

Third, liberalism consists in engaging in communities that have developed a vocabulary that facilitates moral reflection and asserts solidarity with others in this community. This vocabulary sensitizes people to each other and encourages those ad hoc activities that mitigate pain and cruelty to others. There is no objective reality to which someone committed to this liberal community can point in order to prove this perspective to be right. There is only the liberalism that is this community to which a person has historically committed herself. To the charge that this sounds like relativism or subjectivism, Rorty replies that such objections are ultimately rooted in the representational worldview that mistakenly compares the reality out there with its correct conceptual mirroring in here.

POSTMODERN THEOLOGIES: PURIFYING, POLITICAL, AND PRESERVING

When Christian thinkers turned to philosophy in the last part of the twentieth century, the resources available were ones that consciously rejected making truth claims about the structure of reality itself. Twentieth-century philosophy was skeptical about such assertions and most thinkers turned to analysis of language.

This was true for the thinkers briefly summarized in the first section of this chapter. These thinkers have been frequent resources for much postmodern theology.

Postmodern theologians can be grouped into three types: purifying, political, and preservationist.[13] The postmodern purifying theologians may best be typified by Mark C. Taylor. Postmodern political theologians cover a wide variety of people, groups, and perspectives. The work of two prominent voices will be summarized here: the theologies of Mary Daly and Sallie McFague. Among the preservationist postmodern theologies the Yale school of theology, as typified by a cluster of thinkers and their students (Hans Frei, Brevard Childs, George Lindbeck, and Paul Holmer) will be summarized.

Purifying Postmodern Theology

Mark C. Taylor (b. 1945) majored in religion at Wesleyan University and followed that with a Ph.D. from Harvard University in philosophy of religion and a doctorate from the University of Copenhagen in philosophy. He has taught at Williams College since 1973, when he began teaching in the department of religion. Over the years his interests have become distinctly cross-disciplinary, moving from religion and philosophy into art, architecture, and the cyber world. Taylor currently is the Cluett Professor of Humanities at Williams College and the only faculty member at the college unattached to a department. At Williams he helped establish, and now directs, the Center for Technology in the Arts and Humanities. The author of fifteen books, Taylor has recently produced "The Real," a futuristic computer game from the University of Chicago Press.

Taylor typifies the category of purifying postmodern theology by his consistent effort to cleanse it from inadequately critical presuppositions and its captivity by church theology. In the foreword to Taylor's book *Deconstructing Theology,* the "death of God" theologian Thomas J. J. Altizer (b. 1927) says that

> Mark C. Taylor is the first American post-ecclesiastical systematic or philosophic theologian, the first theologian free of the scars or perhaps even the memory of Church theology, and the first theologian to address himself solely to the purely theoretical or cognitive problems of theology. All too significantly, Taylor began his professional work with an intensive study of Kierkegaard, the very Kierkegaard who is almost universally regarded as the primal religious thinker of modernity, but also the Kierkegaard who while inspiring the early dialectical Barth, was abandoned by Barth when Barth embarked upon the *Church Dogmatics. . . .* Through these studies Taylor has not only recaptured but recapitulated the actual genesis of modern theology, and done so in an intellectual

and cultural situation wherein theology is free of the Church, and thereby free of the very power and ground which theological thinking itself negated in realizing its modern epiphany.[14]

In *Deconstructing Theology* Taylor discusses the differing ideas of religious selfhood in Kierkegaard and Hegel, tracing Hegel's thought through Hegel's use of the three traditional proofs for God's existence (ontological, cosmological, and teleological). Taylor argues that Hegel provides a way to understand that "self" and "other" are mutually establishing opposites that establish both difference and unity through the process of relating. This is true of "God" and "self" as well, but that road must ultimately lead through deconstruction.

The central chapters of *Deconstructing Theology,* particularly "Toward an Ontology of Relativism," assert an absolute, reject nihilism, do not deny a correspondence idea about truth, and affirm authorial intention in literary works.[15] By contrast, the opening section, called "Pretext," invokes many of the postmodern thinkers we have mentioned—Barthes, Foucault, and especially Derrida, as well as others. At the end of "Pretext" Taylor says that

> writing books, after having absorbed the insights of Deconstruction, is as difficult as writing theology, after having interiorized the death of God. Honesty compels us to admit the possibility that neither task can any longer be complete. . . . It is, of course, undeniable that not only this "Pretext," but this entire volume remains a Pretext—a pre-text to a text not yet written . . . a postmodern atheology."[16]

Erring: A Postmodern A/theology completed the deconstuctive task that *Deconstructing Theology* left unfinished.[17] *Erring* has absorbed the thought of Derrida, and in it Taylor argues for the deconstruction of Western theology as we have known it. Key concepts such as God, self, and history erode away upon examination. For Taylor, once modernity had rid itself of the traditional supernatural God, it substituted its own god—the human self, solitary, stable, untouched, and reigning over a world that it would bring to a progressive fulfillment. Classical views about God were simply transferred to the human self.[18]

By contrast, without the ultimate center, God, the self as such disappears since it was modeled on the old vision of God. Language is entirely intertextual and interpretation about other interpretations; there is no independent, ultimate referent for our signs. Truth becomes relative, having no direct correspondence to reality since there is no ultimate truth or "reality" out there as traditionally conceived.[19] Binary opposites such as God and self, good and evil, past and present are all overcome by embracing nihilism so radically that nihilism itself is overcome in a way that something profoundly religious appears.[20] And so, not surprisingly perhaps, Taylor begins his conclusion ("Interlude . . .") by citing Hegel, saying, "If Alpha and Omega are One, 'movement is the circle that returns into itself, the circle that presupposes its beginning and reaches it only at the end.'"[21]

Whether Taylor can remain internally consistent through these arguments cannot be treated here, and will be briefly discussed later. Of more interest at the moment is that a continual charge of "nihilism" has been leveled against Taylor's ideas, a charge that he has grown weary of hearing.[22] Historically speaking, however, the "text" of Taylor's work was far from being completed. If Taylor sometimes compared his nihilism to Christian selflessness or Buddhist emptiness, we might think of *Erring* as the "dark night of the soul" in Taylor's journey. Purification eventually leads toward insights that could not be glimpsed prior to those places of darkness. Taylor's work since *Erring* has brought him from a deconstructive, "death of God" theology to that of a creative "philosopher of culture" (to use his own self-description).

In *Altarity* Taylor examines Hegel, Heidegger, Merleau-Ponty, Lacan, Bataille, Kristeva, Levinas, Blancot, Derrida, and Kierkegaard, rethinking "the difference and otherness that lie 'beyond absolute knowledge.'" Taylor seeks to find that creative seam where religion reappears through the presence of the Other whose otherness is beyond the "other" that pairs with the "same," beyond both transcendence and immanence.[23] Taylor continues this search for religion at the seam by turning to art, architecture, and religion. In *Disfiguring: Art, Architecture, Religion* Taylor argues that art and architecture in the twentieth century have paralleled theology.[24] True postmodern thought (which has not postured for a utopia) and postmodern aesthetics must take up the radically negative call, the call from the Other, which cannot be properly named.

Two more recent books developed in their own way from these arguments. In *Nots* Taylor pursues "negative theology," so to speak.[25] He explores the "not" in Anselm, Hegel, Derrida, and the Buddhist writer Keiji Nishitani. Taylor discusses the "not" in pop art and artists such as Madonna; and the "not" in issues of immunology and AIDS. Taylor then produced the boundary-crossing, imaginative *Hiding*, which from the start was done with a high level of artistic input.[26] Meant to be on the interface of text and web hyper-text, *Hiding* ought to be read by not reading but "surfing," so to speak. The book is cyber-looking and reading, with each chapter done differently and with neon abounding. We find chapters on body piercing, fashion, and interfacing. Las Vegas is seen as a logical endpoint of the ideas from the late eighteenth century at the University of Jena where Hegel taught. The center of human life is creativity, especially in art, and Las Vegas embodies the imagination and image made real. As Taylor says (and this can only be misrepresented in the format of this book as compared to how it appears in *Hiding*), "As reality is virtualized, we gradually are forced to confess that real has always been imaginary."[27] A creative coming together of the many worlds that Taylor inhabits, *Hiding* gives us a glimpse of the constructive aspect at which *Erring* hinted—the Other wafts out from the seams, the tears, and the rebinding that happens as we reconstrue meaning.

Political Postmodern Theologies

While Taylor represents the major and most creative voice in the purifying category of postmodern theologians, the political category is represented by a wide range of voices. Who to discuss and who to leave out? I've chosen to discuss briefly the work of Mary Daly and Sallie McFague. Where are Cornell West, Delores Williams, James Cone, Ada Maria Isasi-Diaz, Gustavo Gutiérrez, Kosuke Koyama, Raimundo Panikkar, and other giants of liberation theology? This is a fair question that has several answers.

First, this essay is not an attempt to introduce people to the splendid variety of currently creative theologians. Anthologies exist that do that quite well. For this study, however, some people will be included and some left out, by the scope of this study itself. Beyond that, as the end of this chapter suggests, the positive comments and the constructive comments that are made generally apply *mutatis mutandis* to theologians within this category.

But why Daly and McFague? Both are high profile American theologians, widely known through academic and church circles, and even through popular culture. Within a few years of each other in age, both are feminist thinkers who made the postmodern "linguistic turn" that we have examined. By contrast, their theological projects go very different directions once that turn has been made, and the differences seem interesting and instructive to compare.

Mary Daly (b. 1928) was born Roman Catholic in upstate New York, receiving a traditional pre-Vatican II Roman Catholic education. Daly did her undergraduate work at the College of St. Rose in Albany, where she majored in English. She earned an M.A. in English at Catholic University, and a Ph.D. in religion at St. Mary's College, Notre Dame, Indiana. Daly then earned two more doctorates, one in theology from the University of Fribourg, Switzerland, with a dissertation on Thomas Aquinas; the other a doctorate in philosophy from Fribourg, with a dissertation on the French philosopher Jacques Maritain (1882–1973).

Daly attended the Second Vatican Council, hoping for real progress within Roman Catholicism. There was reason for hope. Many at the council had a vision for theology, church, and worship that conceived of the church as built from the bottom up through the Spirit-inspired ministry of the baptized, not built from the top down through the pope and bishops all modeled on Christ.

Daly was optimistic about the role of women in the Roman church and, having been inspired by the French philosopher and feminist Simone de Beauvoir (1908–1986), Daly wrote her famous first challenge to the Roman Catholic Church, *The Church and the Second Sex*.[28] In careful and vigorous argument, Daly takes up the questions of women's ordination, birth control, and the historical role of women in religious communities.

From today's vantage point, *The Church and the Second Sex* reads straightforwardly and honestly, without bitterness and filled with hope. Consider, for instance, the historically accurate and simple beginning of chapter 3, "Winds of Change":

> With the death of Pius XII the Catholic Church acquired as pope a man entirely different from his predecessors in temperament and stamp of mind. With Pope John XXIII came opened windows and an on-rushing *aggiornamento* which lasted throughout his brief reign. It has become abundantly clear, despite a few discouraging setbacks, that the Church cannot return to its condition before the advent of Pope John and Vatican II.
>
> It is not surprising that one of the signs of new life in the church is an increasing awareness of the need to take an objective and reappraising look at the situation of women. The first startling breakthrough on the ideological level came from Pope John himself, in the encyclical *Pacem in Terris* in 1963. He wrote: "Since women are become ever more conscious of their human dignity, they will not tolerate being treated as mere material instruments, but demand rights befitting a human person both in domestic and in public life."[29]

Elsewhere Daly cited two famous theologians, Teilhard de Chardin (1881–1955) and Paul Tillich (1886–1965), who agreed that a literal reading of the fall diminished Christianity.[30] For Daly the story of the fall connects to a misogyny present in the church and Western culture that has become "divinely inspired." Who could be upset by such arguments? Well, the Jesuit school where she taught, Boston College, fired her immediately. (She was given a term-limit contract.) She became famous and people rallied to her cause. Boston College then rehired her. (She was given promotion and tenure.) Perhaps when we now read (or re-read) *The Church and the Second Sex,* the lesson is not how far we have come but how deep the patriarchy truly was and continues to be today. Consider, for instance, the uncivil treatment that John Paul II accorded Dr. Nafis Sadik, undersecretary of the UN Conference on Population and Development. His unpleasantness to Dr. Sadik was surpassed only by his assertion to her that third world women were at fault for their husbands raping them and making them pregnant, or infecting them with the HIV virus: "Don't you think that the irresponsible behavior of men is caused by women?"[31]

Faced with such Christian patriarchy it was no wonder that Daly's next book was post-Christian. The problem is not this or that church prelate, or some particular piece of Christian doctrine. The problem is an entire worldview, complete with its own language and rituals to instantiate it, that is hierarchical, patriarchal, and violent to women. In her next book, *Beyond God the Father: Toward a Philosophy of Women's Liberation,* Daly argues that Christianity as a whole, from its language to its doctrines to its rituals, forms a world within which women could not come to liberating health.[32] There she pens perhaps the single most famous line of women's liberation theology: "If God is male, then the male is God."

One year after *Beyond God the Father,* the publishers of *The Church and the Second Sex* decided to reprint that earlier book; but Daly had now moved immeasurably beyond her first work. Now that she was post-Christian she had the problem of what to do. Her decision was to write a new post-Christian introduction, which would begin her older, feminist Christian book. In the new 1975 introduction Daly writes about *The Church and the Second Sex* after having recently written *Beyond God the Father:*

> The journey in time/space that took place between the publication dates of the two books *[The Church and the Second Sex* and *Beyond God the Father]* could not be described adequately by terrestrial calendars and maps. Experientially, it was hardly even a mere trip to the moon, but more like leap-frogging galaxies in a mind voyage to further and further stars. Several woman-light years had separated me from *The Church and the Second Sex,* whose author I sometimes have trouble recalling . . .
>
> Opening the book at random, I found myself in Chapter Seven, "Toward Partnership: Some Modest Proposals." I read a few pages and discovered that the author was proposing that there be equality between men and women in the Church (*sic,* with a capital "C"). Why, I wondered, would anyone want "equality" in the church? In a statement that I had given to the press only three or four woman-light years distant from now, I had explained that a woman's asking for equality in the church would be comparable to a black person's demanding equality in the Ku Klux Klan.[33]

The freedom that came from *Beyond God the Father* was only the starting point for new galactic journeys for Daly. Freeing herself from the old worldview means freeing into some other universe, one that she would be instrumental in constructing for herself and for other women.

With her third groundbreaking book, *Gyn/Ecology: The Metaethics of Radical Feminism,* Daly gives a new direction for feminist theology. Women need the power to name and use language that generates life, and Daly spins out new language and a new universe:

> The play is part of our work of unweaving and of our weaving work. It whirls us into another frame of reference. We use the visitation of demons to come more deeply into touch with our own powers/virtues. Unweaving their deceptions, we name our Truth. Defying their professions we dis-cover our Female Pride, our Sinister Wisdom. Escaping their possession we find our Enspiriting Selves. Overcoming their aggression we uncover our Creative Anger and Brilliant Bravery. Demystifying/demythifying their obsessions we re-member our Woman-loving Love. Refusing their assimilation we experience our Autonomy and Strength. Avoiding their elimination we find our Original Be-ing. Mending their imposed fragmentation we Spin our Original Integrity.[34]

Gyn/Ecology broke ground for the book *Pure Lust: Elemental Feminist Philosophy.*[35] *Pure Lust* is divided into the first realm, Archespheres; the second realm, Pyrospheres; and the third realm, Metamorphospheres. *Pure Lust* has a creative universe of language—an index is given at the back of the book—and it has mythic characters, both good and bad.

> We are: Augurs, Brewsters, Dikes, Dragons, Dryads, Fates, Phoenixes, Gorgons, Maenads, Muses. We are Naiads, Nixes, Gnomes, Norns, Mymphs. We are Oceanids, Oreads, Orishas, Pixies. We are Prudes, Salamanders, Scolds, Shrews, Sibyls, Sirens. We are Soothsayers, Sprites, Stiffs, Sylphs, Undines. We are Viragos, Virgins, Vixens, Websters, Weirds.[36]

On the other side of the cosmic battle are villains who inhabit Stag-nation. They are identified as snools, bores, botchers/butchers, cocks, danglers, dicks, drones, fakes, fixers, slashers, framers, frauds, hacks, hucksters, jabbers, jerks, jocks, plug-uglies ("among the grosser snoolish incarnations"), pricks, prickers, rakes, rippers, shams, sneaks, sniffers, snitches, snookers, snoops, snot boys, snudges, snuffers, studs, and wantwits.[37]

Does this new universe of language seem too far out there? One could always look up the terms in *Webster's First New Intergalactic Wickedary of the English*

Language.[38] The problem, seen from Daly's perspective, is not her language but my pillaging of the terms from another galaxy, and then standing them up apart from their living topography as weird creatures to be mocked. It is exactly this type of book, that I write right now, that Daly's language is meant to overturn.

Sallie McFague (b. 1933) graduated from Smith College and Yale Divinity School, and from Yale Graduate School from which she received her Ph.D. in 1964. Her doctoral dissertation *Literature and the Christian Life* was published in 1966 and set the course for her future work in theology.[39] Learning from the work of Ricoeur, McFague pursued the issue of metaphor and religious language in her 1975 book, *Speaking in Parables: A Study in Metaphor and Theology.*[40] In her central chapter on metaphor, "Metaphor: The Heart of the Matter," McFague draws from a wide range of literary critics and philosophers of language and theologians, including Ian Ramsay, David Burrell, Fredrick Ferré, Ernst Cassirer, Owen Barfield, Paul Ricoeur, Elizabeth Sewell, and Ian Barbour. McFague concludes by arguing that

> metaphor, as we have described it, is *the* way of human knowing. It is simply not a way of embellishing something we can know in some other way. There is no other way. If this is so, then human knowledge (of whatever sort) is tentative, relativistic, multi-layered, dynamic, complex, sensuous, historical, and participatory.[41]

In the subsequent chapter, "The Parable: The Primary Form," McFague extends the discussion of metaphor into parable, which she argues is

> an *extended* metaphor—the metaphor is not in discrete images which allow for a flash of insight (a purely aesthetic or intellectual, "Aha!"), but it is a way of believing and living that initially seems ordinary, yet is so dislocated and rent from its usual context that, if the parable "works," the spectators become participants, not because they want to necessarily or simply have "gotten the point" but because they have, for the moment, "lost control" or as the new hermeneuts say, "been interpreted."

Then, borrowing from Robert Funk and Leander Keck, McFague describes Jesus as God's parable and thus "*was* the kingdom" encountering people "through a juxtaposition of the ordinary within a startling new context."[42] What McFague understands through this "study of parables and of Jesus as the parable of God is a model for theological reflection that insists on the metaphoric quality of language, belief, and life."[43] This assertion becomes the foundation for the unfolding journey that can be traced in her subsequent books.[44]

In *Metaphorical Theology: Models of God* McFague makes several important steps in her unfolding theological project. First, she moves from metaphor to model. McFague argues that

> metaphor always has the character of "is" and "is not: an assertion is made but as a likely account rather than a definition. That is, to say "God is mother," is not to define God as mother, not to assert identity between the terms "God" and "mother," but to suggest that we consider what we do not know how to talk about—relating to God—through the metaphor of mother. The assumption here is that all talk of God is indirect: no words or phrases refer directly to God, for God-language can refer only through the detour of a description that properly belongs elsewhere. To speak of God as mother is to invite us to consider some qualities associated with mothering as one partial but perhaps illuminating way of speaking of certain aspects of God's relationship to us.[45]

A model is a developed metaphor, "a metaphor with 'staying power,' that has gained sufficient stability and scope so as to present a pattern for relatively comprehensive and coherent explanation."[46] McFague cites Derrida's comment that metaphor is somewhere between "nonsense" and "truth" so that theology is always "at risk." We could be closer to nonsense than truth, but that is a risk worth taking. No metaphors, and thus models, are privileged, and some may have seen their most useful days come and go, needing to be replaced by other models.

Second, McFague proposes three alternative models to the traditional hierarchical models that have been on the theological field for so long: God as mother, as love, and as friend. These strictly personal models, taken from the deep experiences of life, lead into her next book, *The Body of God: An Ecological Theology.* Here McFague turns her insight of deeply personal models for God to a seemingly natural conclusion. The most appropriate model by which to conceive of the universe is as God's body. Here not only is the transcendent, hierarchical model of God overcome, as it was in *Metaphorical Theology,* but it is turned on its head, so to speak: the transcendence of God is through the radical immanence whereby the world is the divine body. The final chapter, "Eschatology: A New Shape for Humanity," begins to draw out the consequences for church and ethics that come from understanding the universe as the divine body.

These ethical consequences then become the concern for the next two books. In *Super, Natural Christians,* McFague argues that we should look on nature as a subject rather than as an object. We need a subject-subject relationship with nature, which might best be nurtured by direct contact with nature in our towns and communities and by involvement with those who care for the earth. In her next book, *Life Abundant,* McFague argues that love for the earth is far from enough. The human species is destroying the earth. What is needed is an ecological theology, a planetary theology that risks our lives for the well-being of the earth and thus for others. A planetary theology inherently has an ecological economic structure to it, which McFague summarizes for lay theology as having "three main rules: take only your share, clean up after yourselves, and keep the house in good repair for future occupants."[47] In short, McFague conceives of a world of shared resources, with appropriate prosperity for all, within a sustainable biosphere that will be passed on to future generations. McFague then develops this into a theology (God radically in and for the world, so that to love the world is also to love God); into a Christology (God in Christ prophetically for all those oppressed, including nature, and God in Christ sacramentally embodied in the universe); and into a theology of the Spirit (to live in the Spirit is to be, borrowing Richard R. Niebuhr's famous description of Schleiermacher's theology, christomorphic, to who we were meant to be prophetically and sacramentally for others, including the universe).

Preserving Postmodern Theology

Perhaps no theologically conservative movement in the late twentieth century has had more impact on both scholars and church life than the Yale school of theology, sometimes called the New Yale School. This term designates not an institution, nor a faculty as such, but a type of theology that in the last third of the twentieth century developed from the work of four theologians at Yale: Hans Frei, George Lindbeck, Paul Holmer, and Brevard Childs. These theologians have not agreed on all points, and for that reason this approach is sometimes called "postliberal" theology, signifying more narrowly the perspectives of Frei and Lindbeck.

The broader phrase, Yale school of theology, seems more apt. While there may be disagreement, for instance, between Lindbeck and Childs over precisely how narratives form communities of faith, Childs's narrative and canonical approach to Scripture can be suitably fitted to a conservative, "postliberal" approach, as the work of Paul McGlasson shows. Indeed, Childs typically writes the forewords for McGlasson's books. This approach might best be thought of as a family type, with varying areas of overlapping agreement on issues. This observation invites two other comments.

Scholars creatively work their way through their training and into their broader careers, choosing and integrating as seems appropriate. This means that although the Yale school of theology has produced a coherent and powerful vision of conserving Christianity, not all Yale-trained theologians have turned out conservative. Among those who have sought to preserve what they believe is the long-standing, traditional view of scriptural authority, sought to preserve doctrinal assertions within the community of faith, and sought the character-creating quality of the Christian community formed by the canon, one can name, for instance, Stanley Hauerwas, who represents the older generation of Yale-trained theologians; Paul McGlasson, who represents a younger generation of Yale thinkers; and other theologians whose theologies find some agreement in approach—William Willimon and Gabriel Fackre, for instance.

By contrast there are traditional, American evangelical theologians, such as Carl Henry, who reject the Yale school of theology because it does not hold to the literal historical accounts of the biblical texts. The Yale school of theology would not only admit to this apparent criticism but insist upon it. Distinguishing the canonical narrative from the "real historical events" that lie behind it is itself exactly the problem shared by both conservative literalists and liberal historical critics: one side fastidiously holds to a correlation between narrative and historical reality, and the other side uses literary and scientific approaches to deny a literal correlation. In so doing, both sides approach the narrative with a modern, scientific consciousness that has lost sight of what biblical narrative was for Christianity during the centuries prior to the Enlightenment—a world-creating encounter with Jesus Christ, who is the subject matter of the text and whose living presence calls for our response.

Hans Frei (1922–1988) was born in Germany and his family emigrated to the United States in 1938. Frei graduated from Yale Divinity School and Yale Graduate School, from which he received his Ph.D., studying under H. Richard Niebuhr. Frei taught at Wabash College, the Episcopal Seminary of the Southwest, and at Yale. Influenced by the theology of Karl Barth and his narrative exegesis of Scripture, Frei's first book was the extremely influential *The Eclipse of Biblical Narrative: A Study in Eighteenth- and Nineteenth-Century Hermeneutics*.[48] Adapting the work of literary critic Erich Auerbach, Frei argued that narrative is "realistic," by which he meant that there is an

> inseparability of subject matter from its depiction or cumulative rendering, literal rather than symbolic quality of human subject and his social context, mutual rendering of character, circumstance, and their interaction—a realistic narrative is like a historical account.[49]

In other words, there is no "true history" behind the narrative that is the point to the Scripture passage, nor is there some "universal truth" that the characters in the narrative exemplify. The narrative makes its own realistic world, which lays claim on the world of the hearer or reader.

George Lindbeck (b. 1923) was the son of American Lutheran missionaries. Lindbeck attended Yale Divinity School and Yale Graduate School, from which he received his B.D. (1946) and Ph.D. (1955). He taught at Yale from 1952 through 1993, with a specialty in medieval thought. Lindbeck represented the Lutheran World Federation at the Second Vatican Council and thereafter became deeply interested in ecumenical dialogue and theology. His influential book, *The Nature of Doctrine: Religion and Theology in a Postliberal Age,* received a positive reading from theologians of various traditions.[50] Lindbeck argues that Christian doctrines do not make first-order statements about reality but rather are rules by which communities of faith organize and understand themselves. As Lindbeck puts it, "the rules 'Drive on the left' and 'Drive on the right' are unequivocal in meaning and unequivocally opposed, yet both may be binding: one in Great Britain and the other in the United States, or one when traffic is normal, and the other when a collision must be avoided."[51] Resolution between conflicting rules may come about not by collapsing them together, or ignoring one or the other, but by understanding when, where, and how they apply. Eucharistic doctrine, argues Lindbeck, might be one such example.

Undergirding this approach, and having an effect on the later work of Hans Frei, was Lindbeck's assertion that religion is a "cultural-linguistic system," in which people understand what their shared lives mean and in which they express such meaning through beliefs and practices. Ruled out is the notion of "unthematic experience," pure or raw experience as such that is at some point free from the cultural-linguistic system in which it is had.

Born to Swedish immigrant parents, and raised a Swedish Lutheran, Paul Holmer (b. 1916) received his B.A. and M.A. from the University of Minnesota, and his Ph.D. from Yale University (1946). He taught philosophy at the University of Minnesota from 1946 to 1960 and then moved to Yale, where he was professor of philosophical theology. Fluent in Danish, Swedish, and Norwegian, as well the usual scholarly languages, Holmer's first and primary love is the thought of Søren Kierkegaard, which he first studied at the University of Minnesota and then was the subject of his Yale dissertation. Later Holmer turned his attention to the work of Wittgenstein, blending insights from Kierkegaard and Wittgenstein into careful analyses of theological concepts and the human heart. Well-known for his own work such as *The Grammar of Faith,* Holmer has had great impact on other scholars, including Brevard Childs and George Lindbeck.[52]

Brevard Childs (b. 1923) received a B.A. and an M.A. from the University of Michigan, a B.D. from Princeton Seminary, and a D.Theol. from the University of Basel. A fellow of the Deutsche Akademische and the American Academy of Arts and Sciences, Childs has taught at Yale since 1958, and since 1992 has been the Sterling Professor of Divinity there.

An expert in traditional scholarly approaches to biblical texts, such as form criticism and redaction criticism, which ask about the type and use of various scriptural passages in their original historical settings, Childs subsumes these approaches within a larger perspective. Above all, argues Childs, the task is to approach the Bible not as layers of literary archaeology from the past but as sacred Scripture in which God continues to address the church with the living word.[53] How human, historical words and contexts can be the vehicle for the word of God addressing the church afresh remains a miracle. Through the work of the Spirit the canon of the Old and New Testaments forms a theological whole, blending together the variety of scriptural voices in all their intertextual relationships into a consistent witness to God's purpose for God's people.

The Yale school of theology takes the basic approach that liberal theology after Schleiermacher generally was "apologetic": it sought to explain Christian claims to the larger world, correlating Christian truths and practices to human emotions and needs. The result was the assimilation of Christianity into a cultural vision of Western progress. Jesus Christ was turned into a merely human person who exhibited whatever form of progress a particular liberal theologian was interested in. The Bible was turned into a historical book in which one could find the truths that supported the liberal project that Jesus had been made to exemplify. Thus the biblical world was thoroughly adapted to some particular modern world and its agenda. The theologian hiding behind this theology is Karl Barth. More than any other Anglo-American theological movement, the Yale school of theology has preserved the powerful influence of Barth's neo-orthodoxy.

The answer to this unacceptable accommodation of Christianity to the modern world is to let God be God by letting the canonical narrative be the canonical narrative. We must recognize that the Scriptures are a particular kind of narrative that lays claim on us, building for us its own world through which God addresses us with its sole living content, Jesus Christ. Since one must apply to a text a method appropriate to that text, a historical critical method that seeks the real historical truth behind the narrative, in order to translate that historical reality for us today, is an inappropriate method.

But more can be said here. Since there is no unthematic experience—no raw or pure experience free from historical context and the language of a given community—there is no possibility of standing in some neutral, public forum in which to examine Scripture. Historical critical methods are thus not unbiased, neutral approaches though they mistakenly claim to be. When these methods supposedly discover an "objective historical Jesus" this Jesus is merely a nose of wax who becomes fashioned according to the liberal theological agenda at hand. And so, for instance, the current liberal agenda is liberation theology and, using supposedly scientific methods, liberal scholars "discover" the liberating Jesus they need to find and build a theology from that Jesus:

> Indeed, because it uses the techniques of modern theology for its critique—in particular the self-construing and self-validating nature of human experience—liberation theology is the *reductio ad absurdum* of liberalism. Theology, to paraphrase Feuerbach, has become ideology.[54]

The alternative is to let the canonical narrative be what it truly is, allowing the Scriptures "to absorb reality" and create the only true world.[55] There we are addressed by God in the encounter with God's Word, the living Christ, and we are called to respond. That the Christ who encounters us liberates human life may be so, but true Christian theology is not liberation theology as such. That the Christ who encounters us does so as the content of the canonical narrative may be so, but Christian theology is not narrative theology as such. That the Christ who encounters us does so when we have an approach most like that of Karl Barth may be so, but Christian theology is not neo-orthodox theology as such. Christian theology comes from and is grounded in the God who encounters us in the Bible. Older evangelical theologians have sometimes criticized the Yale school of theology for not grounding Scripture in a traditional doctrine of scriptural inerrancy. This may be an accurate description, but given the assertion that the Bible absorbs reality and becomes our world, how stronger a doctrine of Scripture could there really be?

ASSESSING POSTMODERN THEOLOGIES

Postmodern theologies of the purifying, political, and preserving type display three related characteristic claims that are shared with postmodern thought. First, human language and thought exists within specific historical contexts (historically conditioned) and makes claims that relate to other claims within that historical context (intersubjective) rather than about the objective structure of the universe. Theological thought is thus interpretive and pluralistic. This means, second, that Christian doctrine formed within specific communities is also historically conditioned and reflects ultimate concerns, meaning, and relationships within Christian communities. Finally, since language and thought are so thoroughly conditioned historically, and function intersubjectively, claims about the structure of reality are considered irrelevant and unhelpful, if not invalid. The first two of these assertions ought to be affirmed by Christian theology. The third ought to be denied.

Christian Language and Thought Are Irreducibly Pluralistic

Christian theology can appropriately credit the insight that language and thought are historically conditioned and that the Christian witness is by necessity irreducibly pluralistic.[56] When Jesus encountered people in Palestine there were three possible types of reactions. For some the encounter with Jesus was a matter of indifference. His words and deeds were not decisive for their existence one way or the other. He was merely a carpenter's son. For some the encounter with Jesus was a negative one. He was crazy. He was Beelzebub. He was a social bandit who ought to be crucified next to two other bandits. But for some the encounter with Jesus was an encounter with the divine.

When encountered by God through the encounter with Jesus, some people gave titles of honor to Jesus, from within their own historical, cultural setting. Such titles reflected who it was they expected to be the divine presence for them, given their background. If someone expected God to be present as the Savior, then Jesus was the Savior. If people expected God to come as the Prophet, then Jesus was the Prophet. If others expected God to come as the Messiah, then Jesus was the Messiah. If someone else apocalyptically expected God to come as the Son of Man, then Jesus was the Son of Man. The New Testament attests to many titles for Jesus beyond these examples: the Son of God, Sophia, the Way, the Christ, the Bridegroom, the Son of David, the Bread from Heaven, the Good Shepherd, the Lord, the King of the Jews, and so on.

In the words of the New Testament scholar Willi Marxsen, "Jesus has many names" and they are irreducibly pluralistic. In some cases, of course, the tradition shows that names were linked in various combinations that provided more adequate proclamation for that community (cf., Mark 8:29 with the adaptation of Mark in Luke 9:20 and Matt 16:16). But gathering titles together did not produce a fuller, truer, more accurate account of "who Jesus really was." Each title was sufficient in its own context to proclaim that to deal with Jesus was to deal with God because, in simplest terms, "Jesus is God."[57] From the very start, Christianity was *historically conditioned* and known through and expressed by *historically conditioned language*. As Marxsen makes clear, from the onset Christianity is a matter of interpretation.

The original Christian diversity continued well into the second century and can be seen in many ways: language, concepts, liturgy, church organization, and so on. One more complex example should suffice, and here I follow an essay by the New Testament scholar Eduard Schweizer. In the writings of the New Testament two very early creeds can be found:[58]

For I handed on to you as of first importance what I in turn had received: that Christ died for our sins in accordance with the scriptures

and that he was buried,
and that he was raised on the third day in accordance with the scriptures
and that he appeared to Cephas, then to the twelve. (1 Cor 15: 3–5)

> He was revealed in the flesh
> vindicated in spirit
> seen by angels
> proclaimed among Gentiles
> believed in throughout the world
> taken up in glory. (1 Tim 3:16)

On Schweizer's analysis, the tradition that Paul cited in 1 Corinthians conceives the world through a temporal structure: what was named in the past (by
the Scriptures) has taken place in the present (Jesus dead, buried, and raised) in
order to save us from the future (God's judgment day). The problem is judgment
day and the solution is the death and resurrection of the person Jesus.

The tradition that 1 Tim cited conceives the world through a spatial structure: the verses have a sequence that goes:

> a (earth): in the flesh
> b (heaven): in the spirit
> b (heaven): by angels
> a (earth): among Gentiles
> a (earth): throughout the world
> b (heaven:) up in glory.

The entire creed shows the pattern of down-up, up-down, and down-up.
The problem here is a cosmos gone out of control, where principalities and powers rule, and the solution is the uniting of heaven and earth into a single body.

These are two distinct, primitive cultural-linguistic systems, each with a different way to understand the world, the fundamental religious problem, and the
fundamental religious solution to that problem. Lumping these two creeds
together does not produce a fuller, more accurate Christianity anymore than
saying "Drive on the left and drive on the right" produces a fuller, better description of driving. Each was fully adequate in its context.

The titles for Jesus and these two early Christian creeds exemplify what
could be shown in many ways. From its inception Christianity was radically pluralistic and the sociopolitical development of a larger, emerging church from the
second through the fourth centuries eventually produced a Christianity far more
uniform in doctrine. The point for the moment is not that later uniformity was

inherently bad but simply that plurality is necessary because Christianity was interpretive from the start.

Christian Doctrines as Historically Conditioned

To continue the discussion of church doctrines as historically conditioned, it is worth examining in some more detail the idea of Jesus' "incarnation." Here we find an example rich in New Testament and early church history, and rich in current church politics as people debate both the issue of the Trinity and the issue of Trinitarian inclusive language ("Father, Son, and Holy Spirit" or something else like "Creator, Redeemer, Sustainer"). As we have seen, Jesus was given many names that expressed the encounter with the divine that people had when they were encountered by Jesus. One of the titles was Son of God.

Here several observations are needed for clarity. First, the title Son of God, as with all the titles for Jesus, came from the religious and social cultures already at hand. Titles already had their own context and historical use. Within Judaism, for instance, one tradition was that the king of Israel was proclaimed and anointed as "God's Son" on behalf of all the people. The words of Psalm 2 reflect this tradition and Mark used them in his baptismal narrative in which God anoints Jesus as "his son." In classical Hellenistic stories, people became God's son by some semi-biological process. Hercules, for example, was the son of Jupiter and the mortal Alcmena.

Some of the people who felt themselves to be encountered by God when they were encountered by Jesus confessed that "Jesus is the Son of God." From their historical context God's Son would be the one who conveyed the divine presence. Over time this original encounter with Jesus, and the original giving of the title Son of God, became something in the past that could only be reported about later. People would say, "Did you hear? John Riggs was encountered by the Son of God," and what was originally *an interpretive experience* became reported as *a fact that had happened* to someone else. Then something else happened. Where originally the movement was from Jesus to the title Son of God so that the encounter with Jesus defined the title, later as the title became reported the direction went from the title backward to Jesus. In a backwash process the title began to define Jesus by transferring to him what had been culturally expected of the "Son of God."

For instance, differing communities of faith began to confess how Jesus could have become God's Son. Historically conditioned answers were given and applied to Jesus. By 50 c.e., to judge by the creedal fragment that Paul cited at the beginning of his letter to Rome, some people had confessed that Jesus was designated "Son of God" by his resurrection (Rom 1:4). The community of Mark has confessed that Jesus became God's Son when God adopted him at his baptism, anointing him with the Spirit according to the model of Psalm 2. The communities of Matthew and Luke confessed that Jesus became God's Son through some miracle of birth. By the end of the first century C.E. the community of John confessed Jesus as God's Son according to a preexistence with God.

Using religious traditions about the "Son of God" that already lay at hand, various communities then applied these traditions to Jesus in order to explain how he had become "God's Son." But in a manner analogous to the names given to Jesus, we do not have a better "objective" life of Jesus by putting together these explanations, as though preexistence, miraculous birth, and baptism were three temporally sequential events in the career of Jesus. These three explanations were just that—alternative and historically conditioned explanations of how Jesus could have been the "Son of God"—and over time these explanations took on the character of "objective events" that themselves needed to be explained. How, for instance, did "the event" of "the incarnation" really happen?

In the early fourth century a very popular church presbyter in Alexandria named Arius argued that Jesus was adopted by God as God's Son, thus becoming the first-born of creatures. This happened because God foresaw that Jesus would grow in obedience to God and thus God had adopted him as Son from the start. The proclamation of Arius was that just as God had foreseen that Jesus would grow in obedience and had therefore adopted him, so God might see us grow in obedience to God and adopt us as sons and daughters of God.[59]

Arius defended his religious claims by using technical theology partly derived from the great early theologian Origen (ca. 185–ca. 254), probably via Antioch and a thinker named Lucian. According to this view, God was radically other than this creation. In terms of matter, nothing of the created order could be of divine substance or emanation. In terms of time, Jesus could not have been co-eternal with God for then he would have been God's "brother" not his "Son." God's Word entered a human body, grew in wisdom and obedience to God's will, and was adopted as Son. Arius's theology was taken up by the Council of Nicaea in 325 C.E., held near the imperial capital, and underwritten by and presided over by Constantine.

The Nicene solution was a political one, offered by the supreme political voice of the empire, the emperor Constantine. The Son, God's Word, was "homoousios" (of the same substance) as the Father. The term was troublesome to many of the bishops; it had been rejected in other theological contexts; it was capable of wide-ranging interpretation (from no distinction between Father and Son to the Father adopting the Son); and it was thought by some to be unscriptural.[60]

Nicene Christianity was defended by Bishop Athanasius, whose own career mirrored the ups-and-downs of the Arian controversy; and careful study of Athanasius and his theology has shown how often he rode the winds of imperial patronage, adjusting his theological stances according to the needs of patronage and power.[61] Athanasius defended Nicaea by taking up a theological tradition also derived from Origen, this by way of Alexandrian traditions. God and God's Word were co-eternal. Only a "Son" who was the divine Word, and thus God, could be a proper mediator between heaven and earth. Likewise only a "Son" who was the divine Word, and thus God, could restore creation and the human soul to its perfection—"God became 'man' that 'man' might become God" said Athanasius in a famous phrase. Only a redeemer who was also the creator could restore creation—what you do not subsume, you cannot redeem.

What then do we make of the great Trinitarian council and its theological defense? What Nicaea does not provide us is an accurate metaphysical description of Jesus' unity in substance with God and thus the basis for conceiving a tri-une God of "three people and one substance." The Nicene language of Jesus being "begotten of the Father" and of "the substance of the Father" constituted a theological explanation about a theological idea ("incarnation"), which itself was an explanation of a confessional title, "Son of God." Even more, imperial politics dictated the language; church conflicts (East versus West, or Antioch versus Alexandria, or debates about Origin) underlay the discussion of the language; and the theological results of the discussion were tied to patronage and power in the empire.

Does this mean that the idea of Trinity as such has no place within Christian theology? Not necessarily, although it does mean that the traditional Trinitarian formula ("three persons and one substance"), based in the Nicene language of Jesus Christ as "the substance of the Father, God of God, Light of Light, true God of true God," is historically conditioned.

Another historically conditioned church teaching is worth considering; in the next chapter it will be rethought. Divine omnipotence, considered simply as the idea that in principle God can guarantee the results of an action if God so desires, also finds its roots in historically conditioned ideas and politics.

The biblical worldview of the New Testament is thoroughly mythological, in the careful meaning given that word by Bultmann and discussed in the first chapter here. One of the ambiguities of that mythological view is that God is seen as having omnipotent power over all things while the human person is called to the radical and freely given faith that is the heart's complete trust in God. Where the biblical narratives show forth this cosmic wizard-type power— God speaking and the guaranteed result happening—they naturally share this view with other religions of the ancient Near East.

In Western theology the idea of divine omnipotence eventually dominated but did not extinguish the idea of human free will.[62] There were always attempts to credit human free will while also crediting divine control over every detail of worldly events. One such attempt was the argument that God could decide not to prevent some act from going against the divine will. In other words, God allowed the act to happen. But when did the idea of complete divine control first gain the upper hand in Western theology? Was it gradual without people noticing or was it partly gradual yet also traceable to forceful theological voices? The answer is the latter.

Above all, Augustine was the person who most instantiated divine omnipotence into Western theological and social culture. Around the year 397 C.E., with the writing of *Ad Simplicianum*, Augustine began to stress the absolute priority of divine grace over human free will. Why? Because Augustine was the first great Christian thinker who read the Genesis accounts of Adam and Eve as the moment of original sin, rather than reading the accounts as concerning Christian freedom, as had been the wide-ranging tradition previously. When Augustine read the Genesis stories as the fall to complete moral bondage he helped give theological justification for imperial, Christian control over both state and church. Christianity would lead humanity out of its humanly irreversible moral depravity toward social stability and religious salvation. Only freely given, omnipotent grace could do this, not human free will.[63]

The Need for Claims about Reality: Evaluating Postmodern Theologies

The unwillingness of these three types of postmodern theology to make claims about reality itself poses several problems, the most serious of which applies to all three—the inability to redeem ethical claims without being self-contradictory, empty, or arbitrary. In order to see how that can be true, I want to summarize the argument found in Franklin Gamwell's *The Divine Good: Modern Moral Theory and the Necessity of God,* whose fundamental argument is that only the divine good can ultimately ground moral claims.[64] How can Gamwell make such a claim?

Gamwell lays out the conceptual possibilities for ethics that are done apart from claims about the structure of reality itself (that is, nonmetaphysical ethical approaches).[65] First, amorality must be rejected because to argue that there are no grounds for moral claims means that one should choose arbitrarily. But this then is a moral principle by which one ought to act, and not to act in an arbitrary manner would be an incorrect choice. Amoralism is self-contradictory.[66]

If we then chose according to a moral principle, without regard to a realizable state of affairs, as Kant argued we ought to do, by what actual content could we judge whether the choice was right or wrong? All that remains is a principle independent of any state of affairs and thus neither right nor wrong. Kant's ethical approach is empty.[67]

Perhaps another significant Western option could be taken, that argued by Aristotle, who thought that the good does entail some state of affairs. The modern philosopher Alasdair MacIntyre turns to this tradition to avoid the emptiness of Kant's ethical approach. According to MacIntyre's approach, virtues are drawn from the traditions of a particular community and its narrative that embody moral intentions. But how is there to be adjudication between different communities and their stories? Such a criterion, argues Gamwell, would have to stand outside the tradition-based communities themselves. In the end MacIntyre's ethical approach is arbitrary because something is virtuous because a community says it is virtuous.[68]

By contrast, Karl-Otto Apel tries to revive the approach of Kant, whose error, argues Apel, is to consider human subjectivity "as solitary, without transcendental relation to other subjects." This leads Kant to an ethics that is empty. When one considers human subjectivity as "necessarily intersubjective" so that there is "essential relations to others," then the moral law upon which one acts has a transcendental character to it. Human moral claims mutually recognize communication partners in an "ideal communication community" where consensus is sought.[69] The problem, argues Gamwell, is how to adjudicate between the diversity of all the participating claims. Only a norm that could include all conceivable state of affairs would suffice. More specifically, only an "'infallible' subject" would suffice because the offer to communicate to fallible subjects presupposes a strictly comprehensive subject, God, who could assent to any and all valid claims.[70] By stopping short of this conclusion Apel's ethical approach remains incomplete. Gamwell then goes on to complete just such a theistic ethic.[71]

This is a brief summary of a book that has been called "one of the best—if not the best—book on moral theory written in several decades."[72] Gamwell's well-reasoned point can be put simply for purchase on postmodern theologies: any ethical claim that does not entail assertions about the structure of reality itself can only remain self-refuting, empty, arbitrary, or incomplete.

For Mark C. Taylor postmodern life is to be lived beyond the usual binary opposites that Derrida argues the West has developed in order to avoid decentering. Such binary opposites have a privileged center and a marginalized other. For Taylor,

> erring thought is neither properly theological nor nontheological, theistic nor atheistic, religious nor secular, believing nor nonbelieving. A/theology represents the liminal thinking of marginal thinkers. The / of a/theology (which, it is important to note, can be written but not spoken) marks the limen that signifies both proximity and distance, similarity and difference, interiority and exteriority. This strangely

permeable membrane forms a border where fixed boundaries disintegrate.[73]

This means for Taylor that the "opposites that Western thought traditionally separates and holds apart appear to be confused: inside/outside, identity/difference, remedy/infection, purity/pollution, propriety/impropriety, good/evil. . . ."[74] Along with the German thinker Friedrich Nietzsche—one of *Erring's* most frequently cited authors—we ought to live beyond such polarities, including that of good/evil.[75]

Nietzsche is typically taken to be one of those thinkers for whom there are no grounds for ethical choices since all rational choices are arbitrary. He is an amoralist and one could read Taylor the same way when he argues that boundaries disintegrate and that an "erring" life is lived in "*radical* purposelessness."[76] In this case Taylor's ethical position would be, on the analysis by Gamwell, self-contradictory.

Taylor, however, may intend something other than amoralism. This deconstructive path for theology and the "serpentine wandering" that is the "erring" way is commended by Taylor. It is the way of "mazing grace" where the polarity of sacred/secular is subverted so that "no-thing is truly sacred and thus nothing is simply profane."[77] Thus at some level Taylor has a principle for human choice, even if that be a principle that is beyond the polarity of principle and nonprinciple. But this would seem to leave Taylor with an ethics that is purely formal and empty in content, since all realizable states of affairs are "radically relative" and thus disconnected to the principled choice.

Taylor's ethics are either self-contradictory or empty. The self-contradictory feature of Taylor's argument occurs elsewhere, as Griffin points out.[78] So, for instance, while Taylor criticizes what he thinks is a modern mistake in understanding consciousness, he does so by assuming *the same position* that he criticizes: namely, that one can know the true nature of something, in this case the nature of "consciousness" as such.[79]

The ethical positions of Daly and McFague fare no better. Recall that for Daly the patriarchal narrative and the world that it forms is so thoroughly oppressive to women that the only alternative, as Daly sees it, is to construct an alternative linguistic galaxy.

For Daly, the appeal to language communities that construct their own worlds seems descriptively accurate but socially misguided. On the social level of varied discourses in the postmodern world, Daly would seem to have created her own form of tribalism. By "tribalism" I have in mind a closed community shaped by its language and rituals and oriented toward its own divine reality, and thus ethical injunctions, who preserves this community over and against other communities and their divine realities. Who in the postmodern world can understand the language of Daly's community and enter into it other than white, lesbian, educated women?

But the ethical issue runs yet deeper. By essentially appealing to communal narrative and the virtues that it embodies, how can there be adjudication between narrative communities when their ideas of the moral good differ? Ethics done this way, as Gamwell so argues, can only be arbitrary. What is good is what the community says is good. But this raises a second difficulty.

As problematic as it seems to be to appeal to dead, privileged white men from antiquity, Plato knew what he was saying in the dialogue *Gorgias:* Admit in principle no universal criteria for the good and the just, and we are then forced to agree with the Sophist Callicles, who admired Xerxes because the great Persian imposed his will upon others by force (d. 483).

Might makes right would be the modern phrase about tribalism and this connects to an historical irony. Historically speaking the appeal to one's tribe and its narrative has typically been the way that conservative communities, bent on oppressing their minorities, have operated. To take some examples from American society, in the ante-bellum South southern culture stood on a tripod: the politics of state's rights, the economics of slavery, and the culture of knighthood drawn from authors such as Sir Walter Scott. The antebellum South had its own distinctive and coherent narrative. According to the standards of tribal theology, the South should have been allowed to secede and we might well have slavery today. By contrast it was the abolitionists who appealed to universal claims about the radical equality of all people.

Here is a more modern example. The armed religious right in America and Europe has been abandoning Christianity as its communal narrative. Why? Because it has understood that Christianity and the foundations of America are too inextricably bound to the universalism present in Christianity and deism. What has emerged instead is "Odinism," with its appeal to the armed, tribal Norse god, and his narratives about preserving his chosen people, the "Wotan's Volk."[80]

When Daly depicts the battleaxe as the symbol of her will to fight for her vision, she and others who share this tribal perspective better be ready to defend themselves with real weapons a great deal more deadly than a symbolic battleaxe. When tribal narratives compete there is no universal and public ground upon which to have dialogue. All too often force wins out. This sadly is no exaggeration: ask the family planning clinics across America about the killings, bombings, kidnapings, continual Anthrax scares, and assorted daily violence done by people with a tribal view of religions and community. The same person who bombed a gay and lesbian nightclub in Atlanta also bombed a reproductive health clinic there. From the Sophists of Socrates' day to the hate groups in modern America and Europe, tribalism begets violence and beckons the loss of civilization in any meaningful sense of the word.

The matter of metaphysics and ethics stands differently with McFague, who has consciously borrowed the approach to language and metaphor found in Ricoeur. Recall that for Ricoeur knowledge is intersubjective; it concerns interpreting the world that we inherit rather than making true claims about the objective world as such.

For McFague, metaphor is the human way of knowing and it describes rather than defines. We have no access to reality, nor therefore to God as the ultimate reality. Metaphor tries to describe the human experience of God, but "when we try to speak of God there is nothing which resembles what we can conceive when we say that word."[81] Language cannot describe God's being but rather constructs a theological model about which we ask questions such as,

> Is it better in terms of our and the world's preservation and fulfillment? Is it better in terms of coherence, comprehensibility, and illumination? Is it better in terms of expressing the Christian understanding of the relationship between God and the world? All these criteria are relevant, for a metaphor that is all or mostly nonsense has tried its chance and failed.[82]

But this raises a problem for McFague's ethical project, which builds on the model of the universe as God's body. Insofar as a model is a metaphor "with staying power," models make no more claim to speak about the structure of reality or the nature of God than do mere metaphors. On what basis then could the model be considered to be *true* about God, in any way other than offering an enduring and coherent pattern of human meanings? Without some literal claim about the structure of reality and about God there would seem to be no way to adjudicate whether the model is true or not.[83] What remains is a linguistically formed community abiding by a model and its narratives, which make no claims about reality as such. Its models are judged according to criteria such as their coherence, their comprehensibility, and their power to illumine the human situation. Different models may be judged more or less adequate according to such criteria, but ultimately they remain arbitrary because they cannot be grounded in anything other than intersubjective communal assent. The quarrel is neither about the model, the universe as the body of God, nor about the theological and ecological ethics themselves, but about the grounds upon which they are held to be valid.

Preserving postmodern theology as exemplified by the New Yale School has a similar struggle. The biblical narrative communicates Christ himself to us, absorbs reality, and forms the Christian community as an alternative to the world. Stanley Hauerwas stands as a leading ethical voice from that tradition and his work has been deeply influenced by the thought of Alasdair McIntyre.[84]

Gamwell's analysis of McIntyre's project applies *mutatis mutandis* to the narrative, tradition-model ethics of Hauerwas. In the end, on what basis can ethics be other than arbitrary? They are true because the tradition of the community, shaped by the biblical narrative, says they are true. For Hauerwas there is no need to be apologetic about this. The Christian community stands over and against the world, and the modern world that hangs on to the Enlightenment project.[85]

> Theology is best done without apology. I therefore have no intention of apologizing for the unapologetic character of this book. That I refuse to offer such an apology puts me at odds with a great deal of modern theology, which has adopted as its task to "explain"—either to our cultural despisers or to what is a growing and more characteristic population, the indifferent—what Christians believe. This explanatory enterprise is undertaken on the presumption that theologians, like Christians in general, will be more or less tolerated if they underwrite views about which agreement prevails.[86]

But there are problems with the preserving postmodernism of the New Yale School, and one of them is the issue of natural theology. Liberal Protestants from Schleiermacher on have appealed to natural theology because the God who decisively revealed through Jesus ("God the Redeemer") is also the same God who reveals in and to human experience as such ("God the Creator"). Thus liberal Protestant apologetic appeal has fundamentally not been a capitulation to culture in order to receive its approbation. Rather, liberal apologetics point out that a humanist commitment made without an appeal to Jesus Christ as the decisive witness to human existence produces a truncated humanism. Schleiermacher knew this. Barth, however, thought Schleiermacher's apologetic task was a capitulation to culture and would have nothing of a natural theology. The New Yale School continues the theological trajectory of Barth.

But how stands it with a natural theology? Is natural theology to be rejected in favor of biblical theology? In a careful study of scriptural texts and the world-view of their authors, James Barr has shown that the Scriptures, both Hebrew and Christian, assume and assert the natural human ability to know about the world and the relationship of humans to God.[87] Thus biblical theology that looks to the canonical narrative, denying that theology has resources naturally from human experience and the world, strangely denies what the authors of the Scriptures themselves assume and assert.

A second and related problem is that of how we know that God has indeed addressed us in the narrative. Without some prior relationship to God by which we could re-cognize God we could not know the One calling us to be God. Appeal to God's original revelation in and to human beings as such would seem requisite, hence the need for some type of natural theology.

Finally we have the problem of tribalism. Internally there is the issue of arbitrariness. If ethical activity must account for intention, and intention is known through the narrative of a particular community and the saints whose virtues one aims at, how do we know such intended virtues are good? We know because they are exemplified in people the community considers good. Externally, there is the irony that while attempting to be an alternative to modern culture, the Christian tribalism that focuses on language and community narrative, rather than on claims about reality as such, merely continues the (most) modern trajectory. It sets up yet another competing narrative in a pluralistic world with no way to adjudicate between the various narrative communities.

In these three areas the fundamental problem is the claim that simply as a human being one cannot make any first-order truth claims about the world and God. To credit some claims about the world and God would: (1) Provide for a biblical theology that was appropriate to the worldview of the biblical authors in which natural theology was a part; (2) Provide a basis for explaining how one knows the address that comes in the biblical narrative to be *God's* address (that is, coming to know would be a form of recognizing that which already was known at least in some fashion); and (3) Avoid the arbitrary and modern tribal quality to the ethical project.

NOTES TO CHAPTER THREE

1. Ludwig Wittgenstein, *Tractatus Logicus Philosophicus* (trans. D. F. Pears and B. F. McGuinness; intro. by Bertrand Russell; London: Routledge, 2001.) Also see, B. F. McGuinness, *Wittgenstein: A Life; Young Ludwig* (Berkeley: University of California Press, 1988); Merrill B. Hintikka and Jaako Hintikka, *Investigating Wittgenstein* (London: Blackwell, 1986); Hans Sluga and David G. Stern, *The Cambridge Companion to Wittgenstein* (Cambridge: Cambridge University Press, 1996).

2. Ludwig Wittgenstein, *Philosophical Investigations* (trans. G. E. M. Anscombe; Oxford: Blackwell, 1963).

3. Ferdinand de Saussure, *Course in General Linguistics* (ed. Charles Bally and Albert Sechehaye in collaboration with Albert Reidlinger; trans. Wade Baskin; London, Peter Owen, 1974).

4. Saussure's structuralism influenced the French author and literary critic Roland Barthes (1915–1980). Barthes applied a structuralist approach to popular culture, and in his 1957 collection of essays, *Mythologies,* he critically examined advertising, consumerism, and the entertainment cultures to show how signs organize everyday life. Barthes's love was semiology—the

science of signs, *how* things mean—and his many essays show how the first level of signs actually involves a social and political meaning, which it then presents naturally. A famous example is the picture of a black soldier saluting the French flag on the cover of the French magazine *Paris-Match*. The picture is the signifier, and the actual soldier is the signified, but this set of signifier-signified is itself a signifier for the "truth" (the signified) that justice prevails for all people in colonial France, an idea that all people ought to salute. For Barthes, this is how myth worked.

5. Jacques Lacan, *The Language of Self: The Function of Language in Psychoanalysis* (trans. with notes and commentary by Anthony Wilden; Baltimore: Johns Hopkins University Press, 1981). See also, Benvenuto Bice and Roger Kennedy, *The Works of Jacques Lacan: An Introduction* (New York: St. Martin's, 1986).

6. See Jeff Collins, *Introducing Derrida* (Duxford, Cambridge: Icon, 2000); John D. Caputo, ed., *Deconstruction in a Nutshell: A Conversation with Jacques Derrida* (New York: Fordham University Press, 1977); Julian Wolfreys, ed., *The Derrrida Reader: Writing Performances* (Edinburgh: Edinburgh University Press, 1998).

7. Jacques Derrida, *Of Grammatology* (corrected ed., trans. Gayatri Chakrovorty Spivak; Baltimore: Johns Hopkins University Press, 1998).

8. Michel Foucault, *Madness and Civilization* (trans. Richard Howard; New York: Pantheon, 1965). See also, Gary Gutting, ed. *The Cambridge Companion to Foucault* (Cambridge: Cambridge University Press, 1994); Paul Rabinow, ed., *The Foucault Reader* (New York: Pantheon, 1984).

9. So, for instance, Michel Foucault, *Discipline and Punishment* (trans. Alan Sheridan; New York: Pantheon, 1977); *The History of Sexuality* (trans. Robert Hurley; New York: Vintage, 1990).

10. Toril Moi, ed., *The Kristeva Reader* (New York: Columbia University Press, 1986); Kelly Oliver, ed., *The Portable Kristeva* (New York: Columbia University Press, 2002); Julia Kristeva, *Tales of Love* (trans. Leon S. Roudiez; New York: Columbia University Press, 1987); idem, *Strangers to Ourselves* (trans. Leon S. Roudiez; New York: Columbia University Press, 1991).

11. Lewis Hahn, ed., *The Philosophy of Paul Ricoeur* (The Library of Living Philosophers, vol. 24; Chicago: Open Court, 1985); Paul Ricoeur, *Essays on Biblical Interpretation,* ed. Lewis S. Mudge; Philadelphia: Fortress, 1980); idem, *Figuring the Sacred* (ed. Mark I. Wallace; trans. David Pellauer; Minneapolis: Fortress, 1995); idem, *Hermeneutics and the Human Sciences* (ed. and trans. John B. Thompson; Cambridge: Cambridge University Press, 1981).

12. Richard Rorty, *Philosophy and the Mirror of Nature* (Princeton: Princeton University Press, 1979). For a good introduction to Rorty, with a format of essays and responses that makes much of Rorty's thought accessible, see Robert B. Brandon, ed., *Rorty and His Critics* (Oxford: Blackwell, 2000).

13. These categories and the analysis of Mark C. Taylor are indebted to David Ray Griffin, William Beardslee, Joe Holland, *Varieties of Postmodern Theology* (Albany: State University of New York Press, 1989). This whole postmodern series edited by Griffin is recommended, especially Griffin et al., *Founders of Constructive Postmodern Philosophy.*

14. Mark C. Taylor, *Deconstructing Theology* (Chico, Calif.: Scholars, 1982), xii.

15. Ibid., see 45–85, esp. 48–49, 62 nn. 20–21, 69, 77.

16. Ibid., xx.

17. Mark C. Taylor, *Erring: a Postmodern A/theology* (Chicago: University of Chicago Press, 1984).

18. Ibid., 22–25.

19. Ibid., prelude, chs. 1–2, 8; esp. pp. 14, 35, 105, 170, 172, 175.

20. Ibid., chs. 6–7.; esp. pp. 140, 166, 170.

21. Ibid., 183.

22. Griffin, Beardslee, and Holland, *Varieties of Postmodern Theology,* 55–56, n. 44.

23. Mark C. Taylor, *Altarity* (Chicago: University of Chicago Press, 1987), xxvii. See for instance, the last section of Taylor's chapter on Kierkegaard, 340–53.

24. Mark C. Taylor, *Disfiguring: Art, Architecture, Religion* (Chicago: University of Chicago Press, 1982).

25. Mark C. Taylor, *Nots* (Chicago: University of Chicago Press, 1993).

26. Mark C. Taylor, *Hiding* (Chicago: University of Chicago Press, 1997).

27. Ibid., 264–65.

28. Daly, *The Church and the Second Sex.*

29. Ibid., 118.

30. Ibid., 185–86.

31. Carl Bernstein and Marco Politi, *Holiness: John Paul II and the Hidden History of Our Time* (New York: Doubleday, 1996), 513–30 ("Eve"), esp. 519–24.

32. Daly, *Beyond God the Father.*

33. Daly, *The Church and the Second Sex,* "Autobiographical Preface to the Colophon Edition," 5–6.

34. Mary Daly, *Gyn/Ecology: The Metaethics of Radical Feminism* (Boston: Beacon, 1978), 423.

35. Daly, *Pure Lust.*

36. Ibid., 12.

37. Ibid., 20–24.

38. *Webster's First New Intergalactic Wickedary of the English Language* (conjured by Mary Daly in cahoots with Jane Caputi; Boston: Beacon, 1987).

39. Sallie TeSelle, *Literature and the Christian Life* (New Haven: Yale University Press, 1966).

40. Sallie McFague TeSelle, *Speaking in Parables: A Study in Metaphor and Theology* (Philadelphia: Fortress, 1975).

41. Ibid., 62.

42. Ibid., 82.

43. Ibid., 86.

44. Sallie McFague, *Metaphorical Theology: Models of God in Religious Language* (Philadelphia: Fortress, 1982); idem, *Models of God: Theology for an Ecological, Nuclear Age* (Philadelphia: Fortress, 1987); idem, *The Body of God: An Ecological Theology* (Philadelphia: Fortress, 1993); idem, *Super, Natural Christians: How We Should Love Nature* (Minneapolis: Fortress, 1997); and idem, *Life Abundant: Rethinking Theology and Economy for a Planet in Peril* (Minneapolis: Fortress, 2001).

45. McFague, Metaphorical Theology, 33–34.

46. Ibid., 34.

47. McFague, Life Abundant, 122.

48. Hans Frei, *The Eclipse of Biblical Narrative: A Study in Eighteenth- and Nineteenth-Century Hermeneutics* (New Haven: Yale University Press, 1974).

49 Ibid., 14.

50. George Lindbeck, *The Nature of Doctrine: Religion and Theology in a Postliberal Age* (Philadelphia: Fortress, 1984).

51. Ibid., 51.

52. Paul Holmer, *The Grammar of Faith* (San Francisco: Harper & Row, 1978). See the collection of essays in his honor: Richard H. Bell, ed., *The Grammar of the Heart: New Essays in Moral Philosophy and Theology* (San Francisco: Harper & Row, 1988).

53. See, for instance, Brevard Childs, *Introduction to the Old Testament as Scripture* (Philadelphia: Fortress, 1979); idem, *The New Testament as Canon: An Introduction* (Philadelphia: Fortress, 1985).

54. Paul McGlasson, *God the Redeemer: A Theology of the Gospel* (Louisville: Westminster John Knox, 1983), 189 n.3.

55. See Wallace, *The Second Naiveté*, 87–110.

56. This section is thoroughly indebted to the work of the New Testament historical critic Willi Marxsen, much of whose work is now in English translation. For an important collection of translated essays, plus an introductory essay and bibliography, see Marxsen, *Jesus and the Church*.

57. Marxsen, *Jesus and the Church*, 1–15.

58. Eduard Schweizer, "Two Testament Creeds Compared," in *Neotestamentica: Deutsche und englische aufsätze, 1951–1963* (Zurich: Zwingli Verlag, 1963), 122–35.

59. See Robert C. Gregg and Dennis E. Groh, *Early Arianism: A View of Salvation* (Philadelphia: Fortress, 1981).

60. See W. H. C. Frend, *The Rise of Christianity* (Philadelphia: Fortress, 1984), pp. 498–99; J. N. D. Kelly, *Early Christian Doctrines* (2d ed.; New York: Harper & Row, 1960), 129-36, 232–37.

61. See Timothy Barnes, *Athanasius and Contantius: Theology and Politics in the Constantinian Empire* (Cambridge, Mass.: Harvard University Press, 1993).

62. For a helpful introduction to the material, see Hartshorne, *Omnipotence*, 10–26.

63. For an excellent analysis, see Elaine Pagels, *Adam, Eve, and the Serpent* (New York: Vintage, 1989).

64. Franklin I. Gamwell, *The Divine Good: Modern Moral Theory and the Necessity of God* (San Francisco: HarperCollins, 1990).

65. See, for example, his chart and summary comments, Gamwell, *The Divine Good*, 155–58.

66. Ibid., 35–36.

67. Ibid., 46–51.

68. Ibid., 67–80.

69. Ibid., 128, 139–43.

70. Ibid., 144–53.

71. Ibid., 155–84.

72. George L. Goodwin, review of Franklin I. Gamwell, *The Divine Good: Modern Moral Theory and the Necessity of God, Process Studies* 21 (1992): 184.

73. Taylor, *Erring,* 12.

74. Ibid., 93.

75. See, just as one example, the discussion in Taylor, *Erring,* 166–67 and his quotation from Nietzche's *Will to Power.*

76. Taylor, *Erring,* 157.

77. Ibid., 149–69.

78. Griffin, Beardslee, and Holland, *Varieties of Postmodern Theology,* 35–40.

79. Ibid., 36–37.

80. For example, see *Intelligence Report* 98 (2000): 25–29. *Intelligence Report* is published by the Southern Poverty Law Center, which carefully monitors hate movements in America and abroad. More directly, seek the Internet sites for Thule Publications, the Order Bruder Schweigen, or David Lane, the man who drove the getaway car in the machine-gunning of Alan Berg, the Denver talk show host. Lane is the legendary author of the famous "fourteen words": "We must secure the existence of our people and a future for white children." The fourteen words have now been taken as the motto of the American Nazi Party.

81. McFague, *Metaphorical Theology,* 194.

82. McFague, *Models of God,* 70.

83. See, for example, the comments by David J. Bromell, "Sallie McFague's 'Metaphorical Theology,'" *JAAR* 61, no. 3 (1993): 485–503.

84. See, for instance, Stanley Hauerwas, *Wilderness Wanderings: Probing Twentieth-Century Theology and Philosophy* (Boulder, Colo.: Westview, 1997), 14, 21 n. 26; also, 82–96, 99–110, passim.

85. Ibid., 1–21, 25–31.

86. Ibid., 1.

87. James Barr, *Biblical Faith and Natural Theology* (Oxford: Clarendon, 1993).

CHAPTER FOUR
TOWARD AN INCLUSIVE LIBERAL THEOLOGY

Chapter 3 traced postmodernism. The work of Saussure, Barthes, Foucault, Wittgenstein, Derrida, and Rorty all showed the anti-rational rationalism of modernity taken to its furthest point yet. Not only were rational claims not made about reality as such, such claims were argued to be invalid. Turning inward, these thinkers reflected on language itself. On the positive side, this movement has shown that knowledge and language are thoroughly conditioned by historical contexts. Language has been all too often used to stifle alternative voices and to project the interests of the powerful as neutral truths to be followed by all. Little wonder that Christian liberation theologians have found resources here. Daly's famous one-line assertion—"If God is male, then the male is God"—can be applied *mutatis mutandis* to other contexts.

The cost of these insights has been philosophical projects doubtfully capable of sustaining ethics or civilization in any meaningful way, to say nothing about a fundamental internal inconsistency: to claim that all language and thought is historically conditioned, and thus part of human cultural-linguistic systems that cannot make transcendental claims about the structure of reality, is itself to make a claim about the nature of reality as such.

Christian postmodern theologians have shared in the strengths and weaknesses of the postmodern resources upon which they drew. The final part of chapter 3 argued that the necessary plurality of voices for which postmodernism argues, and the historically conditioned nature of theological concepts, are features to be credited. Examples from apostolic Christianity were given. By contrast, all three forms of postmodern theology (purifying, political, and preserving) suffered from the inability to make claims about reality.

Can such claims be meaningfully made? And if so, what might an inclusive, liberal, Christian theology that credited such claims look like? And how might such an approach treat ethical and ecumenical issues that currently are much debated: sexual ethics, reproductive rights, and interreligious dialogue?

THE CHARACTER OF CLAIMS ABOUT REALITY ITSELF

Are there ways to talk about reality that, though arising in some particular context, fundamentally concern any conceivable context? Here the work of the philosopher Charles Hartshorne leads in a helpful direction. The son of an episcopal clergyman, Hartshorne was raised to worship divine love and to think critically about religion. Hartshorne received his Ph.D. in philosophy from Harvard, did a postdoctorate in Europe where he listened to the lectures of Husserl and Heidegger, and then returned to Harvard as a research fellow. During this period at Harvard, he helped edit the papers of Peirce and he worked as a teaching assistant for Whitehead. Hartshorne then went on to teach philosophy at the University of Chicago, working mostly out of the Divinity School. He later taught at Emory University and finished his career as the University of Texas.

Influenced by Whitehead and Peirce, among others, Hartshorne argued that certain claims could be made about reality as such, claims that were strictly necessary because they could not fail to apply to any conceivable context. Hartshorne put the matter in this way:

Metaphysical truths may be described as such that no experience can contradict them, but also such that any experience must illustrate them. Let us take this as an example: "The present is always influenced by the past." Could any experience conflict with this? We cannot know that we are uninfluenced by the past, for to know the past is, in one's state of knowledge, to be influenced by it.[1]

A little later he offers some other examples:

Take the sayings, "Life has a meaning," or "There are real values," or "Some ways of thinking and acting are better than others." In no case can these affirmations rightfully be denied, for if life itself is never worthwhile, then neither is the denial of life's worthwhileness ever worthwhile, since this denial itself is a piece of life, an act of a living being. And to say that no way of thinking is better than any other is to say that the way of thinking thus expressed is no better than the contra-dictory way, and such a manner of talking nullifies itself.[2]

Such assertions are, in Hartshorne's words, "metaphysical truisms." They cannot be meaningfully denied and at the same time they are affirmed by any experience. Other metaphysical truisms would be "Something exists," or "Life is important." These are claims about reality that cannot "rightfully be denied." Any conceivable attempt to deny that something exists would itself be something that existed. Any conceivable attempt to deny the importance of life would itself show that life was important enough to attempt to deny its importance. In both cases no concrete state of affairs is ruled out by these types of assertions.[3] They merely assert that any conceivable state of affairs must exemplify the features that "something exists" and that "life is important."

These truisms refer to the character of reality itself ("metaphysical truisms") and Hartshorne spent most of his academic work discussing metaphysical issues as well as the idea of God, which he thought an adequate metaphysics must entail.[4] At the end of the essay on metaphysical assertions, from which citations have just been given, Hartshorne concludes by saying that

> metaphysics gives us no fact, ordinary or superior, but it gives us the key to fact, on both levels, the clue or ideal by which factual experience is to be interpreted. It gives us a sense of what a German theologian has called the accompanying melody, *Begleitmelodie,* of all existence. The import of the word "God" is no mere special meaning in our language, but the soul of significance in general, for it refers to the Life in and for which all things live.[5]

Simply put, the humanist commitment as defined in the introduction here—that of critical reflection according to human experience and reason—must lead to critical thinking about God.

The works of one of Hartshorne's theological students, Schubert Ogden (b. 1928), have exemplified just this project. In his classic essay "The Reality of God," Ogden argues that the ineradicable human faith in the ultimate meaning of life implies the reality of God. In an argument that echoes Hartshorne's insistence that "life has a meaning," or Whitehead's assertion that beneath knowledge and sense experience "the glimmering of consciousness reveals, something that matters,"[6] Ogden argues that reflection on human experience as such reveals an ineradicable confidence in the worth of any conceivable decision.

> Always presupposed by even the most commonplace of moral decisions is the confidence that these decisions have an unconditional significance. No matter what the content of our choices may be whether for this course of action or for that, we can make them at all only because of our invincible faith that they somehow make a difference which no turn of events in the future has the power to annul.[7]

Even should we try to deny there is any significance in the choices we make, such denial displays the confidence that the denial itself somehow makes a difference. This can be demonstrated, argues Ogden, even when someone makes an articulated effort to show the basic absurdity of life. Analyzing the story by Albert Camus, "The Myth of Sisyphus," Ogden shows that ultimately Camus can only display exactly what the story is meant to disprove-that there is inherent meaning to human choices.[8]

The entire second section of "The Reality of God" is an extended argument for theism based on Ogden's analysis of human faith in the ultimate meaning of life.[9] After the discussion that any choice presupposes a confidence in its unconditional significance, Ogden then identifies what on the objective side (so to speak) correlates to that feature of basic confidence revealed by analysis on the subjective side.

> I hold that the primary use or function of "God" is to refer to the objective ground in reality itself of our ineradicable confidence in the final worth of our existence. It lies in the nature of this basic confidence to affirm that the real whole of which we experience ourselves to be parts is such as to be worthy of, and thus itself to evoke, that very confidence. The word "God," then, provides the designation for whatever it is about this experienced whole that calls forth and justifies our original and inescapable trust, thereby meaning existentially, as William James once said, "You can dismiss certain kinds of fear." From this it follows that to be free of such fear by existing in this trust is one and the same thing with affirming the reality of God.[10]

In sum, there is an ineradicable confidence in the worth of existence whose most adequate explanation is that such confidence is the aspect of the human experience of self, world, and the whole, whose objective side is the reality of God itself.

We are now in a position to return to the postmodern assertion of radical plurality and crediting such plurality in the Jesus encounter that marked the beginning of Christianity. The analysis in this first section will help show how such an encounter with Jesus was for some an encounter with the divine. The issue of plurality and universal claims about reality will be seen to be features of this encounter. Second, reflection on how Jesus' word and deeds functioned in the encounter with Jesus will provide a basis for understanding interreligious dialogue in a new way. And finally, by starting with this encounter with Jesus, and understanding it by way of original confidence, a personal view of God can be developed that provides the basis for ethics.

ANALYZING THE ENCOUNTER WITH JESUS
Plurality and Original Confidence

According to the New Testament scholar Willi Marxsen, the positive encounters with Jesus resulted in several types of reaction. Sometimes particular words or deeds of Jesus were reenacted as a summons to response. Through such activity people passed Jesus on to others. Other times such enacted words or deeds were connected with explanatory religious language such as "God's rule" or "the finger of God." Finally, in some cases people transferred titles of honor to Jesus to explain how it was that they had been encountered by the divine when they were encountered by Jesus.[11]

Chapter 3 argued that such conferring of titles was interpretive according to the context of the one who had been encountered by Jesus. If someone expected God to be present as the Christ, then Jesus was the Christ. In another context, if someone expected God to be present as the Messiah, then Jesus was the Messiah. If someone apocalyptically expected God to be present as the Son of Man, then Jesus was the Son of Man. From its inception Christianity was interpretative. This is Marxsen's (postmodern) insight. But interpretive of exactly what?

Every person who met Jesus unfailingly had as a feature of human experience that ineradicable confidence in the ultimate meaning of human life. Such a feature to human life cannot be meaningfully denied but rather is presupposed and affirmed by any and every human act. As such this claim is not context bound but rather is a feature or aspect of human existence. This also means, on the analysis of Ogden, that no one who met Jesus could be without a prior immediate relationship with God already as a feature of her or his existence simply as a human being. However, awareness of such a relationship, which would require language and thus be mediated, is in no way required by the assertion that the immediate experience of God already is present. Being unaware of something in no way implies its absence. As a crude example, when someone says that "you can feel your heart beating" you then become aware of an immediate internal experience you were having but were not aware that you were having.

And so in the encounter with Jesus that was for some an encounter with the divine, the immediate experience of God's relationship to them came to awareness, and could *only* have done so through the particular language and context that was theirs. There was no awareness other than in and through the particular, language-determined context of that particular person. Christianity was thus *necessarily* interpretive from the start. At the same time, any such interpretation had to presuppose the original confidence that was the human side of the divine-human relationship. The plurality of original Christian interpretation necessarily goes hand in hand with that ineradicable feature of human experience, original confidence.

Jesus's Words and Deeds: Revelation as Representation

In this view, what was decisive about Jesus ("decisive revelation") was not that God constituted in Jesus some new way of being that established a saving relationship not already there. Rather what was decisive about Jesus was that his words and deeds re-presented externally and objectively the relationship with God that no one could already be without ("original revelation"). Ogden has a useful example of the contrast between Jesus constituting the divine offer of grace and Jesus re-presenting such a divine offer. Consider a conservation between three baseball umpires:

> The youngest and least experienced umpire allows, "I call 'em as I see 'em." Whereupon the second umpire, being older and more sure of himself, claims, "I call 'em as they are." But to all this, the oldest and shrewdest umpire responds with complete self-confidence, "They ain't nothing till I call 'em." By an event constitutive of the possibility of salvation I mean an event that is like the third umpire's calls, in that the possibility of salvation is nothing until the event occurs. On the contrary, what I mean by an event representative of the possibility of salvation is an event similar to the calls of the second umpire, in that it serves to declare a possibility of salvation that already is at it is—is already constituted as such—prior to the event's occurring to declare it.[12]

Simply put, Jesus is decisive revelation precisely because he re-presents, presents again, the offer of God's saving love already present in and to human experience by virtue of God's already existing relationship to all people.

God as a Personal Reality

Who then is this God that Jesus decisively represented through his words and deeds? When we begin with Jesus as the one whose words and deeds were for some people the encounter with God, then the apostolic witnessing to this encounter stands as the norm for interpreting God. We all want to hand on what we in turn have received,[13] which means by the logic of tradition that the apostolic testimony to Jesus stands at the headwaters of Christian tradition. In this sense, Christianity is built "upon the foundation of the apostles and prophets, with Christ Jesus himself as the cornerstone," as the author of Ephesians put the matter (2:20). And what do we find when we take this approach? A strictly personal God.[14]

For one thing, *the agent* of divine revelation, Jesus, is personal. Not a way of life, nor a book, nor a set of philosophical teachings, but personal words and

116

deeds were the agent of revelation. Furthermore, *the agency* of this agent is also personal. The earliest apostolic witnesses uniformly use language such as for-giveness, justification, reconciliation, redemption, healing, love, and so on. Since both the agent and agency of God's revelation are strictly personal, an explicit authorization exists to consider God as strictly personal. This raises two key areas that can only be outlined briefly here: how to think about God's nature and God's power.

If we are authorized to conceive God as strictly personal then the divine nature would show a structure analogous to social beings.[15] First of all, there would be some aspect or aspects that remain unchanging for every conceivable moment of life. For instance, John Riggs has blue eyes. Or Andrew Riggs has John Riggs and Cindy Bumb as his parents. Or Abigail Riggs also has blue eyes, and has John Riggs and Cindy Bumb as her parents.

So likewise there are unchanging aspects to the divine life. God's absolute and unchanging aspect is redeeming love. Such redeeming love accounts for the original confidence in the ultimate meaning of all that we do. Notice that this love itself depends on no circumstance whatsoever. It is simply a given feature of the divine life at any conceivable moment.

Personal life not only has an unchanging aspect or aspects, it also has a chang-ing aspect as well. Who I concretely am right now involves integrating actualized past and anticipated future into a new moment as I compose this sentence. So too God has a changing aspect to the divine life. If God experiences all things exactly as they creatively become, and loves them exactly as they come to be in each new moment, then God continually grows as the universe continually becomes.

This contrasts with classical theism in which God could not literally grow and for whom changelessness was the perfection. But why should absolute changelessness be the divine perfection? Why should absolutely perfect sensitiv-ity, and therefore perfect growth, not be the perfection?[16] We certainly seem to think sensitivity and growth are virtues, and rightly so. Growing with perfect sensitivity to all things, and in perfect integration of these experiences into a meaningful whole, seems a proper divine perfection. In this sense, God is imma-nent in the world as the perfectly sensitive One who experiences all and inte-grates such experiences into a whole; just as God is also transcendent to the world as unchanging grace, which itself depends on nothing for its existence. God is both immanent and transcendent.

What then of divine power? In chapter 3 we saw that divine power, con-ceived as omnipotence that guaranteed its own results, stemmed from some mythological features of the biblical worldview embodied soundly in the church for political as well as religious reasons during the time of Augustine. By con-trast, how might divine power be conceived when the encounter with Jesus is taken as the starting point?

Since God is to be conceived as personal so also God's power must be conceived as personal. Personal power cannot guarantee results because it works by influence, not omnipotent coercion. You may love someone, but that does not guarantee he or she will take such love to heart. You may forgive someone, but that does not guarantee he or she will take such forgiveness to heart. You may be angry with someone, but that does not mean he or she will take such anger to heart. Personal power works through people, not over them as though it were a cloudburst cutting wadis through the desert.

While it may seem a politically correct nod to postmodernism to speak of divine power as personal, the apostolic narratives of Christianity suggest precisely the opposite. We see biblical authors asserting divine social power over and against the cultural (and thus politically correct) notion of divine wonders. Paul proclaimed that the cross was a stumbling block because people wanted signs and wonders. Mark constructed a narrative designed to counter the idea of Jesus as a "divine man," proclaiming instead the way to the cross. John's Gospel used as a resource a preexisting "signs-source" but made clear that blessed are the ones who believe but have not seen. John's Gospel recast this signs-source within an entire gospel devoted to faith as trusting God.

LIFE IN POSTMODERNITY: ETHICS AND TRUE RELIGIONS

The Structure of Christian Ethics

To begin the ethical discussion I want to indicate a structure for Christian existence that has long been noticed in the writings of the apostle Paul. Paul's basic ethical structure had two aspects that scholars have named, using grammatical terms, "the indicative" and "the imperative." The indicative points to what God has done on our behalf; the imperative points to what we ought to do because of what has already been done for us.[17]

Paul's letter to the Romans illustrates this pattern. The situation there was conflict between Jewish and Gentile members of the community. From chapter 1 through chapter 11 Paul describes in great detail what God has done for both the Jews and the Gentiles. At the end of the eleventh chapter, Paul gives a doxology that ends this "indicative" section: "For from him [sic] and through him and to him are all things. To him be the glory forever. Amen" (Rom 11:36).

Paul then begins his "imperative" section of the letter with the following verse from the beginning of chapter 12: "I appeal to you therefore, brothers and sisters, by the mercies of God, to present your bodies as a living sacrifice, holy and acceptable to God, which is your spiritual worship." In other words, because the God from whom and through whom and to whom all things are has done such great things (indicative), you therefore should act toward each other and the world in a way that takes such divine activity seriously (imperative). Paul's indicative-imperative structure appropriately adapts to an ethical approach that understands God as a personal reality.

The moral indicative begins with the assertion that the world is comprised of individuals who at each moment integrate their actualized past and their anticipated futures into a new creative self. Because such individuals are at the most basic level not substance-like billiard balls but continually creative acts of integration, these individuals comprise a world in which individuals influence each other and so become a part of each other's ever-new creative synthesis. As Ogden says,

> I know myself most immediately only as an ever-changing sequence of occasions of experience, each of which is the present integration of remembered past and anticipated future into a whole new moment of significance. My life history continually leads through moments of decision in which I must somehow determine what both I and those with whom I am related are to be. Selecting from the heritage of the already actual and the wealth of possibilities awaiting realization, I freely fashion myself in creative interaction with a universe of others who also are not dead but alive.[18]

This world creatively becoming is experienced by God, who creatively integrates all experiences into the divine reality. And so, the moral indicative is simply that our lives not only make a difference to each other, but make an everlasting difference to God's divine life. This objective reality has as its subjective feature "the ineradicable confidence in the final worth of our existence."

The moral imperative follows from this moral indicative. We ought to act so that we maximize the creative individuality of each individual in such a way that we also maximize the creative individuality of all, and thus the divine life as well. Or, to say this in the traditional narrative that we first find in Mark's Gospel:

> Jesus answered, "The first is, 'Hear, O Israel: the Lord our God, the Lord is One; you shall love the Lord your God with all your heart, and with all your soul, and with all your mind, and with all your strength.' The second is this, 'You shall love your neighbor as yourself.' There is no commandment greater than these." (Mark 12:29–31, NRSV)

With this basic structure for ethical decisions in place I want to turn to two ethical issues under discussion within Christianity today. The first is that of same gender sexual ethics, the second is that of abortion rights.

Same Gender Sexual Ethics

It may be worth a moment to clear some scriptural notions about sex out of the way prior to proceeding to the ethical norm that has been laid out and what it means for same gender sexual ethics. Historical perspective often helps relativize what we thought had to be in order to see better what truly applies.

The ancient world of the Hebrew and Christian Scriptures was almost indescribably odd and different from today. Most Americans who picture the time of Jesus have scenes like those from *Ben-Hur* in mind. While *Ben-Hur* has fine historical accuracy the movie scenes themselves are clean and almost modern looking. By contrast, although *The Last Temptation of Christ* has a most strange story, the oddity of the ancient world seems somehow captured there. This type of world was the context for those parts of the Hebrew and Christian writings that relate to human sexuality. As a way of illustrating the difference between their world and ours consider some of the following practices and passages.

In the ancient Near East the practice was known of swearing an oath by giving verbal commitment while holding the penis ("thigh") of the patriarch of the household. Where today we seal a deal with a handshake, these ancients sealed it with a penis-shake:

> Now Abraham was old, well advanced in years; and the Lord had blessed Abraham in all things. Abraham said to his servant, the oldest of his house, who had charge of all that he had, "Put your hand under my thigh, and I will make you swear by the Lord, the God of heaven and earth, that you will not get a wife for my son from the daughters of the Canaanites, among whom I live, but will go to my country and to my kindred and get a wife for my son Isaac." (Gen 24:1–4 NRSV. See also, Gen 47:29–31)[19]

This passage is an excellent illustration of the interrelation between sexual perspective and patriarchal power and relationships. Or taking a very different passage, what about God being the author of "soft-core porn," which is what we would have to conclude if we thought God authored the Bible. Consider this passage from the Song of Songs, which is not an allegory about God and Israel, or about Jesus and the church, but an erotic love song. Take a careful look at the commentary on the Song of Songs done by the philologist and Old Testament scholar Marvin Pope. Pope's work includes illustrations of art work and artifacts from the ancient world.[20] Here is Pope's translation of 5:4–5:

> My love thrust his "hand" into the hole,
> And my inwards seethed for him.

I rose to open for love,
And my hands dripped myrrh,
My fingers liquid myrrh,
On the handles of the bolt.

We can find soft-core pornography used in a demeaning way as God describes Samaria and Jerusalem as two whoring sisters, Oholah and Oholibah (Ezek 23). Oholibah had played the whore in Egypt where she had sought out lovers whose penises were like donkeys and whose ejaculations were like stallions (23:20).

This ancient world was different from ours. In the ancient Near East of Judaism and very early Christianity sexual activity was a matter of power and property, where the bodies of women belonged to the male head of their households, or sexual activity was a matter of ritual purity. We cannot lift out biblical passages, turn to Webster's Dictionary to define the practice so named in our English translations, and apply some rule to human behavior today.

Several years ago Planned Parenthood asked that I speak to a subcommittee of the Missouri legislature on behalf of a very sensible bill that would help give human sexuality guidelines for school systems developing human sexuality material for their students. I began by describing the ways that sexual activity in the ancient world of Judaism and primitive Christianity was connected to issues of property rights and purity. After the meeting a woman ran up to me and asked incredulously, "Do you mean that adultery isn't the same now as it was then?" And I replied that was exactly what I was saying. Adultery was a property violation that occurred when a woman who was the wife of a male head of household had sex with some other man.[21] But sex between a married man and an unattached woman, or between an unmarried man and a woman not the property of some man, fell under no moral prohibitions.

In the early New Testament, when we look at Jesus and Paul, we see that the issue of clean and unclean had disappeared as matters of external dirt or contagion. Issues of purity were matters of internal moral intent. As for the issue of property, we see that Jesus overturned the basic family structure of the ancient world, both Jewish and Greek, and thus family members as property of the male head of household. Paul retained the sense of property—adultery was still a matter of coveting someone else's property, though the sin was the covetousness, strictly speaking—but Paul saw sex in the larger sense of all people being the personal property of the Lord Jesus who was immanently returning to take his people home. The matter of sex was fundamentally how to orient one's life properly toward God.[22]

As the church developed over the coming centuries, it borrowed concepts from Stoicism and particularly Neoplatonism to explain its theology. The Neoplatonic worldview brought with it the inherent sense that the human body was problematic and that human spiritual life reflected the divine life. Generally speaking sexual activity was for procreation—sheer biological theology—and marriage was seen as the way both to cure bodily lust and ensure procreation. Monasticism had arisen, in great measure to return to primitive Christian ideals once the church and empire had enmeshed, and celibacy was soon taken as a superior state of human existence. Christian history was then bequeathed a negative view of sex in which sexual activity other than abstinence had to be justified.[23]

Scripturally speaking we need not, indeed ought not, to have such a view. While the scriptural texts on sex give us little guidance, other than to understand how our attitudes have developed, the ethical perspective that has been developed in this chapter is grounded in reflection on the apostolic testimony to the encounters with Jesus. Appropriately understanding God as personal, Christian ethics has the Pauline structure of indicative-imperative: *the world is* comprised of individuals who by their creative becoming literally become part of each other and part of a greater creative whole that contributes to God. *We therefore ought* to maximize every individual's creative becoming in order to ultimately maximize the divine life that experiences the creative becoming of all individuals.

Here the creative becoming of the self and the other are positive features of human life. To view sexual activity from this perspective is to encourage the creativity of the self and the other for the enrichment of others and the divine life. We should be open and accepting of the creative becoming of others, drawing a boundary on sexual activity only where it is obviously destructive to self and others. Notice that this basic approach to sexual ethics stands on its head the Christian pattern that has historically developed in which celibacy was the ultimate norm and any sexual activity had to seek justification.

Let me include two further comments here. First, this view of human sexual relations looks to the enrichment of both the proximate and ultimate persons involved. Does the activity enrich the other person in such a way that helps maximize the creative self-realization of others? And ultimately, does this activity contribute to the creative well-being of God? Notice, second, that this perspective coheres with the attitudes of Jesus and Paul that we find witnessed in the Gospels and Pauline letters. People are no longer property (except of "the Lord's," as Paul saw it), and all people ought to orient their entire lives toward the gracious God who has unconditionally cared for them.

How then to view same gender sexual relations? The first thing to say—and here I speak as a heterosexual, middle-aged, happily married man with two kids, so I speak with some hesitation and hope to speak out of love—is that nothing else needs to be said. The ethical structure developed from our apostolic appeal to Scripture applies to homosexual sexual relations as well as heterosexual sexual relations. Does the sexual activity try to maximize the creative self-becoming of the other, and do so in a way that helps maximize the creative self-becoming of others and the actuality of God?

However, given the current climate in which many Christians are to my mind inexplicably homophobic, turning Scripture and religion against those men and women whose sexual lives are oriented toward the same gender, two more comments need to be said. First, and above all, the abuse and oppression that the church has heaped upon lesbian women and gay men ought to be a matter of repentance. And given this situation we ought to be particularly open to hearing the voices and claims of these, our friends, families, and neighbors. There is the obligation to go as far as we can to listen to these voices.

Second, we ought to refrain from the truly illegitimate uses of Scripture that continue to harm lesbian women and gay men. For instance, we ought to stop plucking out passages from Leviticus that connect to ancient purity laws and applying them willy-nilly to same gender sexual activity. From its inception the Christian church has relativized Leviticus as not pertinent to Christianity. We wear clothes illicitly made of two fabrics. And no one on the so-called religious right calls for America to have a jubilee year and forgive debts and return property. Furthermore, the Leviticus 18 texts about same gender sexual relationships are considered issues of purity and are "abominations" because they are ritually unclean, not morally evil.[24] These texts ought not be applied either. Or to take an example that is sometimes cited as normative for sexual pairing: if we turn to the two creation stories in Genesis where male and female were created, why should these be applied to gay men and lesbian women? The church has never applied these passages to celibacy, condemning monks and nuns as people who lived contrary to the divinely instituted natural moral order.

Finally, sexual relations between men and women of the same gender that are characterized by the basic approach described above ought to be celebrated as a divine gift, both from God as creator and to God as the consummator who receives all human activity into the divine reality. How would God know and experience the creative joy of such relationships if women and men did not have these relationships in the first place?

Abortion Rights

For the first eighteen centuries of Christianity we can find some theologians, writings, and councils that forbade induced abortion.[25] However, a rule must always be understood according to the reasons given and in the context in which it is given. "Drive on the right side" is an excellent rule and one that I follow, so long as I am in the United States. One night when my wife and I were in the

British West Indies I forgot where we were and forgot that the rule there was "drive on the left."

The prohibition for abortion during these eighteen centuries was never given as the "sacredness of fetal life." The prohibition of abortion was typically related to (1) wrongful sexual activity that did not aim at producing children; (2) contraception since this promoted sexual activity for reasons other than procreation; or (3) the social reality that offspring were property and belonged to the male.

In the early church, the North African theologian Tertullian wrote about the whole person being contained in the seed, here accepting ancient biology that continued through the medieval period. The woman thus bore the man's progeny, his fruit, contributing nothing but fertile soil. But this connects to ancient biology and property rights, not to the modern issue of whether the fetus is a true human person yet ("hominization"). The greatest North African theologian, Augustine, typified the position of the early church. Abortion was condemned because it interfered with procreation as the goal of sex, but the development stage of the fetus was important. If it was early in the pregnancy, prior to a soul being given to the fetus, feticide (the killing of a fetus) was punished by a fine. Only when the fetus had been "ensouled" could one consider feticide to be homicide (the killing of a *hominum—human person*). The view that the fetus was not inherently a human person but became "hominized" by the addition of the soul sometime later in the pregnancy continued through the medieval period. Aquinas, for instance, opposed abortion because it went against marriage and was a form of contraception, and thus abortion interfered with sex having procreation as its goal. However, abortion was not homicide since the fetus first had a vegetative soul, then an animal soul, and only later a human soul.

In sum, for eighteen centuries the idea that a fertilized ovum was a fully human person was not the reason behind those times and places where induced abortion was forbidden. Rather, abortion was linked to larger questions of illicit or adulterous sex, contraception, and procreation. At the same time a wide variety of sources continued to insist that the fetus in its early stages was not hominized; feticide at this point was not homicide; and at some later point the fetus was formed by the addition of a human soul and thus became a human person. All this was to change after the seventeenth century.

Using innovations such as crude microscopes, seventeenth-century scientists thought that they saw in fertilized eggs miniature versions of the full-grown animal. Such miniatures were complete and simply grew bigger and bigger until birth. The human miniature was called the "homunculus."[26] This false biological discovery affected both science and religion, and it was to have fateful consequences in the late twentieth and early twenty-first centuries. In

1869 Pius IX wrote in *Apostolicae Sedis* that abortion was homicide and that the penalty for abortion at any point during pregnancy was excommunication. By these assertions, Pius completely ignored the long standing, Catholic position that hominization occurred at some period past the fertilization of the ovum. Thus began the "fetus is a human person" argument, an argument without which violence directed at reproductive health clinics, their clients, and medical staff, including doctors, would never have begun. By the early twentieth century Roman Catholic canon law called for the excommunication of doctors and nurses who participated in abortions. The Second Vatican Council in its 1965 *Gaudium et Spes* linked abortion with infanticide and thus prohibited abortion not on the older basis of concealing sexual sin but on the basis of protecting life.

What happened historically is that after the 1973 *Roe v. Wade* Supreme Court decision, the Roman Catholic Church was stunned it had been living in its own world and hardly imagined that others thought differently. An active and aggressive grass roots movement was begun in local Roman Catholic parishes. The nonsectarian National Right to Life Committee was formed. By the end of the decade a broad grouping of Protestant evangelical churches also had become active in the effort to find some way to overturn *Roe v. Wade* and prohibit abortion.[27] The net result has been a coalition of conservative Christians from various traditions, spearheaded by the Roman Catholic Church, so confident of their position that "holocaust" language has become prevalent and an ethos of violence has surrounded reproductive health clinics across America.

The history of prohibiting abortion shows that anti-abortion arguments have fallen into two distinct categories. By far the longest standing objection to abortion has been that of sexual ethics. Abortion destroyed the normal movement from sexual intercourse to procreation. Whether to hide illicit sexual activity, or adulterous activity, or as contraception, the only acceptable end for sex, procreation, had been destroyed. The framework for sexual ethics constructed in the last section effectively removes the sexual ethics argument. Sexual activity ought to aim at the creative becoming of the self and the other, contributing to the creative becoming of God. This activity may include the goal of procreation but need not include it.

The more recent argument against abortion, historically rooted in the primitive biology of the seventeenth century, has been the "fetus is a full human person" argument. To kill a fertilized egg is not ovicide but homicide. To kill a fetus is not feticide but homicide. All abortions are homicide so that, for instance, the Roman Catholic Church prohibits its hospitals to provide emergency contraception for rape victims since such measures might interfere with a fertilized ovum and be abortifacient in such a view. Let me cite at length a reporter's questioning of Cardinal Edward Egan at a press conference in Albany, New York:

I pointed out, in what became a surreal exchange with the cardinal, that the American Medical Association requires that victims be told about pregnancy prevention options, including EC [emergency contraception]; and that if a hospital does not provide that information, and the rape victim becomes pregnant, there is legal precedent for a malpractice suit. "Given those realities," I asked Cardinal Egan, "why should Catholic hospitals that deliver a secular service to the general public with public money be allowed to refuse to abide by recommended medical practice?"

The cardinal obviously had no idea what I was talking about. "That preamble would have to be looked at rather carefully," he said. "I don't know the ins and outs of all that . . . Your question would be one I'd like to see submitted in a letter and then allow me to bring forward people who can . . . see whether or not any of that is so." Then he added: "Let me put something before us that is generic. You and I would agree, I believe, that there is something within the woman, some kind of being." Focused as I was on emergency room standards of care, the question took me aback. "After a sexual assault?" I asked.

"Yes," he said.

"*Sperm*" I heard myself say. "Sperm might be there."

Now the cardinal was taken aback. "Well then," he retorted, his face a holy crimson, "if there's only sperm, the egg and the sperm didn't get together, is that what you're saying?"

"Yes," I said, and on he went: "At a certain point, rather early in the development of that something, it gives indication that it might be a human being—beating hearts and fingers and toes and things like that certainly suggest that there may be something there that is a human being with an in-aaalien-able right to liiiive," said the cardinal, lapsing into an Irish brogue as he gave a staggeringly inaccurate account of what happens in the hours after intercourse. [28]

In the year 2002 the fundamental idea of the "homunculus" still lived. Egan's "staggeringly inaccurate" biology aside, the basic position taken by the Roman Catholic hierarchy is that a fertilized ovum is a human person. Does this idea bear merit?

Consider the idea that the self is not strictly identical over time. For example, the adult at age forty has experiences that she did not have, and in principle could not have had, when she was sixteen. Likewise the human adult contains within herself all the experiences she had as a fetus, but the fetus in principle did not contain the experiences that the adult has had. The fact that a human fetus may become a human person in no way means that a human fetus is a human person. The fact that A becomes B in no way means that B is strictly self-identical with A. No one thinks an acorn is an oak tree or that a fertilized chicken egg is a rooster. So here with the fetus and the human adult.

Does this mean that the death of an aborted fetus does not mean loss of human life? No, of course not. It means the loss of human fetal life but not the killing of a human person. There is other loss, of course—the loss of possibilities. The fetus had a literally endless combination of possibilities that as a human person it might have made concrete, choosing some possibilities and ruling out others. Made concrete these human possibilities would have had the chance to make their contribution to others and thus to God as well. The death of a fetus is the end of these possibilities and, as such, is the loss of something abstract that would have happened in some way always to remain undetermined. The concrete loss, however, was of a creative fetal life not particularly different than that of any other mammal at that fetal stage. To call this infanticide, or murder, or the killing of a child, is misleading at best and deceptively inflammatory at worst.

Naturally one then asks when human personal life begins. With the fertilized ovum? Broadly speaking most scientific and medical experts do not think so. This human cellular life may become a human person, but prior to the implantation of the fertilized ovum in the womb pregnancy, medically speaking, has not even occurred. Perhaps hominization occurs when the fertilized egg becomes implanted, sometime in the first several days or so. But so far the implanted fertilized egg has not developed a brain with an integrated central nervous system. Perhaps hominization occurs with the development of a central nervous system that becomes integrated and working in the third trimester. Here mammal-like sentience and reason might first be attributed sensibly to the fetus.[29] But at this point there is still a human life form living entirely attached to, dwelling within, and receiving all life sustenance from an adult human person.

Perhaps hominization occurs with birth, which has been the predominant teaching of Judaism from the earliest days we have records.[30] (Presumably so with Mary, Joseph, Jesus, and the disciples, all of whom were Jews.) Only two biblical passages deal directly with inducing abortion or premature termination of a pregnancy. In Num 5:11–31 the priest can test for a woman's sexuality fidelity to her husband by means of a ritual, part of which is drinking a cup that can induce an abortion (vss. 18–28). Here God's chosen priest is put in the role of abortionist:

> Then the priest shall make her take an oath, saying: "If no man has lain with you, if you have not turned aside to uncleanness while under your husband's authority, be immune to this water of bitterness that brings the curse. But if you have gone astray while under your husband's

authority, if you have defiled yourself and some man other than your husband has had intercourse with you,"—let the priest make the woman take the oath of the curse and say to the woman—"the Lord make you an execration and an oath among your people, when the Lord makes your uterus drop, your womb discharge; now may this water that brings the curse enter your bowels and make your womb discharge, your uterus drop!" And the woman shall say, "Amen. Amen." (5:19–22 NRSV)

Exod 21:22–25 speaks about the premature death of a fetus when a women is accidentally injured by another person during a fight. If there is only a miscarriage, then property has been lost and a monetary payment is owed to the woman's husband. But if there is personal harm to the woman, the laws applying to personal injury apply. Rabbinic teaching in the early decades and centuries of the common era confirmed this approach. The Mishnah makes clear that a fetus became a person when half the body, or if breach half the head, passed out of the birth canal. Later Jewish authorities confirmed this perspective. This leads to the further consideration that personhood in any meaningful sense occurs when the human being first is able to distinguish itself from the world, and thus know itself as having some particular project, if even a merely biological or primitive one. Of course some animals do this as well, so maybe personhood occurs when the human being no longer lives according to the biological needs of the body, but puts the body in service of some greater good. Some animals may sacrifice for each other, or the group, but so far as we know no animal chooses to drink hemlock for the sake of "truth."

There is no consensus about where to draw precisely the point of humanization, which hardly frees us from making such a hard decision. Perhaps we could take a more practical approach, as the U.S. Supreme Court did, by appealing to the viability of the fetus rather than trying to decide when human fetal life becomes human personal life. This has some merit. Viability always concerns a particular pregnant woman and that particular fetus. Very few abortions are performed after the twentieth week—a point at which the central nervous system has not yet fully developed and integrated. (Note also that fetal life is measured from the first day of the last period of the woman. This means that the actual time a twenty-week-old fetus has been gestating might be as little as eighteen weeks, although the fetus is medically called twenty weeks old.) As Gorney points out, "neonatologists consider twenty weeks too early for any fetus to be considered truly 'viable,' or able to survive outside the womb."[31]

We might want to step back, however, and ask at this point whether there is anything forgotten so far. Has as important issue not been raised? How about the woman? The discussion so far sounds almost "homonculus" oriented, as though we had a small fetus that by being dropped in water, or popped in a warm oven, would expand into the full-sized version of the human person it already was. But the fetus has no life outside that of the woman who grows this partially symbiont human life form from her own body, providing environment and nourishment.

In the West, this relationship between woman and her fetus has always occurred in the context of women as the property of men; more recently in a modified form of that patriarchy in which the white, able-bodied, heterosexual male is the norm, and all others are measured against him. It is worth noting that the anti-choice movement historically coincides with the second great feminist movement in America. As women have slowly begun to take their rightful place as fully equal citizens in America, the efforts at controlling their bodies has increased. Put the other way around, is it any coincidence that denominations that have historically ordained women as ministers (the Unitarian Universalists and the United Church of Christ, for instance) have also been active in the struggle for women's reproductive rights? Or that those traditions that refuse to ordain women (the Roman Catholic Church and most evangelical Protestant churches, for instance) have most actively tried to control women's reproductive rights? Given this context we ought to lean over as far as possible to hear the voices of women who express the desire to make sound, heart-felt, and even religious choices about their bodies and reproduction.

In sum, three things must be said about abortion rights. First, the moment when human personal life begins can be viewed differently. At the early end, the moment of fertilization is surely too early. The fertilized ovum is hardly more *concretely* developed than the fertilized ova of other mammals; and the potential for personal life not much greater than the potential contained in the woman's eggs, since they have human personal life as their potential. A fertilized ovum can hardly be the beginning of human personal life, and medically speaking a fertilized ovum does not signal pregnancy since implantation has not yet occurred. But neither the moment of implantation nor the development of a functioning brain are adequate moments either. Personal life must also include living apart from the woman, or at least the potential for living apart from the woman ("viability"), to say nothing about what really makes human life personal: the ability to differentiate oneself from the environment, and so be an "I" relative to the world; or the ability to order one's body according to a creative project.

Given that both these last two criteria concern the human person as what she or he really is, a social reality, birth seems the most adequate point to consider the beginning of human personal life. At birth a baby comes to be and joins her community. This accords well with the early history of Christianity, which (1) was surely faithful to its Jewish heritage that has always understood personal life coinciding with birth, and (2) rejected the commonplace practice of infant exposure. If one wanted to include prematurely born babies, then viability at approximately the twenty-fourth week of fetal life might be taken as the place where human personal life begins.

Second, to take birth, or perhaps viability as the beginning of human personal life, accords fairly well with the insistence that a woman has a moral obligation to make her own reproductive choices—in community with others and, if a religious person, in community with her God. Such choices may or may not prove to be moral, depending on how they maximize the creative individuality of all concerned, but ultimately such choices rest with the woman who makes them.

Third, and more broadly speaking, anyone who has followed the discussion so far ought to be, or have become, pro-choice. Why? Not because everyone who hears or reads the arguments will agree, but because the discussion given here is carefully made with consideration for fetus, woman, society, and God. It represents a sound moral position that can be taken and which ought to be left open as a possibility. To be pro-choice is not to be pro-abortion but rather to recognize that different religions, and different people within the Christian religion, hold articulate, heart-felt, but differing views. The pro-choice position is, therefore, *already* the middle-ground compromise position, acknowledging that there are significantly different positions for which people on both sides of the issue ought to be respected and have the right to actualize.

Put from the other direction, the only way that there could be only one, single, concrete ethical choice about abortion rights that would be infallibly right would be for divine intervention that told human society what that ethical choice would be. Only omnipotent intervention can give such an option, otherwise all religious ideas, including choices about abortion rights, derive from historically conditioned understanding of the one ultimate religious truth-that all people are unfailingly related to a personal, divine reality who influences all things for the good but omnipotently controls nothing.

Oddly, since on the Roman Catholic side the prohibition against abortion has never been, technically speaking, an infallible decision, and since on the evangelical Protestant side the only biblical passages about abortion as such sees fetal life as something less than full personal life, and even sees the priest as an abortionist, one would think even those who oppose abortion would recognize that no infallible moral teaching exists about the issue. Sadly, such is not the case. What is difficult to communicate to people who have not actively discussed these issues with those who oppose abortion rights is that those in opposition to abortion believe it absolutely self-evident that the human fetus is a human person. For those whose personal lives do not include such (often spirited) discussion, Gorney's remarkable book on the history of the abortion debate can illustrate over and over how completely self-evident it seems to those who are anti-choice that to talk about a fetus is to talk about a human person.

Finally, since to be pro-choice is to not to be pro-abortion as such—I know many articulate and outspoken people in the pro-choice movement and know no one who is pro-abortion—one would think that preventing unwanted pregnancies and working on family planning would be a great common ground for both sides. This rarely works out. Why? Because the basis of the anti-choice perspective is that full human personal life exists at the moment of fertilization. Since some standard birth control methods can prevent implantation, and are thus seen as abortifacients that must be rejected, artificial birth control is rejected at the family planning level.

The complicated, communal, but finally personal decision about abortion begins with reflecting on what would maximize the creative good for the woman, so that her life thereby contributed to the maximum creative good of others concerned, thus contributing to the divine reality. The process starts with the good of the woman, and the decision finally can be made only by her, but it encompasses a wide range of issues. Yes, the life of the fetus must be considered, but fetal human life is not the same as the personal human life of the woman, or the persons in the family, faith community, and wider society. Yes, the death of a fetus means loss to the wider community. But, as we have seen, such loss is itself abstract since it is the loss of some potential not known and never to come to be.

Naturally, if one believes that the human fetus is a full human being, so that the killing of a fertilized ovum or of a developing fetus is homicide, then the ethical approach of indicative-imperative suggested here would take a different shape. The ethical imperative would be to maximize the creative self-becoming of the fetus, which cannot yet speak for itself so that its life would help maximize the creative self-becoming of others and thus the divine life. This hardly abrogates the approach to ethics suggested here. It only indicates that, absent divine intervention that dictates concrete content, there is no pre-specified, infallible ethical position. It also indicates the importance of deciding whether one believes the human fetus is a fully human person.

Christianity and Other Religions

On the issue of the relationship between Christianity and other religions, I want to summarize in part the argument put forth by Ogden in his work *Is There Only One True Religion or Are There Many?* Ogden's approach is both insightful and thoroughly compatible with the theological approach taken in this chapter.

Most commonly Christians have taken three approaches to other religions: exclusivism, inclusivism, and pluralism. In the postmodern world pluralism has become a common way that Western people think about religions. Pluralism may even be the way that many Christians think about religions other than Christianity. Pluralism argues that there are many alternative ways to think about human life and ultimate reality. Many of these alternatives may be true so that we can say there are a plurality of true religions.

Pluralism contrasts to exclusivism, which is the way that many Christians traditionally have thought, and do think, about other religions. Exclusivism argues that outside Christianity, and thus also outside the church since it bears the offer of salvation, there can be no possibility of salvation. Only Christians inside the church participate in the salvation that God offers. Thus a primary role of the church is the spread of the gospel throughout the world so that others might have the chance to be saved. The great age of conquest, as Spain and Portugal seized new lands in the Americas, often had this view of Christianity as one of the reasons for such conquest. The Spanish conquerors and colonists posed this as such a good, for instance, that the practice of *encomienda* was conceived. The conquerors would teach the indigenous peoples the true religion (Christianity) and, as payment for such a great gift, the people then became indentured servants of the colonizers. The great missionary efforts of the nineteenth century, and the great growth of missionary societies, partly owe their existence to an exclusivistic view about Christianity and other religions.

Exclusivism has two principal difficulties. First, is it really believable? Can we believe that some people can be saved, while others are hopelessly lost without salvation simply by an accident of birth? What of the countless millions who lived and died prior to Jesus Christ? Christians have sometimes appealed to the connection between the old dispensation given to the Jews and the new dispensation given in Jesus Christ. The new dispensation fulfills, or completes, the old dispensation given to Abraham and his descendants. Thus the Jewish people are included in the dispensation that began with them. But the Hebrew writings themselves are neither prophecies about Jesus nor the preamble to the Christian church, and Christians would be better off not pillaging them as though they were resources to justify Christianity. And what of those people who lived prior to Jesus Christ who were not Jews? Were they in principle without the possibility of salvation?

More broadly speaking, some Christians have appealed to God's omnipotent saving work. God saves whom God wills. For this argument to amount to anything more than divine capriciousness one would have to conceive of omnipotent, universal salvation. But does that perspective not itself mitigate against exclusivism?

Finally, Christians may say theirs is the true religion and that they have known salvation, but on what logical basis could they deny such salvation elsewhere? And by what means could they ascertain that such a denial were true?

A second problem with exclusivism is that it hardly seems Christian, where Christian means being appropriate to the apostolic testimony to Jesus. As we have seen, such testimony supports a personal view of God who relates to all people as the One who values them and desires that they take such valuing as their ultimate orientation in life. But how could we take that affirmation seriously if we were to conceive of a divine offer of salvation that some people, in principle, could never know simply by an accident of their birth?

The third option has been inclusivism. The basic idea is that the salvation that God revealed in Jesus Christ is offered to all people and thus other religions may, in fact, be making such an offer in and through their own religious systems. We already have seen Justin Martyr argue that the Word or Logos cast his presence (seeds) throughout creation so that his light shone here or there amid the darkness. This same Word was then incarnated as Jesus Christ. In recent times one of the twentieth century's greatest theologians, Karl Rahner (1904–1984), offered a very sophisticated modern version of this type of argument. Rahner's basic point was that since God eternally had salvation through Jesus Christ as the final goal for the world, nothing that was created could have come to be without this eternal, supernatural reality as a natural part of its existence.[32]

The central problem with inclusivism is that it remains fundamentally akin to exclusivism. There is ultimately only one true religion, established by God's acts in Jesus Christ, and ultimately only one true salvation, that offered through Jesus Christ. Other religions are true and possess the offer of salvation only insofar as they participate, implicitly, in the Christian religion, which is the explicit manifestation of the true religion and offer of salvation. In this respect pluralists view inclusivists as well-intentioned, but needing to come over to pluralism in order to avoid exclusivism and credit the religious pluralism they want to credit.

What then of pluralism? Does it remain an option? Several problems arise with pluralism, the gravamen of which is how one would judge that some other religion were indeed the true religion. To make such a claim a pluralist would have to have some criterion by which to decide that another religion were true. But where would such a criterion come from, other than from one's own religion or from some philosophy that dealt with religions? In that case the pluralist is no different from the inclusivist because both make a particular religion the norm by which others are judged.

Furthermore, the exclusivist claim is that a religion other than Christianity *cannot* be true. The pluralist claim is that religions other than Christianity *are* true. These two claims both cannot be true, but both could be false. Indeed the argument has been made here that both ought to be rejected. The complete opposite claim (strictly speaking, the contradictory claim) to the exclusivist claim that a religion other than Christianity *cannot* be true is the claim that

133

some other religion *can* be true. Whether such other religion *is* true is another matter.

Thus there is another option worth taking in interreligious dialogue (here implicitly rejecting the option that no religion can be true): Christianity is a true religion and other religions also can be true. Ogden calls this the "fourth option." How might we think about this option?

As this chapter already argued, the cause of God's saving grace is nothing other than God's own existence as grace. This simply is who God is and, on this view, the words and deeds of Jesus did not serve to *constitute* that saving reality for us but rather to *re-present* that saving reality. Other religions can therefore be true, if the mediator upon which they are built truly represents the unfailingly present ultimate reality that we Christians call God. This fourth option avoids the problems of exclusivism, inclusivism, and pluralism, while still allowing for the possibility of other true religions and while respecting the claims of these other religions and the people making such claims.

NOTES TO CHAPTER FOUR

1. Charles Hartshorne, *The Logic of Perfection* (LaSalle, Ill.: Open Court, 1962), 285.
2. Ibid., 286–87.
3. This is what Hartshorne means by the word "necessary" when it applied to metaphysical claims. "Metaphysics we may now define as the search for necessary and categorical truth— necessary in that, unlike empirical truths or facts, it excludes no positive possibility, and thus imposes no restriction upon the process of actualization, and categorical in that (unlike mathematics interpreted as deduction from unasserted postulates) it applies positively to any actuality." Hartshorne, *Logic of Perfection*, 285.
4. See, for instance, the assertion by John B. Cobb Jr., "Hartshorne's Importance for Theology," in *The Philosophy of Charles Hartshorne* (Library of Living Philosophers 20; ed. Edwin Hahn; LaSalle, Ill.: Open Court, 1991), 171, that "Hartshorne knew that arguments for God's existence could be convincing only if the idea of God for which they argued was itself intelligible. His primary contribution, therefore, has been in the introduction of a way of thinking of God that fits well with clear thinking about the world."
5. Hartshorne, *Logic of Perfection*, 297.
6. Alfred North Whitehead, *Modes of Thought* (New York: Free Press, 1968), 116.
7. Ogden, *The Reality of God*, 36.
8. Ibid., 41–42. For the Camus story, see Albert Camus, *The Myth of Sisyphus and Other Essays* (trans. Justin O'Brien; New York: Vintage, 1955). Also see Ogden's essay, "The Strange Witness of Unbelief," in *The Reality of God*, 120–43.
9. The second section of Ogden's essay "The Reality of God" has the title, "The Reality of Faith," *The Reality of God*, 21–43.
10. Ibid., 39.

11. For a discussion of Marxsen's views on the reactions to Jesus, see the essay by Philip E. Devenish in Marxsen, *Jesus and the Church*, xi–xxxv, esp. xvi–xxiv.

12. Schubert M. Ogden, *Doing Theology Today* (Valley Forge, Pa.: Trinity Press International, 1996), 182.

13. See, for instance, Paul's comments in 1 Cor 11:23; 15:3.

14. For a technical discussion from which the following argument derives, see Philip E. Devenish, "The Sovereignty of Jesus and the Sovereignty of God," *ThTo* 53 (1996): 63–73.

15. See the helpful and concise discussion in Ogden, *The Reality of God*, 57–61.

16. Note the comments by Ogden, *The Reality of God*, 59–60, n. 97.

17. See Victor Paul Furnish, *Theology and Ethics in Paul* (Nashville: Abingdon, 1968), esp. 224–27.

18. Ogden, *The Reality of God*, 58.

19. On this passage see, for instance, Gerhard von Rad, *Genesis: A Commentary* (trans. John H. Marks; Philadelphia: Westminster, 1961), 249-50; Claus Westermann, *Genesis: A Practical Commentary* (trans. David E. Green; Grand Rapids, Mich.: Eerdmans, 1987), 171; Bruce Vawter, *On Genesis: A New Reading* (Garden City, N.Y.: Doubleday, 1977), 266–67.

20. Marvin H. Pope, *Song of Songs* (The Anchor Bible; Garden City, N.Y.: Doubleday, 1977).

21. For an extended discussion of various texts, see L. William Countryman, *Dirt, Greed, and Sex* (Philadelphia, Fortress, 1988), 148–59.

22. See Countryman, *Dirt, Greed, and Sex*, 190–220, esp. 190–202, 213–14.

23. See, for example, Vern L. Bullough, *Sexual Variance in Society and History* (New York: John Wiley, 1976), 159–201; Vern L. Bullough and Bonnie Bullough, *Sin, Sickness and Sanity* (New York: Garland, 1977), 10–40; Richard Posner, *Sex and Reason* (Cambridge, Mass.: Harvard University Press, 1992), 37–50; John Boswell, *Christianity, Social Tolerance, and Homosexuality* (Chicago: University of Chicago Press, 1980), 91–166. Also see Peter Brown, *The Body and Society: Men, Women, and Sexual Renunciation in Early Christianity* (New York: Columbia University Press, 1988).

24. See, for example, Boswell, *Christians, Social Tolerance, and Homosexuality*, 99–102; Countryman, *Dirt, Greed, and Sex*, 28–32.

25. This section on abortion rights is indebted in various ways to Daniel Dombrowski and Robert Deltete, *A Brief, Liberal, Catholic Defense of Abortion* (Urbana, Ill.: University of Illinois Press, 2000), 1–78; John B. Cobb Jr., *Matters of Life and Death* (Louisville: Westminster John Knox, 1991), 69–93; Beverly Wildung Harrison, *Our Right to Choose* (Boston: Beacon, 1983), 119–53; Charles Hartshorne, "Concerning Abortion: An Attempt at a Rational View," *ChrCent* 98 (1981): 42–45; idem, *Omnipotence*, 99–103.

26. For seventeenth-century developments on the issue of hominization, including a discussion (and picture) of the homunculus, see Dombrowski and Deltete, *Defense of Abortion*, 34–42.

27. Cynthia Gorney, *Articles of Faith* (New York: Simon & Schuster, 1997), esp. 161–93, 308–76.

28. Angela Bonavoglia, "Cardinal Sins," *MS* 11 (June/July 2002): 43.

29. See the discussions in Dombrowski and Deltete, *Defense of Abortion*, 42–47, 55–58.

30. For a helpful introduction and summary of the perspective of Judaism on abortion, and specifically the status of fetal life, see the essay by Rabbi Raymond A. Zwerin and Rabbi

Richard J. Shapiro entitled "Judaism and Abortion." This essay can be found at the website for the Religious Coalition for Reproductive Choice, under the link to Educational Series (see www.rcrc.org/religion/es/judaism.html).

31. Gorney, *Articles of Faith*, 409.

32. Rahner has an articulate, progressive Roman Catholic perspective from the era of the Second Vatican Council, which cannot be adequately dealt with here. See his *Theological Investigations* (Baltimore: Helicon, 1961), 5:97–114, 115–124; 12:161–78; 14:280-94; 16:199–224; and 17:39–50.

CHAPTER FIVE
SUMMARY

This chapter pulls together the various strands from the previous chapters and makes summary comments on them, situating this study historically and theologically. The first section traces the arguments from the first three chapters. How did we get to postmodern theologies? What do they look like? And in what ways are they adequate and inadequate as Christian theologies? The second section suggests how the inclusive liberal theology sketched in chapter 4 credits the insights that postmodern theologies have to offer while avoiding the primary problem with such theologies. As such it offers a theology that is contextual without being relativistic and a theology that credits universal claims without being authoritarian. The third section briefly situates this theology in its theological traditions.

POSTMODERN THEOLOGY AND ITS HERITAGE

Christian Theology

Situated in rural Palestine, and beginning as a reform movement with Judaism, Christianity had a primitive structure of wandering charismatic preachers and householders who put them up and opened their homes and table to them. The ministry of Jesus, which was comprised of teaching, healing, and table sharing, was continued by these early "Jesus theologians" of the Jesus Movement.

Over time Christian missionaries carried this tradition throughout the Mediterranean basin. As Christianity survived and then mainstreamed into the Greco-Roman world it needed conceptual tools to explain what its proclamations meant and how they might be true. In the middle of the second century Justin Martyr turned to Stoicism with its idea of a divine reason embodied in reality itself. Around the year 200 C.E. the North African thinker Tertullian borrowed from Roman property law to explain ideas about Scripture, Christ, and the Trinity. Principally from Alexandria came the use of Neoplatonism to explain Christian claims. In some ways this was a good conceptual fit because the spiritual realm of Neoplatonic thought, which consisted of a radically other

One, an Intellect that contained the organizing principles of reality, and the World Soul, neatly correlated to God, Jesus Christ the Logos of God, and the Spirit. Neoplatonism had a religious fit to Christianity as well. The longing of the world to return back to the One found an echo in the experience of the Christian heart and its longing for the one home that would give it rest—God.

The Neoplatonic Christianity of Augustine was formative for Christianity, and in the Western, Latin church was supplanted only when Thomas Aquinas modified its insights by wedding Augustinian theology with the thought of Aristotle. This synthesis, known as Thomism, held in careful balance grace and nature, revelation and reason, theology and philosophy, and church and state. Thomism was challenged in numerous ways during the fourteenth and fifteenth centuries, most dramatically by late medieval nominalism such as that of William of Ockham. Applying the now-famous "Ockham's razor," which itself had intellectual predecessors in the medieval church, Ockham refused to postulate more complex ideas when more simple ones would work. Experience, unrelenting logic, and the reading of Scripture produced a theology known as the *via moderna*—as compared to the *via antiqua* of Aquinas and others—and it was influential on the Reformers.

Two other late medieval traditions influenced the Reformers. Luther, Calvin, and many of the so-called radical Reformers, were influenced by the mysticism of the late medieval period. A divergence came where the medieval tradition thought that only "like can know like" so that the mystic had to become like God in some way—such as conforming one's will to Christ's will—in order to know immediately the grace of God's presence. For the Reformers it was exactly as sinners, with troubled consciences, that we could know this divine presence.

Humanism also influenced Protestantism through its return to the original scriptural languages and texts, its interest in history and criticism, and its concentration on rhetoric, grammar, and even literacy itself. The human person was able to be empowered, be critical, and think for herself. Here, too experience, conscience, and biblical texts were important.

It was characteristic of classical Protestantism to blend humanistic study, the inward experience of piety, and appeal to Scripture as the external, religious norm because the Scriptures witnessed to Christ. As the Lutheran and Reformed traditions moved from the late sixteenth century through the seventeenth century, Protestantism took a different shape. Protestant orthodoxy shaped Protestant Christianity into richly detailed and thoroughly argued doctrinal systems, all based on a theory of Scripture not held by the classical Reformers themselves: a biblical infallibility grounded in verbally inspired texts. The Word of God had all but become the words of God. In reaction to what was perceived as a Protestantism overly concerned with doctrine and the organization of church and its beliefs, pietism began in the last third of the seventeenth century and emphasized

Christianity as a religion of the heart. It was organized around small groups that studied Scripture, oriented toward an irenic acceptance of other Christians, and urged a pastorate trained more effectively in the pastoral arts.

Alongside Orthodox Protestantism and the developing pietist streams in Protestantism came the Enlightenment, which classical Protestantism helped nurture by its own embrace and transmission of Renaissance humanism. In their critical judgment, some Enlightenment thinkers, such as Hume, rejected Christianity while other thinkers, such as Kant, ended up with an oddly traditional form of Christianity.[1]

When Kant was in his later years, a young theologian in Berlin named Schleiermacher was beginning to synthesize a critical Enlightenment approach to Christianity, a pietist encounter with Jesus, and a thorough knowledge of Greek and the New Testament. Schleiermacher produced a synthesis exactly the same shape as that of classical Protestantism, just more adequately expressed for a new context. The encounter with Jesus, which one had when encountered by the church, called forth the prior, always existing relationship with God that no one could fail to be without. In so doing, the encounter with Jesus named and shaped this relationship with God, giving one's religious experience a character no longer one's own but that of the redeemer.

> If it be the essence of redemption that the God-consciousness already present in human nature, though feeble and repressed, becomes stimulated and made dominant by the entrance of the living influence of Christ, the individual on whom this influence is exercised attains a religious personality not his before.[2]

From this starting point of Jesus Christ and the Christian piety formed by Christ in the encounter that one had with him, Schleiermacher worked out the great doctrines of Christianity for his modern world.

By the early twentieth century the modern theology inaugurated by Schleiermacher had in some quarters devolved into a Western cultural religion. God was the kindly Father. Jesus was the moral example that showed us by his life what our hearts really knew. And under the guidance of such a God and Savior the West was making progress as Christianity helped bring civilization to the world. To this form of cultural Christianity Karl Barth responded with a resounding "No!" God was radically other and in sovereign freedom had chosen to redeem us through the covenant of grace embodied in Jesus Christ the Savior, not mere teacher, of humankind. The gospel was thus radically other than any form of culture, bringing a divine ethical challenge to humankind.

However much Barth stood against the liberal Protestantism of his day, he shared with it certain assumptions: the use of historical criticism in Scripture scholarship; the critical use of conceptual tools from philosophy; and the insistence that theology ought to be an ellipse with two foci, God and humankind. In fact, Schleiermacher and Barth share these assumptions with most of the Protestant reformers who applied humanist approaches to the Scriptures, borrowed philosophical tools within the limits of Christian piety, and had the divine-human relationship as the basic structure for their theologies.

During the twentieth century, these fundamental assumptions were taken in other directions as well. Rudolf Bultmann began with Barth by arguing for the radical otherness of God, who summons us to obedient lives. But Bultmann's project was the two-sided task of demythologizing the gospel. Our world is not that of the ancients so we cannot take their worldview as ours. We must, however, look to the divine call that comes through this ancient worldview and then, constructively, express what that means to us today. In the last third of the twentieth century, theologians applied modern Scripture scholarship, critical tools from philosophy and the social sciences, and the divine-human relationship to construct theologies of liberation. Such theologies de-ideologized the gospel by moving theological discussion out of the realm of those thinkers and institutions that used it as a means of subjection and moving it into the realm of the lived experiences of those whom God's Savior, Jesus, had come to liberate.

The Heritage of Postmodern Philosophy

Since postmodern Christianity has shared with all prior Christian theologies the need to borrow conceptual systems in order to express what it means and why its claims should be true, chapter 2 briefly surveyed Western philosophy from the pre-Socratics through postmodern thinkers. Socrates had argued against the Sophists that certain ideas had to hold true across context for there to be anything such as truth, beauty, or goodness. Absent such universal ideas everything became, as the Sophists argued, a matter of local human convention: "Man is the measure of all things." Truth is relative and subjective. Socrates' great student Plato then conceived a philosophical system in which these ideas were given actual form in the created order, a spiritual realm shaping this physical realm. The human soul had a preexistent memory of this world of forms and thus Plato accounted for truth, beauty, goodness, and human knowledge. Plato's great student Aristotle was the son of a physician, raised with what was concretely living, changing, and perishing. Aristotle conceived of universal forms as aspects of concrete things themselves in whose image things grow, as they move from potential to actual, lured on by the presence of a purely actualized being, God, whose only contemplation was the beautiful contemplation of the divine actuality itself.

One of the significant countervoices to this Socratic lineage was that of Skepticism, whose founder, Pyrrho, was a generation younger than Aristotle.

Skepticism argued that we could not actually know things in themselves and that the way to true happiness was to suspend the hopeless attempt to know reality itself when all we know are the conventions of our own contexts. The only extant Skeptical writings are those of the physician Sextus Empiricus, who lived during the third century of the common era. The senses reveal no universal truths since they are grounded in particular contexts. This applied to ethics, as well as physics and mathematics.

Neoplatonism became the dominant philosophical voice of the West from the third century onward as its fundamental structures were borrowed by theologians of that relatively new religion, Christianity, which was to dominate the Latin West. There the universals that Plato had considered so thoughtfully were now conceived to be in the divine mind, the Logos, which illumined every human mind. All knowledge ultimately came from illumination by the Logos, through the universals, as the mind was stimulated by the outward senses and turned inward for understanding. When in the thirteenth century Thomas Aquinas blended the Neoplatonism of Augustine with the philosophy of Aristotle the new Christian theology called Thomism was born. There too universals were ultimately real and in the mind of God, although they occur (as with Aristotle) as features of concrete things themselves. All knowledge comes from the mind abstracting the universal from the individual entity and actively applying it back to that which had been experienced.

In the late medieval period nominalist thinkers such as William of Ockham, and his followers such as John of Mirecourt and Nicholas of Autrecourt, denied the reality of universals. Applying relentless logic, and holding to the concept that the simple is better than the complex, these thinkers argued that we know by simple observation. From our concrete experiences we have memories and new thoughts that make more complex ideas. We can know how these ideas fit the world as we experience it. Both modern science and the writing of modern history have been attributed to this approach. Modern skepticism also has one of its origins here as causality itself was questioned.

These thinkers had the effect of driving philosophical and religious thought away from the structure of reality itself. On the negative side, the gap between what reason could know through reflection, and what faith could know through revelation, seemed to widen. On the positive side, the appeal to experience and reason, and the appeal to biblical concepts for God, reinforced the idea of God as the personal, covenanting God rather than the Unmoved Mover of earlier theological traditions.

For the Protestant reformers, this personal God who values was externally attested to by God's revelation in Jesus Christ and internally known in the experience of piety. The Protestant reformers also were influenced by humanism, with its insistence on human experience and critical judgment, and especially with the insistence on the return to original texts, languages, and their historical contexts. Christian mysticism played its own role in crediting the experience of piety for doing theology.

The Enlightenment thinkers of the seventeenth and eighteenth centuries were the inheritors of late medieval skeptical theology, critical humanist thought and approaches, and the Protestant legacy of critical and personal approach to God and self. To some twentieth-century thinkers, such as Etienne Gilson, this was a great loss as compared to the thought of Thomas Aquinas. Thomas had held together faith and reason, theology and philosophy, and church and state, in a unified vision of reality. Beginning with the impoverished theology of the late medieval nominalists, the West had begun a slow decline into two realms, one sacred and the domain of revelation, the other secular and the domain of reason, which needed no religion. This Gilsonian overview cannot be entirely gainsaid.

Modern thinkers, with only some exceptions, have primarily taken the structure of reality as some kind of given, and reflected either on its cause and effects (science) or on our physical sensation of it and reflections on that sensation (philosophy). The structure of reality, in and of itself, has much less been the object of philosophical or theological reflection. The work of Leibniz was a notable exception, and chapter 2 paused to observe the Enlightenment ridicule of him. In the eighteenth century the German idealists Fichte, Schelling, and Hegel also stood out in their attempt to talk about the structure of reality and to give a unified vision of reality that included both God and creation.

By contrast the overall philosophical development in the West prescinded from such projects, generally concentrating on what we experience through the senses and what if anything we can know from such experiences. The postmodern deconstructive turn to language and politics has merely carried this philosophizing another step in the same direction. The focus has moved not just to what we might know, but to who knows and in what context someone knows. Not surprisingly one well-known philosopher of religion, David Ray Griffin, has critically but aptly called such approaches "mostmodern" rather than "postmodern."

Finally, some time was spent on four of the major voices that were alternatives to the general direction of modern theology—Charles Peirce, William James, Henri Bergson, and Alfred North Whitehead. These four thinkers were notable for swimming upstream in the Western philosophical river, arguing for certain structures of reality itself within which the human person and the divine reality both found a home.

Postmodern Theologies

Postmodern theologies can be divided into three types. Purifying postmodern theology, such as that of Mark C. Taylor, has worked to remove from theology the church accretions that have stuck it in traditional categories and domesticated it from the radical approach of thinkers such as Kierkegaard. Political postmodern theology, such as that of Mary Daly and Sally McFague, has argued that theological language as used by the socially dominant voices has stifled diverse alternative voices and helped to destroy the world as such. New ways to use language in service of some ultimate reality and human liberation have been conceived. Preserving postmodern theology, such as found in the New Yale School, has argued that the canon and the worldview its narrative creates is the encounter with the living Christ, who brings the alternative world commanded by the God who sovereignly reveals in Jesus Christ.

These three approaches, it was argued, tend to share two insights that ought to be credited and one that ought to be challenged. First, theology is really about theologies since all theological thinking is bound to particular contexts, inherently interpretative, and thus irreducibly pluralistic. Second, the rise of Christian doctrines are tied to specific contexts and thus are historically conditioned ways that language has functioned within those settings. Third, these theologies either deny, or see as inappropriate, claims that talk about the structure of reality itself. This third claim undercuts any attempt to have an ethics that is meaningful and avoids being self-contradictory, empty, arbitrary, or incomplete. It fails to credit what scriptural writers everywhere assume or assert. And, finally, this claim can be shown to be conceptually inadequate since some "metaphysical truisms" cannot help but be made—in fact, they are assumed by everything that we do and so cannot be meaningfully contravened, even by their denial.

TOWARD AN INCLUSIVE LIBERAL THEOLOGY

Chapter 4 began with the work of Charles Hartshorne and focused on the claims he called "metaphysical truisms." These claims cannot be denied because they are necessarily presupposed by any conceivable activity. For Hartshorne such claims led to the idea of God. Schubert Ogden argues that "the primary use or function of 'God' is to refer to the objective ground in reality itself of our ineradicable confidence in the final worth of our existence."[3] For Ogden as well as Hartshorne critical reflection on human experience as such leads one to theism. Put the other way around, a humanist commitment that does not entail metaphysical truisms and theism remains truncated.[4] Here, it would seem that Christianity has something to teach postmodernism about its own humanist commitment. These metaphysical assertions, therefore, can bridge the distance between Christianity and postmodern culture, and they do so not as a capitulation to secular culture but as a challenge to secular culture.

These assertions also bridge the distance between postmodern Christianity that seeks plurality and more traditional Christianity that seeks universal assertions. By starting with the encounter that people had with Jesus, in which the already present revelation of God was decisively re-presented, Christian theology from its inception proves to have both universal and contextually interpretive aspects. No one could be without the original confidence that marks the internal pole of the relationship whose external pole is the gracious divine reality. At the same time, this relationship to God only comes to awareness and makes its claim on a person within a specific, culturally-conditioned language.

This approach to Christian theology yields another bridge—this one between those forms of postmodern Christianity that argue that ethics are culturally—conditioned, and thus context bound, and the various forms of Christianity that seek universal ethical claims in order to avoid moral perspectivism.

Reflection on the encounter with Jesus suggested a divine reality that was personal: both the agent of revelation (Jesus) and the agency of revelation (love, forgiveness, reconciliation, and so on) were personal. The divine reality can be appropriately conceived as a structure that is both transcendent and immanent, both unchanging and changing. That God is related to all and experiences all is itself the transcendent, unchanging character of God. Who God is in a given, concrete moment, experiencing all things and incorporating them in the divine self is the immanent, changing divine life.

Borrowing the Pauline ethical structure of indicative-imperative, Christian ethics has the indicative claim that all that we do creatively fashions not just ourselves but others, as they also creatively fashion us, so that the divine reality itself experiences the creative whole. All individuals have their mutually and divinely created lives given ineradicable meaning as they become part of the divine reality. The imperative then grows from the indicative of divine grace: we ought to act as though this were so and maximize the creativity of each, for the maximal creativity of all, and thus the divine life.

There exists, therefore, a universal moral claim, with an indicative-imperative structure, whose origin is reflection on the apostolic encounter with Jesus. Does this claim specify ahead of time the moral content of an act? No, but neither does it lack a Christian moral principle without which choices made would be merely arbitrary. On this basis chapter 4 examined same-gender sexual ethics and abortion rights.

Finally, this approach suggests a way can be seen for interreligious dialogue that focuses not on the mediator, with all the tribal exclusivity that such focus brings, but on the ultimate reality that the mediator re-presents as decisive for human existence as such. No claim is made that other religions cannot be true. Nor is the claim made, unverifiable by experience and without a meaningful norm by which to specify, that other religions are true religions. Rather a middle ground is argued that other religions can be true, whether or not they are true, while the criteria by which such judgment is to be made remains open for dialogue between traditions as they sort out what is meant by the ultimate reality for each religion.

SITUATING THIS INCLUSIVE LIBERAL THEOLOGY

Finally a few observations about the perspective this book offers in order to help locate it on the theological landscape that has been outlined: As the comments on late medieval nominalism and on modern theology reveal, this study is somewhat Gilsonian. There was indeed a disruptive loss when the synthesis of Thomas Aquinas gave way to a Western philosophy whose reflection on sensation and knowing was disconnected to arguments about the structure of reality as such. At the same time, the turn to the historical and the human critical capacities that shook off all inherent external authorities was liberating and for the good. Christianity deserves our allegiance not because we are told it is true, or told to believe, but because from our own contexts and experiences we know its claims to be true and give ourselves to it. Here Protestantism and the Enlightenment find accord.

In this regard the theology sketched here also shows the tradition of Schleiermacher. Schleiermacher has been dubbed, and rightly so, a liberal evangelical. It was the encounter with Jesus that made him who he was and out of which he did his theology. Yet because he was a child of the Enlightenment, the old ways of thinking, which were historically conditioned and understandable in their times and places, no longer sufficed. New, more credible ways of conceiving Christian theology were needed.

Furthermore, in his *Speeches on Religion* Schleiermacher argued that to be interested in the human condition without being interested in religion was to end up with an insufficient view of the human person. Religion was at the heart of being human, and organized religion fundamentally concerned the religious association that people had since the human person was fundamentally social. Schleiermacher was, so to speak, a humanist Christian. Note that the substantive is the world "Christian" and the modifier the word "humanist"—that is, humanist Christian not Christian humanist. So, too, this study argued that an aspect of being human is the ineradicable confidence that all that we do has ultimate meaning. Upon reflection this feature turns out to be the human side of the divine-human relationship so that to consider what it means to be human without considering God is to have a truncated humanism.

Finally, this theological approach is also indepted to Whitehead, Hartshorne, Ogden, and Cobb, among others. Some people may therefore dismiss the arguments as "process theology" or "merely" process thought. That would be a mistake.

The only interest anyone ought to have in doing Christian theology is in doing a *Christian* theology. The theological enterprise ought to take its starting point from the encounter with Jesus and nowhere else, least of all to be beholden ahead of time to this or that particular philosophical system. From the critique of postmodern theology at the end of chapter 3, to the sketching of an inclusive liberal theology in chapter 4, the starting point has always been the encounter with Jesus. From this encounter, and what it said about the agent and agency of redemption, and what it evoked and called forth already present in human experience as such, the claim was made that the divine reality ought best be conceived as personal.

Now if theology is to turn to philosophy for conceptual tools, as it has done for two thousand years, then the twentieth century saw the development of certain conceptual tools quite appropriate to the Christian witness. The trajectory of a valuing, creative, ultimate character to reality was seen in Peirce, James, Bergson, and Whitehead, as well as others mentioned along the way, such as Schelling and Hartshorne. One turns to Whitehead, Hartshorne, Ogden, and Cobb because the conceptual resources used and developed by these thinkers have the most appropriate fit to the Christian witness of faith. Central to these thinkers is the notion that the divine reality may be most aptly described as personal:

Essential to Christian faith, as I understand it, is belief in the reality of God as distinct from and more than the reality of the world, taken either in its individual parts or as the collection thereof. God in the Christian sense is neither a mere part of the word not all of its parts together, but is a distinct center of activity and reactivity, and so a genuine individual in his [sic] own right. At the same time, Christian faith involves the belief that God is the beginning and the end, the ground and the consequent, of ever other individual whatever, so that he himself is not merely an in individual, but the individual, the one whose own reality coincides with reality itself or as such. Whatever is, or is so much as even possible, has its beginning and end in God's love for it and, but for reality of his love, would have neither being nor value in any public or objective sense. Thus while God as individually distinct from the world is believed to transcend it, he is also believed to be immanent in the world as its primal ground, even as it is immanent in him as its ultimate end.[5]

Since the encounter with Jesus revealed both an agent and agency of divine revelation that was personal, the assertion that God is the one strictly universal self is fully warranted by apostolic testimony to Jesus. A metaphysics that argues for a personal divine reality, as does that of process theology, thus shows itself to be both appropriate to this apostolic testimony to Jesus and the most adequate conceptual system available, given the anti-metaphysical postmodern philosophical context, for expressing the meaning and truth of Christian claims.

NOTES TO CHAPTER FIVE

1. See the discussion by Hartshorne, *Insights and Oversights*, 170–88.
2. Friedrich Schleiermacher, *The Christian Faith* (Philadelphia: Fortress Press, 1976), §106.1, 476.
3. Ogden, *Reality of God*, 37.
4. This is precisely what Gamwell shows in his discussion of non-theistic ethics in *The Divine Good*. See the discussion in chapter 3.
5. Schubert M. Ogden, "The Meaning of Christian Hope," in *Religious Experience and Process Theology: The Pastoral Implications of a Major Modern Movement*, (ed. Harry Cargas and Bernard Lee; New York: Paulist, 1976), 196.

BIBLIOGRAPHY

Ameriks, Karl, ed. *The Cambridge Companion to German Idealism.* Cambridge: Cambridge University Press, 2000.

Armstrong, A. H. *Introduction to Ancient Philosophy.* 3d ed. Westminster, Md.: Newman, 1957.

Barnes, Jonathan, ed. *The Cambridge Companion to Aristotle.* Cambridge: Cambridge University Press, 1995.

Barnes, Timothy. *Athanasius and Contantius: Theology and Politics in the Constantinian Empire.* Cambridge, Mass.: Harvard University Press, 1993.

Barr, James. *Biblical Faith and Natural Theology.* Oxford: Clarendon, 1993.

Barth, Karl. *Church Dogmatics.* 1, no. 2. Translated by G. W. Bromiley. Edinburgh: T & T Clark, 1975.

Barthes, Roland. *A Barthes Reader.* Edited and with an introduction by Susan Sontag. New York: Noonday, 1982.

———. *Elements of Semiology.* Translated by Annette Lavers and Colin Smith. New York: Noonday, 1968.

———. *Image, Music, Text.* Selected and translated by Steven Heath. New York: Hill &Wang, 1977.

———. *Mythologies.* Selected and translated by Annette Lavers. New York: Noonday, 1972.

Bell, Richard H., ed. *The Grammar of the Heart: New Essays in Moral Philosophy and Theology.* San Francisco: Harper & Row, 1988.

Bernstein, Carl, and Marco Politi. *Holiness: John Paul II and the Hidden History of Our Time.* New York: Doubleday, 1996.

Bevan, Edwyn. *Stoics and Skeptics.* Oxford: Clarendon, 1913.

Bevans, Stephen. *John Oman and His Doctrine of God.* Cambridge: Cambridge University Press, 1992.

Bice, Benvenuto, and Roger Kennedy. *The Works of Jacques Lacan: An Introduction.* New York: St. Martin's, 1986.

Boff, Leonardo, and Clodovis Boff. *Introducing Liberation Theology.* Maryknoll, N.Y.: Orbis, 1989.

Bonavoglia, Angela. "Cardinal Sins." MS 11 (June/July 2002): 43.

Bonner, Gerald. *St. Augustine of Hippo: Life and Controversies.* London: SCM Press, 1963.

Boswell, John. *Christianity, Social Tolerance, and Homosexuality.* Chicago: University of Chicago Press, 1980.

Bouwsma, William. "Renaissance and Reformation: An Essay in Their Affinities and Connections." Pages 127–49 in *Luther and the Dawn of the Modern Era: Papers for the Fourth International Congress for Luther Research.* Edited by Heiko Oberman. Leiden: E. J. Brill, 1974.

Brandon, Robert B., ed. *Rorty and His Critics.* Oxford: Blackwell, 2000.

Bréhier, Émile. *The Philosophy of Plotinus.* Translated by Joseph Thomas. Chicago: University of Chicago Press, 1958.

Brinton, Crane. "Enlightenment." Pages 519–24 in *The Encyclopedia of Philosophy.* 8 vols. Edited by Paul Edwards. New York: MacMillan, 1967.

Bromell, David J. "Sallie McFague's 'Metaphorical Theology.'" *Journal of the American Academy of Religion* 61, no. 3 (1993): 485–503.

Brown, Peter. *Augustine of Hippo: A Biography.* Berkeley: University of California Press, 1967.

———. *The Body and Society: Men, Women, and Sexual Renunciation in Early Christianity.* New York: Columbia University Press, 1988.

Bullough, Vern L. *Sexual Variance in Society and History.* New York: John Wiley, 1976.

Bullough, Vern L., and Bonnie Bullough. *Sin, Sickness, and Sanity.* New York: Garland, 1977.

Bultmann, Rudolf. *Existence and Faith: Shorter Writings of Rudolf Bultmann.* Translated by Schubert M. Ogden. New York: Meridian, 1960.

———. *New Testament and Mythology: And Other Basic Writings.* Selected, edited, and translated by Schubert M. Ogden. Philadelphia: Fortress, 1989.

Calvin, John. *Institutes of the Christian Religion.* 2 vols. Edited by John T. McNeill. Translated by Ford Lewis Battles. Library of Christian Classics 20–21. Philadelphia: Westminster, 1960.

Cameron, Euan. *The European Reformation.* Oxford: Clarendon, 1991.

Camus, Albert. *The Myth of Sisyphus and Other Essays.* Translated by Justin O'Brien. New York: Vintage, 1955.

Caputo, John D., ed., *Deconstruction in a Nutshell: A Conversation with Jacques Derrida.* New York: Fordham University Press, 1977.

Chappell, Vere, ed. *The Cambridge Companion to Locke.* Cambridge: Cambridge University Press, 1994.

Childs, Brevard. *Introduction to the Old Testament as Scripture.* Philadelphia: Fortress, 1979.

———. *The New Testament as Canon: An Introduction.* Philadelphia: Fortress, 1985.

Christ, Carol P., and Judith Plaskow. *Womanspirit Rising: A Feminist Reader in Religion.* San Francisco: Harper & Row, 1979.

Cobb, John B., Jr. "Alfred North Whitehead." Pages 165–95 in *Founders of Postmodern Constructive Theology: Peirce, James, Bergson, Whitehead, and Hartshorne.* Edited by David Ray Griffin, John B. Cobb Jr., Marcus P. Ford, Peter A. Y. Gunter, and Peter Ochs. Albany: State University of New York Press, 1993.

———. *Matters of Life and Death.* Louisville: Westminster John Knox, 1991.

Collins, Jeff. *Introducing Derrida.* Duxford, Cambridge: Icon, 2000.

Cone, James H. *A Black Theology of Liberation.* Twentieth anniversary edition. Maryknoll, N.Y.: Orbis, 1995.

Copleston, Frederick. *A History of Medieval Philosophy.* New York: Harper & Row, 1972.

———. *A History of Philosophy.* 9 vols. London: Burns, Oates & Washbourne, 1947–1975.

Cornford, Francis M. *Before and After Socrates.* Cambridge: Cambridge University Press, 1932.

Cottingham, John, ed. *The Cambridge Companion to Descartes.* Cambridge: Cambridge University Press, 1992.

Countryman, L. William. *Dirt, Greed, and Sex.* Philadelphia: Fortress, 1988.

Courtney, William J. "Nominalism and Late Medieval Religion." Pages 26–58 in *The Pursuit of Holiness in Late Medieval and Renaissance Religion.* Edited by Charles Trinkhaus and Heiko Oberman. Leiden: E. J. Brill, 1974.

Crossan, John Dominic *The Historical Jesus.* San Francisco: HarperSanFrancisco, 1991.

Daly, Mary. *Beyond God the Father: Toward a Philosophy of Women's Liberation.* Boston: Beacon, 1973.

———. *The Church and the Second Sex.* New York: Harper Colophon, 1975.

———. *Gyn/Ecology: The Metaethics of Radical Feminism.* Boston: Beacon, 1978.

———. *Pure Lust: Elemental Feminist Philosophy.* San Francisco: HarperSanFrancisco, 1984.

Derrida, Jacques. *Deconstruction in a Nutshell: A Conversation with Jacques Derrida.* Edited with commentary by John D. Caputo. New York: Fordham University Press, 1977.

———. *Glas.* Translated by John P. Leavey Jr. and Richard Rand. Lincoln: University of Nebraska Press, 1986.

———. *Of Grammatology.* Corrected edition. Translated by Gayatri Chakrovorty Spivak. Baltimore: Johns Hopkins University Press, 1998.

Devenish, Philip E. "The Sovereignty of Jesus and the Sovereignty of God." *Theology Today* 53 (1996): 63–73.

Dombrowski, Daniel, and Robert Deltete. *A Brief, Liberal, Catholic Defense of Abortion.* Urbana, Ill.: University of Illinois Press, 2000.

Duling, Dennis C., and Norman Perrin. *The New Testament* 3d ed. New York: Harcourt Brace, 1994.

Fatio, Olivier. "Reformierte Orthodoxie." Pages 485–97 in *Theologische Realenzylkopädie* 25. Berlin: Walter de Gruyter, 1995.

Ford, Marcus P. "William James." Pages 89-132 in *Founders of Postmodern Constructive Theology: Peirce, James, Bergson, Whitehead, and Hartshorne.* Edited by David Ray Griffin, John B. Cobb Jr., Marcus P. Ford, Peter A. Y. Gunter, and Peter Ochs. Albany: State University of New York Press, 1993.

Ford, Marcus Peter. *Willaim James's Philosophy: A New Perspective.* Amherst: University of Massachusetts Press, 1982.

Foucault, Michel. *The Archeology of Knowledge* Translated by A. M. Sheridan Smith. New York: Pantheon, 1972.

———. *The Birth of the Clinic.* Translated by A. M. Sheridan Smith. New York: Vintage, 1994.

———. *Discipline and Punishment.* Translated by Alan Sheridan. New York: Pantheon, 1977.

———. *The History of Sexuality.* Translated by Robert Hurley. New York: Vintage, 1990.

———. *Madness and Civilization.* Translated by Richard Howard. New York: Pantheon, 1965.

Frei, Hans. *The Eclipse of Biblical Narrative: A Study in Eighteenth- and Nineteenth-Century Hermeneutics.* New Haven: Yale University Press, 1974.

Frend, W. H. C. *The Rise of Christianity.* Philadelphia: Fortress, 1984.

Fuller, B. A. G. *A History of Philosophy.* Rev. ed. 2 vols. New York: Henry Holt, 1945.

Furnish, Victor Paul. *Theology and Ethics in Paul.* Nashville: Abingdon, 1968.

Gamwell, Franklin I. *The Divine Good: Modern Moral Theory and the Necessity of God.* New York: Harper Collins, 1990.

Gay, Peter. *The Enlightenment: An Interpretation.* 2 vols. New York: Knopf, 1966–1969.

George, Timothy. *Theology of the Reformers.* Nashville: Broadman & Holman, 1988.

Gerrish, B. A. *Grace and Gratitude: The Eucharistic Theology of John Calvin.* Minneapolis: Fortress, 1993.

———. *The Old Protestantism and the New.* Chicago: University of Chicago Press, 1982.

———. *A Prince of the Church*. Philadelphia: Fortress, 1984.

———. *Tradition in the Modern World: Reformed Theology in the Nineteenth Century*. Chicago: University of Chicago Press, 1978.

Gerson, Lloyd P. *Plotinus*. London: Routledge, 1994.

———. ed. *The Cambridge Companion to Plotinus*. Cambridge: Cambridge University Press, 1996.

Gilson, Etienne. *The Christian Philosophy of Saint Augustine*. Translated by L. E. M. Lynch. New York: Octagon, 1960.

———. *The Christian Philosophy of St. Thomas Aquinas*. Translated by L. E. M. Lynch. New York: Random House, 1960.

———. *History of Christian Philosophy in the Middle Ages*. New York: Random House, 1955.

———. *Reason and Revelation*. New York: Charles Scribner's Sons, 1938.

———. *Wisdom and Love in St. Thomas Aquinas*. Milwaukee: Marquette University Press, 1951.

Gilson, Etienne, and Thomas Langan. *Modern Philosophy: From Descartes to Kant*. New York: Random House, 1963.

Gilson, Etienne, Thomas Langan, and Armand Maurer. *Recent Philosophy: Hegel to the Present*. New York: Random House, 1962.

Goodwin, George L. Review of Franklin I. Gamwell, *The Divine Good: Modern Moral Theory and the Necessity of God*. *Process Studies* 21 (1992): 184.

Gorney, Cynthia. *Articles of Faith*. New York: Simon & Schuster, 1997.

Grane, Leif. *Peter Abelard: Philosophy and Christianity in the Middle Ages*. Translated by Frederick and Christine Crowley. New York: Harcourt, Brace & World, 1970.

Gregg, Robert C., and Dennis E. Groh. *Early Arianism: A View of Salvation*. Philadelphia: Fortress, 1981.

Griffin, David Ray, William Beardslee, Joe Holland. *Varieties of Postmodern Theology*. Albany: State University of New York Press, 1989.

Griffin, David Ray, John B. Cobb Jr., Marcus P. Ford, Peter A. Y. Gunter, and Peter Ochs. *Founders of Postmodern Constructive Theology: Peirce, James, Bergson, Whitehead, and Hartshorne*. Albany: State University of New York Press, 1993.

Grube, G. M. A. *Plato's Thought*. With new introduction, bibliographic essay, and bibliography by Donald J. Zeyl. Indianapolis: Hackett, 1980.

Gunter, Peter A. Y. "Henri Bergson." Pages 133–63 in *Founders of Postmodern Constructive Theology: Peirce, James, Bergson, Whitehead, and Hartshorne*. Edited by David Ray Griffin, John B. Cobb Jr., Marcus P. Ford, Peter A. Y. Gunter, and Peter Ochs. Albany: State University of New York Press.

Guthrie, W. K. C. *The Greek Philosophers*. New York: Harper & Row, 1975.

Gutiérrez, Gustavo. *A Theology of Liberation: History, Politics, and Salvation.* Rev. ed. Edited and translated by Sister Caridad Inda and John Eagleson. Maryknoll, N.Y.: Orbis, 1990.

Gutting, Gary, ed. *The Cambridge Companion to Foucault.* Cambridge: Cambridge University Press, 1994.

Guyer, Paul. *The Cambridge Companion to Kant.* Cambridge: Cambridge University Press, 1992.

Hahn, Lewis, ed. *The Philosophy of Charles Hartshorne.* Vol. 20 of *Library of Living Philosophers.* Chicago.: Open Court, 1991.

———. *The Philosophy of Paul Ricoeur.* Vol. 24 of *The Library of Living Philosophers.* Chicago: Open Court, 1985.

Hartshorne, Charles. *Anselm's Discovery.* LaSalle, Ill.: Open Court, 1965.

———. *Aquinas to Whitehead: Seven Centuries of Metaphysics of Religion.* Milwaukee: Marquette University Publications, 1976.

———. "Concerning Abortion: An Attempt at a Rational View." *Christian Century* 98 (1981): 42–45.

———. *Creative Synthesis and Philosophic Method.* LaSalle, Ill.: Open Court, 1970.

———. *Creativity in American Philosophy.* Albany: State University of New York Press, 1984.

———. *The Darkness and the Light.* Albany: State University of New York Press, 1990.

———. *Insights and Oversights of Great Thinkers: An Evaluation of Western Philosophy.* Albany: State University of New York Press, 1983.

———. *The Logic of Perfection.* LaSalle, Ill.: Open Court, 1962.

———. *Omnipotence and Other Theological Mistakes.* Albany: State University of New York Press, 1984.

Hartshorne, Charles, and Creighton Peden. *Whitehead's View of Reality.* New York: Pilgrim, 1981.

Hartshorne, Charles, and William Reese. *Philosophers Speak of God.* Chicago: University of Chicago Press, 1979.

Hauerwas, Stanley. *Wilderness Wanderings: Probing Twentieth-Century Theology and Philosophy.* Boulder, Colo.: Westview, 1997.

Hintikka, Merrill B., and Jaako Hintikka. *Investigating Wittgenstein.* London: Blackwell, 1986.

Holmer, Paul. *The Grammar of Faith.* San Francisco: Harper & Row, 1978.

Horsley, Richard A., with John S. Hanson. *Bandits, Prophets, Messiahs.* Harrisburg: Trinity Press International, 1999.

Jolley, Nicholas, ed. *The Cambridge Companion to Leibniz.* Cambridge: Cambridge University Press, 1995.

Jungmann, Joseph. *The Mass of the Roman Rite.* 2 vols. Translated by Francis A. Brunner. Westminster, Md.: Christian Classics, 1986.

Kelly, J. N. D. *Early Christian Doctrines.* 2d ed. New York: Harper & Row, 1960.

Kelsey, David. *To Understand God Truly.* Louisville: Westminster John Knox, 1992.

Kemp, John. *The Philosophy of Kant.* Oxford: Oxford University Press, 1968.

Koester, Helmut. *History, Culture, and Religion of the Hellenistic Age.* 2d ed. Berlin: Walter de Gruyter, 1995.

Kretzmann, Norman and Eleonore Stump, eds. *The Cambridge Companion to Aquinas.* Cambridge: Cambridge University Press, 1993.

Kristeller, Paul O. *Renaissance Thought: The Classic, Scholastic, and Humanist Strains.* New York: Harper, 1961.

Kristeva, Julia. *Desire in Language.* Edited by Leon S. Roudiez. Translated by Thomas Gora, Alice Jardine, and Leon S. Roudiez. New York: Columbia University Press, 1980.

———. *The Kristeva Reader.* Edited by Toril Moi. New York: Columbia University Press, 1986.

———. *The Portable Kristeva.* Edited by Kelly Oliver. New York: Columbia University Press, 2002.

———. *Strangers to Ourselves.* Translated by Leon S. Roudiez. New York: Columbia University Press, 1991.

———. *Tales of Love.* Translated by Leon S. Roudiez. New York: Columbia University Press, 1987.

Lacan, Jacques. *Écrits: A Selection.* Translated by Alan Sheridan. New York: Norton, 1977.

———. *The Language of Self: The Function of Language in Psychoanalysis.* Translated with notes and commentary by Anthony Wilden. Baltimore: Johns Hopkins University Press, 1981.

Leff, Gordon. *The Dissolution of the Medieval Outlook.* New York: New York University Press, 1976.

———. *William of Ockham: The Metamorphosis of Scholastic Discourse.* Manchester: Manchester University Press, 1975.

Lindbeck, George. *The Nature of Doctrine: Religion and Theology in a Postliberal Age.* Philadelphia: Fortress, 1984.

Long, A. A. *Hellenistic Philosophy: Stoics, Epicureans, Skeptics.* 2d ed. Berkeley: University of California Press, 1986.

———. ed., *The Cambridge Companion to Early Greek Philosophy.* Cambridge: Cambridge University Press, 1999.

Luther, Martin. *Luther's Works.* Vol. 31. Edited by Harold J. Grimm. Philadelphia: Fortress, 1957.

Malherbe, Abraham J. *Social Aspects of Early Christianity.* 2d ed. Philadelphia: Fortress, 1983.

MacMullen, Ramsay. *Paganism in the Roman Empire.* New Haven: Yale University Press, 1981.

———. *Roman Social Relations.* New Haven: Yale University Press, 1974.

Marxsen, Willi. *Jesus and the Church: The Beginnings of Christology.* Selected, translated, and introduced by Philip E. Devenish. Philadelphia: Trinity Press International, 1992.

Mattias, Markus. "Lutherische Orthodoxie." Pages 464–85 in *Theologische Realenzylkopädie* 25. Berlin: Walter de Gruyter, 1995.

Maurer, Armand A. *Medieval Philosophy.* New York: Random House, 1962.

McFague, Sallie. *The Body of God: An Ecological Theology.* Philadelphia: Fortress, 1993.

———. *Life Abundant: Rethinking Theology and Economy for a Planet in Peril.* Minneapolis: Fortress, 2001.

———. *Metaphorical Theology: Models of God in Religious Language.* Philadelphia: Fortress, 1982.

———. *Models of God: Theology for an Ecological, Nuclear Age.* Philadelphia: Fortress, 1987.

———. *Super, Natural Christians: How We Should Love Nature.* Minneapolis: Fortress, 1997.

McGlasson, Paul. *Another Gospel: A Confrontation with Liberation Theology.* Grand Rapids, Mich.: Baker, 1994.

———. *God the Redeemer: A Theology of the Gospel.* Louisville: Westminster John Knox, 1983.

McGrade, Arthur. *The Political Thought of William of Ockham.* Cambridge: Cambridge University Press, 1974.

McGuinness, B. F. *Wittgenstein: A Life. Young Ludwig.* Berkeley: University of California Press, 1988.

McIntyre, John. *St. Anselm and His Critics.* Edinburgh: Oliver & Boyd, 1954.

Meeks, Wayne A. *The First Urban Christians.* New Haven: Yale University Press, 1983.

Moody, Ernest. *The Logic of William of Ockham.* London: Sheed & Ward, 1935.

Moxnes, Halvor. "Patron-Client Relations and the New Community in Luke-Acts." Pages 241–68 in *The Social World of Luke-Acts.* Edited by Jerome H. Neyrey. Peabody, Mass.: Hendrickson, 1991.

Muller, Richard A. *Christ and the Decree: Christology and Predestination in Reformed Theology from Calvin to Perkins.* Durham, N.C.: Labyrinth, 1986.

Neusner, Jacob. *From Politics to Piety.* Englewood Cliffs, N.J.: Prentice-Hall, 1973.

———. "The Pharisees: Jesus' Competition." Pages 45–61 in *Judaism in the Beginning of Christianity.* Philadelphia: Fortress, 1984.

Niebuhr, Richard R. *Schleiermacher on Christ and Religion*. New York: Charles Scribner's Sons, 1964.

Norton, David Fate, ed. *The Cambridge Companion to Hume*. Cambridge: Cambridge University Press, 1993.

Oberman, Heiko. *The Dawn of the Reformation*. Edinburgh: T & T Clark, 1986.

———. *Forerunners of the Reformation*. New York: Holt, Rinehart & Winston, 1966.

———. *The Harvest of Medieval Theology*. Cambridge, Mass.: Harvard University Press, 1963.

———. *Luther: Man between God and the Devil*. Translated by Eileen Walliser-Schwarzbart. New Haven: Yale University Press, 1989.

Ochs. Peter. "Charles Sanders Peirce." Pages 43–87 in *Founders of Postmodern Constructive Theology: Peirce, James, Bergson, Whitehead, and Hartshorne*. Edited by David Ray Griffin, John B. Cobb Jr., Marcus P. Ford, Peter A. Y. Gunter, and Peter Ochs. Albany: State University of New York Press, 1993.

Ogden, Schubert M. *Christ without Myth*. New York: Harper, 1961.

———. *Doing Theology Today*. Valley Forge, Pa.: Trinity Press International, 1996.

———. *Faith and Freedom: Toward a Theology of Liberation*. Revised, enlarged edition. Nashville: Abingdon, 1989.

———. *Is There Only One True Religion or Are There Many?* Dallas: Southern Methodist University Press, 1992.

———. "The Meaning of Christian Hope." Pages 196–212 in *Religious Experience and Process Theology: The Pastoral Implications of a Major Modern Environment*. Edited by Harry Cargas and Bernard Lee. New York: Paulist, 1976.

———. *On Theology*. San Francisco: Harper & Row, 1986.

———. *The Point of Christology*. San Francisco: Harper & Row, 1982.

———. *The Reality of God and Other Essays*. New York: Harper & Row, 1966.

O'Meara, Thomas. *Romantic Idealism and Roman Catholicism: Schelling and the Theologians*. Notre Dame, Ind.: University of Notre Dame Press, 1982.

Ozment, Steven E. *The Age of Reform*. New Haven: Yale University Press, 1980.

———. *Mysticism and Dissent: Religious Ideology and Social Protest in the Sixteenth Century*. New Haven: Yale University Press, 1973.

———. *The Reformation in the Cities*. New Haven: Yale University Press, 1975.

———. *Protestants: The Birth of a Revolution*. New York: Doubleday, 1992.

———. *When Fathers Ruled: Family Life in Reformation Europe*. Cambridge, Mass.: Harvard University Press, 1983.

Pagels, Elaine. *Adam, Eve, and the Serpent*. New York: Vintage, 1989.

Pope, Marvin H. *Song of Songs*. The Anchor Bible. Garden City, N.Y.: Doubleday, 1977.

Popkin, Richard H. *The High Road to Pyrrhonism*. Indianapolis: Hackett, 1993.

————. *The History of Scepticism from Erasmus to Spinoza.* Berkeley: University of California Press, 1979.

————. ed. *The Columbia History of Western Philosophy.* New York: Columbia University Press, 1999.

Portalié, Eugène. *A Guide to the Thought of St. Augustine.* Chicago: Regnery, 1969.

Posner, Richard. *Sex and Reason.* Cambridge, Mass.: Harvard University Press, 1992.

Putnam, Ruth Anna, ed. *The Cambridge Companion to William James.* Cambridge: Cambridge University Press, 1997.

Rabinow, Paul, ed. *The Foucault Reader.* New York: Pantheon, 1984.

Rad, Gerhard von. *Genesis: A Commentary.* Translated by John H. Marks. Philadelphia: Westminster, 1961.

Radford Ruether, Rosemary. *Gaia and God: An Ecofeminist Theology of Earth Healing.* San Francisco: HarperSanFrancisco, 1992.

————. *Sexism and God-Talk.* Boston: Beacon, 1983.

Ragland-Sullivan, Ellie, and Mark Bracher, eds. *Lacan and the Subject of Language.* New York: Routledge, 1991.

Rahner, Karl. *Theological Investigations.* 23 vols. Baltimore: Helicon, 1961–.

Raposa, Michael L. *Peirce's Philosophy of Religion.* Bloomington, Ind.: Indiana University Press, 1989.

Redeker, Martin. *Schleiermacher: Life and Thought.* Translated by John Wallhauser. Philadelphia: Fortress, 1973.

Ricoeur, Paul. *Essays on Biblical Interpretation.* Edited with an introduction by Lewis S. Mudge. Philadelphia: Fortress, 1980.

————. *Figuring the Sacred.* Edited by Mark I. Wallace. Translated by David Pellauer. Minneapolis: Fortress, 1995.

————. *Hermeneutics and the Human Sciences.* Edited, translated, and introduced by John B. Thompson. Cambridge: Cambridge University Press, 1981.

Riggs, John W. *Baptism in the Reformed Tradition.* Columbia Series in Reformed Theology. Louisville, Ky.: Westminster John Knox, 2002.

————. "Protestants Speaking the Gospel into Postmodern Ears" *Concordia Journal* 27 (2001): 124–33.

————. "The Sacred Food of Didache 9-10 and Second-Century Ecclesiologies." Pages 266–67, in *The Didache in Context.* Edited by Clayton N. Jefford. Leiden: E. J. Brill, 1995.

Rorty, Richard. *Objectivity, Relativism, and Truth.* Cambridge: Cambridge University Press, 1991.

————. *Philosophy and the Mirror of Nature.* Princeton: Princeton University Press, 1979.

———. *Philosophy and Social Hope.* London: Penguin, 1999.

———. *Truth and Progress.* Cambridge: Cambridge University Press, 1998.

Rorty, Richard, ed. *The Linguistic Turn.* Chicago: University of Chicago Press, 1967.

Ross, W. D. *Aristotle.* New York: Barnes & Noble, 1956.

Saussure, Ferdinand de. *Course in General Linguistics.* Edited by Charles Bally and Albert Sechehaye in collaboration with Albert Reidlinger. Translated by Wade Baskin. London: Peter Owen, 1974.

Schleiermacher, Friedrich. *The Christian Faith.* Philadelphia: Fortress, 1976.

Schweizer, Eduard. "Two Testament Creeds Compared," Pages 122–35 in *Neotestamentica: Deutsche und englische aufsätze, 1951–1963.* Zurich: Zwingli Verlag, 1963.

Seeburg, Reinhold. *Text-Book of the History of Doctrines.* 2 vols. Translated by Charles E. Hay. Grand Rapids, Mich.: Baker, 1964.

Sherburne, Donald W., ed. *A Key to Whitehead's Process and Reality.* New York: Macmillan, 1966.

Sluga, Hans, and David G. Stern. *The Cambridge Companion to Wittgenstein.* Cambridge: Cambridge University Press, 1996.

Stump, Eleonore, and Norman Kretzmann, eds. *The Cambridge Companion to Augustine.* Cambridge: Cambridge University Press, 2001.

Tamburello, Dennis E. *Union with Christ: John Calvin and the Mysticism of St. Bernard.* Columbia Series in Reformed Theology. Louisville, Ky.: Westminster John Knox, 1984.

Taylor, A. E. *Epicurus.* London: Constable, 1911.

Taylor, Mark C. *Altarity.* Chicago: University of Chicago Press, 1987.

———. *Deconstructing Theology.* Chico, Calif.: Scholars, 1982.

———. *Disfiguring: Art, Architecture, Religion.* Chicago: University of Chicago Press, 1982.

———. *Erring: A Postmodern A/theology.* Chicago: University of Chicago Press, 1984.

———. *Hiding.* Chicago: University of Chicago Press, 1997.

———. *Nots.* Chicago: University of Chicago Press, 1993.

Tentler, Thomas N. *Sin and Confession on the Eve of the Reformation.* Princeton: Princeton University Press, 1977.

TeSelle, Sallie (McFague). *Literature and the Christian Life.* New Haven: Yale University Press, 1966.

———. *Speaking in Parables: A Study in Metaphor and Theology.* Philadelphia: Fortress, 1975.

Vawter, Bruce. *On Genesis: A New Reading.* Garden City, N.Y.: Doubleday, 1977.

Vignaux, Paul. *Philosophy in the Middle Ages.* Translated by E. C. Hall. Westport, Conn.: Greenwood, 1973.

Wallace, Mark I. *The Second Naivetè: Barth, Ricoeur, and the New Yale Theology.* Macon, Ga.: Mercer University Press, 1990.

Weinstein, Donald. "In Whose Image and Likeness? Interpretations of Renaissance Humanism." *Journal of the History of Ideas* 33 (1972): 165–76.

Westermann, Claus. *Genesis: A Practical Commentary.* Translated by David E. Green. Grand Rapids, Mich.: Eerdmans, 1987.

Wheelwright, Philip, ed. *The Presocratics.* New York: Odyssey, 1966.

Whitehead, Alfred North. Alfred North Whitehead, *Modes of Thought.* New York: Free Press, 1968.

———. *Religion in the Making.* New York: Macmillan, 1926.

———. *Science and the Modern World.* New York: Macmillan, 1926.

Wildung Harrison, Beverly. *Our Right to Choose.* Boston: Beacon, 1983.

Wittgenstein, Ludwig. *Philosophical Investigations.* Translated by G. E. M. Anscombe. Oxford: Blackwell, 1963.

———. *Tractatus Logicus Philosophicus.* Translated by D. F. Pears and B. F. McGuinness with an introduction by Bertrand Russell. London: Routledge, 2001.

Wolfreys, Julian, ed. *The Derrrida Reader: Writing Performances.* Edinburgh: Edinburgh University Press, 1998.

Wolfson, Harry A. *Philo: Foundations of Religious Philosophy in Judaism, Christianity, and Islam.* Rev. ed. 2 vols. Cambridge, Mass.: Harvard University Press, 1948.

Wood, David C. *Derrida: A Critical Reader.* Oxford: Blackwell, 1992.

Young, Pamela Dickey. *Feminist Theology/Christian Theology.* Minneapolis: Fortress, 1990.

Zachman, Randall C. *The Assurance of Faith: Conscience in the Theology of Martin Luther and John Calvin.* Minneapolis: Fortress, 1993.

INDEX

Abelard, Peter, 50–51, 68n. 10
abortion
    abortifacients, 131
    abortion rights, 8, 123
    abortionist, 127
    anti-choice, 131
    pro-choice, 130–31
Absolute Spirit, 63–64
absolution, 19, 20
abstinence, 122
Actium, battle of, 45
Adam, 19, 49, 55, 100
adultery, 121
aesthetics, 26
Africa, 12
Age of Reason, 59, 60–61
agriculture, 12, 20
AIDS, 20, 83
Alexander the Great, 10, 44–45
Alexandria, 15, 45, 48, 137
Altizer, Thomas J.J., 81
American nazi party, 110n. 80
Ameriks, Karl, 71n. 43
amoralism, 102
amorality, 100
Anaximander, 42
Anaximenes, 42
Anselm of Canterbury, 50, 68n. 10, 83
ante-bellum South, 103
Anthrax scares, 103

anti-speculative rationalism of modernity, 7, 59–60, 61, 67
anxiety, 20, 31
Apel, Karl-Otto, 101
apostolic testimony to Jesus, 15–16, 116, 133, 147
Aquinas Institute of Theology, ix
Aquinas, Thomas, 18, 51–52, 56, 69n. 11, 84, 124, 138, 141–42, 145
arete (skill at living, how-to), 43
Aristotle, 17, 18, 19, 24, 42, 44–45, 50–51, 101, 140
Arius, 98
ascending desire, 48
ascetic practices, 22
Assyrians, 10
Athanasius, 48, 98–99
Athens, 44
atonement of Christ, 50
Auerbach, Erich, 91
Augustine of Hippo, 17, 19, 48–49, 51–52, 54, 100, 138, 141
Aurelius, Marcus, 46
Avignon, 49
awareness, 19, 26,115, 144
Ayer, A.J., 64

Babylonians, 10
Bakhtin, Mikhail, 78
baptism, 14, 19, 97–98

Wheelwright, Philip, 68n. 6
Whitehead, Alfred North, x, 15, 37n. 7, 41–42, 66–67, 68n. 2, 72n. 46, 73, 112, 134n. 6, 142, 146, 146
William of Champeaux, 51
William of Ockham, 52, 60, 68n. 12, 138, 141
Ockham's razor, 138
Williams, Delores, 84
Willimon, William, 91
Wilmore, Gayraud, 33
Wisdom literature, 41
Wittengenstein, Ludwig, 64, 67, 73–74, 106nn. 1, 2, 111
family resemblances, 74
language games, 74
Philosophical Investigation, 74
Wolfreys, Julian, 107n. 6
Wolfson, Harry S., 37n. 9

Wolleb, Johannes, 23
Womanspirit Rising, 31
wondrous communion with Christ, 55
Word (Christ), 49
Word of God *see* Logos of God
works-righteousness, 30
World Soul, 48, 138
Wotan's Volk, 103
Wurzberg, 62

Yahweh, 10

Zachman, Randall C., 38n. 21
Zadok, 13
Zanchius, Jerome, 24
Zeno the Stoic, 46
Zwerin, Raymond A., 135n. 30
Zwingli, 23, 57